PENGUIN ANANDA

DANCING IN THE BREEZE

Osho defies categorization. His talks, which run into thousands, cover everything from the individual quest for meaning to the most urgent social and political issues facing society today. Osho's books are not written but are transcribed from audio and video recordings of his extemporaneous talks to international audiences. As he puts it, 'So remember: whatever I am saying is not just for you . . . I am talking also for the future generations.'

Osho has been described by *Sunday Times* in London as one of the '1000 Makers of the 20th Century', and by American author Tom Robbins as 'the most dangerous man since Jesus Christ'. *Sunday Mid-Day* (India) has selected Osho as one of ten people—along with Gandhi, Nehru and Buddha—who have changed the destiny of India.

About his own work Osho has said that he is helping to create the conditions for the birth of a new kind of human being. He often characterizes this new human being as 'Zorba the Buddha'—capable both of enjoying the earthy pleasures of a Zorba the Greek and the silent serenity of a Gautama the Buddha.

Running like a thread through all aspects of Osho's talks and meditations is a vision that encompasses both the timeless wisdom of all ages past and the highest potential of today's (and tomorrow's) science and technology.

Osho is known for his revolutionary contribution to the science of inner transformation, with an approach to meditation that acknowledges the accelerated pace of contemporary life. His unique OSHO Active Meditations™ are designed to first release the accumulated stresses of body and mind, so that it is then easier to take an experience of stillness and thought-free relaxation into daily life.

Two autobiographical works by the author are available: *Autobiography of a Spiritually Incorrect Mystic*, St Martin's Press, New York (book and e-book), and *Glimpses of a Golden Childhood*, OSHO Media International, Pune, India.

OSHO

DANCING IN THE BREEZE

THE DISCIPLINE OF TRANSCENDENCE

PENGUIN
ANANDA

PENGUIN ANANDA
Published by the Penguin Group
Penguin Books India Pvt. Ltd, 7th Floor, Infinity Tower C, DLF Cyber City, Gurgaon 122 002, Haryana, India
Penguin Group (USA) Inc., 375 Hudson Street, New York, New York 10014, USA
Penguin Group (Canada), 90 Eglinton Avenue East, Suite 700, Toronto, Ontario, M4P 2Y3, Canada
Penguin Books Ltd, 80 Strand, London WC2R 0RL, England
Penguin Ireland, 25 St Stephen's Green, Dublin 2, Ireland (a division of Penguin Books Ltd)
Penguin Group (Australia), 707 Collins Street, Melbourne, Victoria 3008, Australia
Penguin Group (NZ), 67 Apollo Drive, Rosedale, Auckland 0632, New Zealand
Penguin Books (South Africa) (Pty) Ltd, Block D, Rosebank Office Park, 181 Jan Smuts Avenue, Parktown North, Johannesburg 2193, South Africa

Penguin Books Ltd, Registered Offices: 80 Strand, London WC2R 0RL, England

First published by OSHO Media International 1976
Published in Penguin Ananda by Penguin Books India 2015

10 9 8 7 6 5 4 3 2 1

ISBN 9780143424918

For sale in the Indian Subcontinent only

Printed at Replika Press Pvt. Ltd, India

A PENGUIN RANDOM HOUSE COMPANY

CONTENTS

PREFACE

I love Gautama the Buddha because to me he represents the essential core of religion. He is not the founder of Buddhism – Buddhism is a by-product – but he is the beginner of a totally different kind of religion in the world. He's the founder of a religionless religion. He has propounded not religion but religiousness. And this is a great radical change in the history of human consciousness.

Before Buddha, there were religions but never a pure religiousness. Man was not yet mature. With Buddha, humanity enters a mature age. Not all human beings have yet entered that, it's true, but Buddha has heralded the path; Buddha has opened the gateless gate. It takes time for human beings to understand such a deep message. Buddha's message is the deepest ever. Nobody has done the work that Buddha has done, the way he has done. Nobody else represents pure fragrance.

Other founders of religions, other enlightened people, have compromised with their audience. Buddha remains uncompromised, hence his purity. He does not care what you can understand, he cares only what the truth is, and he says it without being worried whether you understand it or not. In a way this looks hard; in another way this is great compassion.

Truth has to be said as it is. The moment you compromise, the moment you bring truth to the ordinary level of human consciousness, it loses its soul. It becomes superficial, it becomes a dead thing. You cannot bring truth to the level of human beings; human beings have to be led to the level of truth.

Osho
The Diamond Sutra

1

THE EIGHTFOLD WAY

MOVE STEP-BY-STEP AND YOU COME HOME

The Buddha said:
Those who follow the way are like unto warriors who fight single-handed with a multitude of foes. They may all go out of the fort in full armor; but among them are some who are faint-hearted, and some who go halfway and beat a retreat, and some who are killed in the affray, and some who come home victorious.
O monks, if you desire to attain enlightenment, you should steadily walk in your way, with a resolute heart, with courage, and should be fearless in whatever environment you may happen to be, and destroy every evil influence that you may come across; for thus you shall reach the goal.

Gautama the Buddha has no leaning toward abstraction, philosophy or metaphysics. He's very practical, down-to-earth practical. He's very scientific. His approach is not that of a thinker; his approach is existential. When he attained and became a buddha, it is said that the god of the gods, Brahma, came to him and asked, "Who is your witness? You declare that you have become a buddha, but who is your witness?" Buddha laughed, touched the earth with his hand, and said, "This earth, this solid earth is my witness."

He is very earthy; he made the earth his witness. He could have said so about the sky, but no; he could have said so about the sun or the moon or the stars, but no. He touched the earth and said, "This solid earth is my witness." His whole approach is like that.

Before we enter into these sutras, his basic steps have to be understood.

Buddha's way is called "the eightfold way." He has divided it into eight parts. Those divisions are arbitrary, just utilitarian. The way is one, it is not really divided. It is divided so that you can understand it easily. This is very fundamental: if you can understand these eight steps or eight divisions of the way, the way will open just in front of you. You are already standing on it, but not aware; your mind is wandering somewhere.

The way is in front of you. So try to understand these eight steps as deeply as possible.

The first is right view.

All these eight steps are concerned with rightness – right view, right intention, right speech, right morality, right livelihood, right effort, right mindfulness, and the eighth, the ultimate, right *samadhi*. The word *right* has to be understood first because the Sanskrit word *samyak* is so meaningful, is so pregnant with meaning that it cannot be translated. *Right* is a very poor translation for it for many reasons.

First, the word *right* immediately gives the idea that it is against the wrong. *Samyak* never gives that idea; *samyak* is not against wrong. Buddha's right is not against wrong because Buddha says wrongs are many, right is one – so how can right be against wrong? Health is one, diseases are many. There are not as many healths as there are diseases, so health cannot be against the diseases – otherwise there would be so many healths. Somebody is suffering from TB and then he becomes healthy, somebody is suffering from cancer and he becomes healthy, and somebody is suffering from flu and he becomes healthy. These three healths are not three healths. The diseases were different, but health is one, and one cannot be against the many.

Exactly the same is true about right and wrong. Right is one. Wrongs are millions. You can go on inventing wrongs, but right cannot be invented; it does not depend on you. Right is a state of affairs where you are in tune with the whole. That is the meaning of health too: when you are in tune with the whole you are healthy. The music flows between you and the whole, there is no obstruction. You feel a well-being, there is no noise, everything is in harmony. When the individual is in tune with the universal, right exists, health exists. When you fall out of tune, then so many wrongs arise there is no limit to them, they are endless. And you can invent new wrongs.

Humanity has invented many new diseases which were not prevalent before. In the old scriptures, ayurvedic scriptures, many diseases are not mentioned. People think they are not mentioned because ayurveda was not enough of a science yet, so it could not diagnose those diseases. That is not true. Ayurveda became a perfect science but those diseases were not in existence, so how could you diagnose a disease which didn't exist? They were nonexistential. There were a few diseases which existed only for rich people, very rich people. They were called royal diseases. Tuberculosis was called "royal," it was not an ordinary disease. Now the whole world has become royal; now the whole world suffers from richness, affluence. Leisure has made many things available, many new diseases available.

Cancer is a very new disease. It can exist only when the mind is very worried, when worry becomes like a wound. And around that subtle wound in the psyche arises a disease in the body corresponding to it. That's what cancer is, that's why cancer seems to be incurable. There is no way to cure it from the body side. It can be cured only from the mind side because basically it arises there.

Each age has its own diseases, each age has its own vices, and each age invents its own sins. But virtue is ageless, timeless. Sainthood has nothing to do with any age, time period. It is not historical – it is existential.

Buddha says right is that which is not your invention. It is already there. If you go away from it you are wrong, if you come close to it you are right. The closer you are, the more right you are. One day when you are exactly home, you are perfectly right. *Samyak* and *samadhi* both come from the same root *sam*. *Samyak* is the step toward *samadhi*. If you don't understand *samyak*, you will not be able to understand *samadhi*.

So seven steps ultimately lead to the final step. *Samadhi* means now everything has fallen in tune with existence; not a flaw exists, the music is utterly perfect. But there is no better word in English than *right*, so you have to understand it. *Right* in the Buddhist meaning of the term means balanced, centered, grounded, harmonious, tranquil – all these things. But the basic thing can be understood even if there is no synonymous term in English to translate it.

Remember, it has nothing to do with wrong. Wrong is a human invention, right is divine. Right is not something that you have to do: You were born right. Wrong is something that you have to do; you were not born wrong. Every child is born in harmony. That's why children are so beautiful. Have you ever seen a baby who is ugly? It doesn't happen. All babies are beautiful, but not all grown-ups are beautiful. So something somewhere must have gone wrong – because all babies are beautiful. They have a grace, a tremendous elegance which has nothing to do with any practice because they have no time to practice anything. They come into the world without any rehearsal. They are just there: so happy, so silent, so harmonious. Such grace surrounds them – as if the whole existence is protective toward them. Then by and by, they learn the ways of man and become wrong. Then ugliness appears. Then beautiful eyes can become horrible; then a beautiful face can become criminal; then a beautiful body can lose all grace. Then a beautiful intelligence... Every child is born intelligent; that's how things are. An intelligent child can become stupid, mediocre. These are human achievements.

Wrong is a human achievement, right is divine. You are not to do anything for it, you have only to stop all that you have been doing to create it. And when there is right, you don't feel you are right. That's why, I repeat again, it is not against wrong. When you are in the right you are simply natural. You don't have any feeling of being righteous, you don't have any feeling that you are a great saint. If you have that feeling then you are still wrong somewhere – because it is a jarring note, it does not allow the music to flow.

Right means balanced, non-tense, centered. You are not a stranger in existence; that's what right means: you are at home, this existence is your family; you are not an alien. In the West, and in the East too, the modern mind continuously talks and thinks about alienation, that man has become an outsider, that man has become a stranger, that we seem to be just like accidents on earth. Existentialists have the right word for it: they say we have been thrown here. Thrown, dumped, expelled, punished – that this existence is against us. You can prove it: so many diseases – death is there, so many frustrations, failures. People go on saying man proposes and God disposes.

So of course man is doomed, doomed from the very beginning, is born with great desires and without any possibility of any fulfillment, ever. How can this existence be your home? It can't be your family.

Right is when you start feeling that you are at home. Nothing is alien, nothing is strange.

Buddha says if you *are*, you are wrong – because whenever you are, you are separate from existence. When you are not, you are right. Listen to this paradox – it is one of the most beautiful paradoxes. Buddha says when you are, you are wrong. Your *being* is wrong. The very separation, that "I am," creates a barrier. Then you don't melt, then you become frozen, then you are like an ice cube: dead, closed. Then you have a boundary.

When you start melting and you start feeling, "Existence is, and I am just a part," and you relax, and there is a let-go – you disappear. Then you are right. When you are not, you are right.

These eight steps are just indicators, step-by-step, of how to come to that tremendous courage, that ultimate courage where you take the quantum leap and you simply disappear. When the self disappears, the universal self arises.

The first is right view.

Buddha says look at things without any opinion, otherwise you never look at reality. Look at things without any philosophy, without any prejudice, without any dogma, creed, scripture. Just look. Look at things as they are. Be factual, don't create a fiction. If you are looking for something with a prejudice you will find it. That is the trouble: if you are already full of a belief you will find it because the mind is so creative, so imaginative, so capable of auto-hypnosis, that whatsoever it believes it can create. Buddha says go into reality without any belief. Belief is the barrier.

You must have seen it. If you are born a Hindu – that means if you are being conditioned from your childhood by Hindus, you are a victim of Hinduism. The same applies to Mohammedans and Christians, Jews, Jainas, communists: the whole humanity is a victim of this school or that, of this prejudice or that, of this belief or that. If you are born a Hindu, have been conditioned in certain dogmas and you start meditating, you will start seeing visions of Krishna, Rama. It depends on what you have been taught, what has been enforced and engraved in your mind – but Christ will never come to you. Christ comes to a Christian, Buddha comes to a Buddhist, Mahavira comes to a Jaina. Mohammed can never come to a Jaina; it is impossible. Even to conceive the idea is impossible. Even in a dream, Mohammed will not come to a Jaina. What is happening? Are these Buddhas, Mahaviras, Christs, really coming, or is your own belief creating them? Your own belief is creating them.

Nobody comes to a communist. His belief is that all religion is nonsense, an opium for the people, a dangerous poison to be got rid of as soon as possible. Then nobody comes. It depends on you. If you have a belief, that very belief becomes a dream; and if you are very, very sensitive, receptive, that dream can look more real than the reality. In fact this happens every day, even to nonreligious people. You dream in the night and when you dream the dream looks so real. And you have dreamed your whole life and every morning you cancel it as unreal. But again next night you dream, and in the dream again it seems real.

The dreaming faculty lives on belief. If you have a strong belief then the dreaming faculty joins with the belief, pours its energy into the belief, makes the belief a reality, and you start having visions. Buddha is not in favor of any visions because he says: "That which is, needs no visions. It needs simply clarity to see." Your mind need not have any dreams, great dreams of great saints, heaven and hell; these are all your creations.

Right view is having no prejudice, having no belief, having no opinion whatsoever. Difficult; Buddha's path is arduous, he demands too much. It almost seems to be a superhuman feat. But it is possible – and that is the only way toward truth.

If you have any opinion you will impose your opinion on the truth. You do it every day. If you come to me with the opinion: "This man is good," you will go convinced that this man is good; if you come with the opinion: "This man is bad," you will go convinced that this man is bad. Your belief will always find that which it wants to find. Belief is very selective.

I have heard...

The boy had been brought into court again charged with stealing auto hubcaps. The magistrate determined to appeal to his father: "See here," said the judge. "This boy of yours has been in this court charged with theft many times, and I am tired of seeing him here."

"I don't blame you, Judge," said the father. "I am just as tired of seeing him here as you are."

"Then why don't you teach him how to act? Show him the right way and he would not be coming here."

"I have already shown him the right way," said the father, "but he just does not seem to have any talent for learning. He always gets caught!"

Now, the right way is different for the judge and for the father. The father himself is a thief. He also wants the boy to learn the right way so that he is never caught again. But his right way is *his* right way.

For a holiday, Mullevy decided to go to Switzerland to fulfill a life-long dream and climb the Matterhorn. He hired a guide, and just as they neared the top the men were caught in a snowslide.

Three hours later a Saint Bernard plowed through to them, a keg of brandy tied under his chin.

"Hooray!" shouted the guide. "Here comes man's best friend."

"Ah," said Mullevy. "And look at the size of the dog that is bringing it!"

Now, for one the dog is the greatest friend of humanity, for the other it is the bottle that he is bringing.

"Ah," said Mullevy. "And look at the size of the dog that is bringing it!"

It depends on how you look at things. You can look at the same thing, and you may not be seeing the same thing. If you are listening to me in trust, you listen differently. If you are listening to me with disbelief, you listen to me differently. If you are listening as a disciple, you listen differently. If you are listening just as an outsider, a visitor – just by the way, may have come with a friend – you listen differently. What I say is the same, but how you interpret it will depend on you. Right listening will be that you listen as nobody: neither for nor against, with no prejudice – just listening. If you can see things without any idea in the mind, then Buddha says it is right view.

Right view needs no conceptualization. That's why Buddha says, "Don't ask me any theoretical question." He does not say anything about God. Not that God is not – he does not say anything about it because it is pointless to create a theory. He tries to open your eyes to it. He says to know the truth, you need eyes – just as you cannot teach a blind man what light is like, howsoever hard you try. You cannot teach a blind man anything about the light. Of course, you can teach as much as you want and he may learn all the information that you deliver to him, but still in reality he will not be able to conceive what light is. He cannot conceive.

It happened…

A blind man was brought to Buddha. He was passing through the village, and the people of the village were tired of the blind man because he was very logical and very philosophical. He was so argumentative that he used to prove that the light exists not.

He would say, "You just bring it, I would like to touch it"; or "You bring it so I can taste it"; or "You bring it, at least let me smell it"; or "You bring it and beat it like a drum so I can hear it." Of course, you cannot beat light like a drum, and you cannot taste it, and you cannot smell it, and you cannot touch it.

The blind man would laugh, laugh with victory, and he would say, "You fools! You are trying to prove something to me which is not. I have got four senses. Prove it. I am ready, I am open."

They could not prove it, so the blind man started thinking that they were just trying to befool him about this light: "The whole business is just a deception, a fraud. In fact, they want to prove that I am blind. They are insulting me. I am not blind because light doesn't exist. So what is the point? If light doesn't exist, eyes need not be there. Eyes are just a fiction." He would say, "You are all blind, but you are dreaming about something that doesn't exist."

They brought the man to Buddha, and Buddha said, "Don't bring him to me. But I know a physician; this man needs no conviction, he needs to see the light. He needs eyes. He needs treatment, he needs no theory about it. But I know a physician."

Buddha had a beautiful, very learned physician. He was given to him by an emperor, to look after Buddha's body. The blind man was taken to the physician. He treated him, and within six months he was able to see.

By that time Buddha had moved to another town. The man came running and dancing. He was ecstatic; He fell at Buddha's feet and said, "You have convinced me."

Buddha said, "Don't talk nonsense. I have not done anything. Your eyes have convinced you, and there is no other way."

Buddha used to say, "I am not a philosopher, I am a physician. I would like to treat your inner eyes, and the first step is right view." Right view really means a mind without views. If you have any view, it is a wrong view. If you don't have any views, then you are simply open, clear. Then your window is completely open, you don't have any hindrance. Whatsoever is available you will be able to see. Buddha never says anything about that which you will see; he only talks about how to treat your blindness, how to get out of your blindness.

Mulla Nasruddin's son, studying political science, asked his father, "Dad, what is a traitor in politics?"

"Any man who leaves our party," said the Mulla, "and goes over to the other one, is a traitor."

"Well, what about a man who leaves his party and comes over to yours?" asked the young man.

"He would be a convert, son," said Nasruddin, "a real convert."

Now, when somebody goes from your party to another party he is a traitor, and when somebody comes from the other party to yours he is a convert. When a Hindu becomes a Christian, to Hindus he is a traitor, to Christians he is a convert; and when a Christian becomes a Hindu, they welcome him: his understanding is back, he has realized what truth is. But to Christians, he is a traitor.

If you live with views, you cannot see the truth of anything. Your view always comes as a barrier. It obstructs, it distorts, it does not allow you to see things as they are. "God" is that which is. To know the real you need not have any views. In fact, if you really want to know the real, you have to drop views. That is the first renunciation Buddha teaches: Drop all views, and right view will arise. All views are wrong views. The Hindu, the Christian, the Buddhist: all views are wrong views. A man without views, a man without opinion, a man with not a thought to cling to, a man who is just a mirror, reflects reality.

The woman heard the preacher go through the commandments, and after every commandment she joined the rest of the audience in shouting, "Amen!"

When he came to the commandment: Thou shalt not commit adultery, she said, "Now he is beginning to meddle."

Something looks absolutely right when it fits with you – as if you are the touchstone of truth, as if you are the criterion of truth. The moment it is not fitting with you it is wrong. This is a wrong approach, and if you have this approach you will never arrive at that which is real. If something is not fitting with you, then don't be in a hurry to settle the matter – that it must be wrong because it doesn't fit with you. It need not fit with you. Existence has no obligation to fit with you. Reality has no obligation to fit with you. If it is not fitting with you, then a man of right understanding will change himself rather than deny the reality.

So whenever it hurts, whenever reality hurts and whenever you feel that you are unfit, it is you who are unfit, not the reality. A man who has no views will never find that there is any conflict between him and the reality. He will always fit with the reality and reality will fit with him – just like a glove fits on the hand. This is right view.

The second step is right intention.

We live result-oriented, we live goal-oriented, we live with intention, with desire: "Things should be like this, then I will be happy. If they are not like this, then I'm going to be unhappy." That's why we are so frustrated. Buddha says your frustration comes from your intentions. Your intentions seem to be going against reality, then you are frustrated.

Drop intentions, drop desires, and just move moment to moment with reality wherever it leads. Become like driftwood, just float with the stream and you will never be frustrated. Frustration comes whenever there is conflict between you and the real. And remember, the real is going to win; you cannot win against the real. Nobody can win against existence; that's not possible, that doesn't happen. You can win only with it. Whenever you succeed, remember: somehow, accidentally, you must have been with existence. All success simply means this: that unknowingly you must have stepped with existence, and that's why you have succeeded. Failure means that unknowingly you must have stepped against it. Failure is an indication, success is an indication.

A man who has learned this drops all his intentions. He has no private desires. He says exactly what Jesus says on the cross: "Thy Kingdom come, thy will be done." He surrenders. Buddha has no concept of God. His approach is more scientific than Jesus'. Jesus is more poetic. "God" is poetry, a beautiful poetry. Buddha is not a poet, he's very mathematical. He says, "There is no need to talk about God. Only one thing can be understood: drop intentions." When you don't have any intentions, you have the right intention. You have to remember this paradox in all the eight steps.

Right intention means no intention on your part. Then the

universe flows through you. Then the universe goes on fulfilling its intention through you. You become a vehicle.

"Please," the little man prayed, "you know me. I am always praying to you and yet I have had nothing but bad luck, misery, sickness and despair all my life. And look at the butcher next door. He's never prayed in his life and yet he has nothing but prosperity, health and joy. How come a believer like me is always in trouble and he is always doing good?"

Suddenly a big booming voice sounded in his ear, "Because the butcher is not always bugging me, that's why!"

Now, your prayer can be a "bugging." What are your prayers? – your prayers are your intentions, the desires that you would like fulfilled. What are your prayers? – your prayers are always against God. Look at the absurdity: you are praying to God, and the prayer is basically against God – because if it is not against God then there is no point in praying. You are ill; if you trust God that means you know that God wants you to be ill. This is how you are at this moment. This is what God's will is – you accept it. Then your prayer is only of gratitude. You don't beg for anything, you simply thank him: "Thank you for making me ill. Thank you because I know it must be needed. I may not understand, but I know you give me whatsoever is needed, whenever it is needed." You don't go to the temple or the church or the mosque and ask for health. If you ask, you are going against God. That which has happened already cannot happen against the will of the whole, whatsoever it is. If it is a dark night, then you must be in need of a dark night.

A Sufi mystic used to say in his prayer every day, "Thank you, my lord – you always give me whatsoever is needed." His disciples were very much annoyed by this because they had been with him many times when he was poor, hungry, nowhere to rest in the night. And still he would pray to God five times a day, and he would say, "Thank you. How grateful I am – whatsoever I need you always give me."

One day it was too much. For three days they had been hungry; nobody had even offered them food. For three days they had been sleeping under the trees, outside a town, and the town was very antagonistic and people were ready to kill them. The morning of the fourth day the mystic was praying again and he was saying, "Thank you. Whatsoever I need you always give me."

One disciple could not contain himself. He said, "Stop all this nonsense. There is a limit to everything. What are you thanking God for? For three days we have been hungry, thirsty, no shelter. Nights are cold and we are getting frozen and you are thanking! For what! What has he given you?"

The mystic laughed and said, "For these three days I needed to be hungry, needed to be without any shelter. It was part of my growth. These three days have done me tremendous good, they have been a great blessing. That's what was needed, and he always gives whatsoever is needed."

In fact, whatsoever he gives is whatsoever is needed. But when you pray, your prayer is always "bugging." You are complaining, you are grumpy, grouchy. You are saying, "Nothing is right, everything is wrong. Put it right, otherwise I will start disbelieving in you; otherwise I am going to become an atheist. If you are, then do these things. If you are not, then I am finished, I am not going to pray anymore."

Is your prayer a sort of bribery? Do you praise him just to persuade him to fulfill your desires? Buddha says the real religious person has no intention of his own – and that is the right intention. He does not live a private life, he does not live a separate life. He moves with the universe, he's one with the universe. He has no separate goal, no separate destiny. The destiny of the whole is his destiny. Then the man becomes holy.

The man who has no intention, of course lives moment to moment. He cannot project into the future. He responds accordingly to whatsoever is needed in this moment. He is spontaneous and he is responsible. When I use the word *responsible* I use it in its original sense. He is response-able; he can respond, and he can respond totally because he has no intention of his own. He can simply say, "Yes," and he can say it totally. He will not hold back anything. His yes will not be a reluctant yes. It will be like a flower blooming, releasing its fragrance to existence.

The man of right intention lives a life without any tension. Look at the word *intention*; it is made of *tension*. All intention will create tension. It is made of two words, *in* and *tension*. When your inner reality is tense, it is in tension. When your inner reality is relaxed and there is no tension – you are not going anywhere, you are not chasing anything, you are not after anything, you are just here and now, relaxed – that state of no tension or no intention is what Buddha calls right intention. Then suddenly the universe starts flowing through you. You become like a hollow bamboo. You become a flute.

The third is right speech.

Buddha says, "Say only that which is. Never move into fictions – only say that which is true and real." Only say that which you have experienced; never talk about others' experiences. If you have not known God, please don't say anything about God – because whatsoever you say will be a falsification, will be sacrilege, will be a sin because whatsoever you say will be wrong. If you have known God, only then; otherwise not. The world will be more beautiful, less confused, if Buddha's dictum is listened to: right speech. He says: "Say only that which you have experienced, which is grounded in your experience, rooted in your experience. Never say anything else."

Just think about it, how many things we go on saying which we have never experienced, which we don't know anything about. We may have heard, we may have read, but that doesn't make you capable of uttering anything. It is all borrowed, and the borrowed is never the truth. Say only that which is. Be factual, not fictitious.

Buddha has not created any mythology. His statements are bare of all poetry and fiction, all ornaments. He never decorates his statements; they are nude, they don't have any dressing. He says if you start playing with fictions, there is no end. And the many religions in the world are ninety-nine percent fiction. Hindus say there is one hell, one heaven. Jainas say there are seven hells and seven heavens. There was a teacher, Gosala, in the days of Mahavira. Somebody asked him, "What do you say? – Because Hindus believe in only one heaven, one hell. And the disciples of Mahavira say that Hindus have not gone deep enough, but their master has gone deeper and he says there are seven hells and seven heavens."

Gosala laughed. He said, "That is nothing! I know there are seven hundred hells and seven hundred heavens."

Now, you can go on playing; there is no end to it, and there is no need to prove it. In the name of religion, fictions can continue. All sorts of foolish things can be said in the name of religion. There is no way to judge whether they are true or not. There is no way to make them valid or invalid: you cannot prove, you cannot disprove. That's why all sorts of nonsense continues. There are three hundred religions on the earth and every religion has its own fiction. They are all fictitious. If they are just fictitious, then there is no problem. Then it is understood; if you want to enjoy a fiction, then enjoy.

Do you know that Krishnamurti goes on reading detective fictions? He never reads the Gita, he never reads the Koran, he never reads the Bible. He goes on reading detective novels. Nobody has asked him why, and he has never answered, but I know why – because it is all the same. Whether you read a detective novel, or you read the Bible or the Koran, makes no difference. There are religious detective novels, there are secular detective novels. You may be surprised that a man of the qualities of Krishnamurti should read detective novels, but it is very indicative. He's simply saying that everything is a fiction, and if you want to read a detective novel then why not read a twentieth-century detective novel? Why go backward and read rotten, primitive things? Why not the new, the latest model?

Buddha says right speech means don't be fictitious, don't be esoteric. Just be absolutely honest and authentic. There were many times when questions were asked of Buddha and he would remain quiet, he would not answer. He would say, "This is not needed for your spiritual growth. This is unnecessary."

Somebody would ask, "Who created the world?"

He would say, "Don't ask – because if *A* created or *B* created or *C* created, what difference does it make to you? Or if nobody created it and it has been there without anybody's making it, creating it, what difference does it make? Just ask something real, empirical. Ask something which can be of some help to you. Don't ask foolish questions."

Now see: he says, "These questions – foolish!" because the

answers won't help you in any way to grow. There are people who go on fighting about these things. Somebody says God created the world in six days. Somebody else says he is still creating, the creation continues, it has never been finished, the full point has not come yet. And they go on fighting and quarreling. It seems they want to fight, so any excuse will do. These are beautiful excuses because there is no way to end them: you can go on and on and on, ad infinitum. Then there are people who ask, "Who created God?" Now they are also asking a pertinent question.

These questions are irrelevant and Buddha says, only say that which you know, and only say that which is helpful, and only say that which is beneficial. Don't be frivolous and don't be fictitious. Be sincere in your utterances.

It happened...

The local political leader was invited to speak to the inmates of a mental asylum. The politician had begun his talk and had been going for about ten minutes when a fellow in the back stood up and yelled, "You don't know what you are talking about! Besides, you are talking too much. Why don't you shut up and sit down!"

"I will wait a minute until you put that man out," the politician said to the superintendent.

"Put him out?" the superintendent asked. "Certainly not! That poor man has been here for eight years and that is the first time he has ever said anything that made any sense, sir."

Have you listened to your politicians' speeches? They go on talking and talking without saying a single thing. That's what diplomacy is: to go on saying things without saying anything, otherwise you will be caught. So people go on roundabout and roundabout. In the end you cannot have any conclusion. There is no conclusion: they simply play with words. Words have their own charm, and if you watch you will be able to see. Sometimes you say a word, then that word leads to another word – the words have their own charm – then you go to the other word that leads you into another word, and finally you end up somewhere you had never wanted to go. Words have their own charm, their own magic. Ask the novelists, poets: they know about it. The novelist starts a story, but it never ends according to him. By and by, the characters start asserting their own personalities. By and by, the words weave in certain ways and lead into certain directions. All great novelists have known it and have said, "It is so – we start the novel but we never end it. It ends in its own way."

Try to write a story. First you plan it in the mind, you have a bare blueprint when you start. The moment you start, things start happening which you never intended. Then you are led astray and astray, and the novel or the story ends somewhere you had not even dreamed about. What happens? Words have a magic of their own. One word leads to another, and one can go on and on.

Buddha says, "Be mindful." Don't be led astray by words. Say that which you really want to say, don't be frivolous.

Just the other night Mrs. Mulla Nasruddin came to me. She said, "Do you know? I can stand at the door and by just looking at my husband's face I can tell whether he is lying or not."

I was surprised. I said, "How on earth can you do that?"

She said, "If his lips are moving, he's lying."

Mulla Nasruddin is a politician. If his lips are moving, that's enough. Then he must be lying. What else can he do?

Remember one thing: you have to be careful about what you take in, and you have to be careful about what you put out. Only then can you have a life which is centered. People are careless: they go on stuffing themselves with whatsoever they find. Anything. They go on stuffing – in the body, and in the mind too. Be careful.

If your neighbor comes and starts gossiping, you listen very attentively. If the neighbor throws some rubbish in your garden you will start fighting, but if he throws some rubbish in your head, you are perfectly welcoming of it. You don't see that once somebody has been allowed to put rubbish in your head, what will you do with it? Sooner or later it will come through your mouth and enter somebody else's head. You cannot keep it inside. That's why people have so much difficulty in keeping a secret. Tell somebody not to tell anybody anything, and you can be certain he will tell. Tell your wife, "This is very secret, don't tell anybody," and you can be certain that within twenty-four hours the whole town will know. Of course she will also say the same thing when she tells the story to the servant: "Don't say this to anybody, it is very secret." And he will say the same to his wife, and it will go on and on and on. Within twenty-four hours you will see the whole town knows about it. There is no better way to spread a thing around; just go on telling people, "Don't say it to anybody." It is certain they will have to say it because whenever there is a secret it becomes difficult to keep it inside. It wants to come out.

Don't go on taking anything in, and don't go on throwing anything out on people. If you are too full of rubbish, go to the riverbank, go to the forest, and just talk to the trees. There will be no harm because they don't listen. You can talk, you can unburden yourself, you can unwind and come back. But don't do that to human beings – they are already too burdened.

Buddha says right speech means very sincere speech.

The Bible says, "In the beginning was the word – and then everything came in." Buddha says if you drop the word, there will be reality – the beginning. If you become silent, then whatsoever you say will have significance.

Have you watched it? If you fast for one day, the next day your hunger has a different passion to it. If you fast, then you have fresh hunger arising in you. If you go on stuffing yourself every day, continuously, and never fast, you completely forget the language of hunger – the freshness, the beauty, the aliveness of hunger. Fast one day, and next day you will have fresh hunger arising, and next day you will have a different sense of taste. The food may be the same, but it will become tasteful because it is hunger that makes it tasteful.

The same happens with words. Keep silent, and then say something and you will see: that something has power in it. Silence is like a fast, it brings life to your words. And in this world only those people who have kept themselves in deep silence have been of tremendous import, and their words have been of lasting eternal value.

Buddha was silent for many months, Mahavira was silent for twelve years. Whenever Jesus would feel that he was tired he would go to the desert and he would say to his disciples, "Leave me. Leave me alone." He would be in silence for forty days, and then he would come back. Then his words would have a value to them: each word would be like a diamond.

If you really want that your words should have value, then learn silence. Keep more and more silent, then one day you will know what right speech is.

The fourth step is right morality.

Buddha says the morality that comes from without is not the right morality. The morality that comes from within is the right morality. All that we think is moral is not really moral. It is just conditioned by the society. You have been taught to behave in a certain way, so you behave in a certain way – but that behavior is the behavior of a slave. It is not that of a free man, it is not out of freedom. And how is morality possible out of slavery?

Buddha says morality is possible only when you are totally free, without any conditioning. It is not that you have to do certain things, not that it is your duty, not that you have to follow a certain rule – but that you have become conscious, you have become aware. And out of that awareness you behave in a certain way. Awareness is right morality, unawareness is wrong morality.

You can be truthful – you may not be a thief, and you may not fool around with others' wives, and you may not be a deceiver – but if it is just because society has forced these things on you, you are not moral. You may be a good citizen, but morality is a greater thing; it is not so cheap. You may be good for the society; society does not want anything more than that. If you don't create any trouble – enough; if you don't create any mischief – enough, you are a good citizen. But to be moral means something more than being a good citizen. It means being a good man. It has nothing to do with society; it has something to do with your inner integrity.

Buddha says, "Become more conscious. Live through consciousness rather than living through conscience."

Conscience is made by the society. If you are born in a Jaina family you will not eat meat, but it does not mean that you are nonviolent. How can you be nonviolent just by not eating meat? Just because from your very childhood you have been taught not to eat meat and it has become nauseating. The Jaina cannot even look at meat; even seeing meat he starts feeling nauseous, he starts feeling sick.

When I was a child, in my home even tomatoes were not allowed. I asked my mother, "Why are tomatoes not allowed?" She said, "They look like meat. One starts feeling sick if one looks at tomatoes."

Tomatoes, poor tomatoes – you cannot find more innocent people than tomatoes. But I did not taste tomatoes for a long time in my childhood. Only when I went to a hostel, only then did I gather courage to eat tomatoes. And the first day I ate them, I could not sleep the whole night. My whole stomach was rumbling, and I was afraid I had committed a great sin. In the morning I vomited – just a conditioning.

The French language has only one word for both consciousness and conscience. That is right; Buddha would have agreed with it. It has only one word for both conscience and consciousness. Buddha also says, "Your consciousness should be your conscience. You should become more aware. You should start seeing more things as they are, and then a nonviolence will arise." It is stupid to kill animals just for your food. It is not sin; it is stupid. It has nothing to do with sin. You are not going to be thrown into hellfire.

I have heard…

A rich man died, a miser – he must have been a *marwari*. They are the Indian Jews. He died. He told his wife, "No need to put any clothes on me because I know where I'm going – I am going to the hot place. I have committed many sins, so I am going to hell. There is no need for clothes, and clothes are costly, and costs are rising higher and higher every day. Keep them. They will be useful for our children." So the wife burned him without clothes.

The next night, in the middle of the night, somebody knocked on the door. So she opened the door. The ghost of her husband was there, and he said, "Give me my woolen clothes!"

"And what is the matter with you?"

He said, "Now those old days are gone. They have air-conditioned hell. I'm shivering!"

Forget all that nonsense – that in hell you will suffer. So many politicians are there, so many scientists are there. It is natural that they have air-conditioned it by now.

Buddha says you should be moral not because of fear, but because of understanding. And you should not be moral because of greed. Your ordinary religions are based on fear and greed – just the ordinary trick of reward and punishment. Just as you do with your children, your religions have been doing with you: if you do this you will go to heaven, if you do this you will go to hell – fear and greed. They are playing on human fear and greed, and they say that one should not be afraid, and one should not be greedy, and their whole structure is based on the same fear and greed.

Buddha says, "Have no fear and have no greed. Just look into things, and out of your awareness responsibility arises." You start behaving gracefully. You don't do foolish things, that's all.

If you are doing things out of fear, you will never be able to be totally moral because deep down, beyond the fear, you will know – and the desire to do the opposite, to be the opposite, will remain there.

It happened...

During a religious meeting an attractive young widow leaned too far over the balcony and fell, but her dress caught on a chandelier and held her suspended in mid air. The preacher, of course, immediately noticed the woman's predicament and called out to his congregation, "The first person who looks up there is in danger of being punished with blindness."

Mulla Nasruddin, who was in the congregation, whispered to the man next to him, "I think I will risk one eye."

An enforced morality cannot be total; one is always willing to risk one eye, at least. Who knows? – it may be true, it may not be true.

The so-called moral people will always need holidays because it will be tiring. It is based on conflict: one part of your being says something and morality says something else. You are divided, you are split. Because of this split the whole of humanity is a little schizophrenic – one part going south, one part going north. You are always in an ambiguity, and you are always undecided, wavering – where to go? What to do? Your instincts are saying something and your conditioning is saying just the opposite. You can enforce anything upon yourself, but really it will never be part of you.

An egoist can be told by the society to become humble, and he can try to become humble. But an egoist is an egoist: now humility will hide his ego.

I have heard...

A rabbi addressed his congregation. They were very moved by his sermon and one man stood up and said, "I'm Joe Smith. I came to this land without a cent. Now I am worth five million, but when I hear your words, I am nothing."

Another man stood up and said, "I started out without a cent, too. Now I am worth ten million, but when I hear your words, Rabbi, I am nothing, absolutely nothing.

Then another man rose and said, "I work for the post office. I make eighty dollars a week, but when I hear your words I am nothing, utterly nothing."

And the first millionaire said to the second, "Look who wants to be nothing."

Just a postman, trying to become nothing? Nothingness needs that you first become a millionaire. That's why in India, such a religious country, not even once has a simple person been declared an avatar, a *tirthankara*. No, not yet; it has not happened because if you are poor, what will you renounce? All the twenty-four *tirthankaras* of the Jainas come from royal families, sons of kings. Buddha himself comes from a royal family; Rama, Krishna – everybody comes from a royal family.

Why? Why not Kabir? Why not Farid? Why not Dadu? Nothing is lacking. Only one thing is missing: they don't have anything to renounce. Look who is trying to be nothing! First you must *have*; to renounce you must have much, you need much, you have to have. A simple person is not really a humble person, only an egoist is a humble person. Then he tries, through his humbleness, to say that he is the greatest humble person in the world. But the same thing continues in a different garb.

Your morality never transforms you. So Buddha says right morality is from within, from awareness – not out of fear, not out of greed.

The fifth step is right livelihood.

Buddha says life should be simple, not complex. Life should be based on needs, not on desires. Needs are perfectly okay: you need food, you need clothes, you need shelter, you need love, you need relationships. Perfectly good, nothing wrong in it, needs can be fulfilled. Desires are basically unfulfillable. Desires create complexity. They create complexity because they can never be fulfilled. You go on and on working hard for them, and they remain unfulfilled and you remain empty.

The first thing about livelihood is: it should be based on needs, not on desires. Then a very small quantity of things is enough.

Secondly: it should not be violent. You should not do something just because you can get some money out of it. You can kill somebody and get some money, you can be a butcher and you can make your livelihood, but that is inhuman – and very unconscious. Better ways are possible. One should be creative in one's livelihood, one should not be destructive.

The businessmen were discussing a compatriot.

"He used to work for me," said the first one. "I wouldn't trust him with my money. He'd lie, steal, cheat; anything for a buck."

"How do you know him so well?"

"How?" said the first. "I taught him everything he knows."

One should be a little more alert. Money is not all, and one should not destroy one's own life just in accumulating money. Poverty can be tremendously beautiful. If you are just living by your needs, poverty can be a tremendous contentment. In fact, you will never find rich people contented. Sometimes you can come across a beggar with a contented face, but never a millionaire.

The more you chase, the more you feel the horizon is faraway. The faster you run, the closer you come to your death, but never to any fulfillment. The shadow of death, the fear of death, the fear that you are going to miss again, destroys all contentment.

The sixth is right effort.

Buddha says, "Never strain and never be lazy. One has to balance between the two. Then there is right effort." Effort that is basically effortless.

Have you seen children playing? They play, but there is no

effort, there is no strain. They enjoy it. Have you seen a painter painting, a poet writing his poetry, a musician playing on his instrument – or a dancer? There is no effort. If there is effort then the dancer is not a real dancer. Then the dancer is just trying to earn something out of it. Then he is result-oriented, goal-oriented. Then the activity itself, the dance itself, is not his joy.

When Buddha says right effort, it means everything that you do should be a joy unto itself. It should be an intrinsic value. It should be playful.

And right mindfulness is the seventh step.

Mindfulness is Buddha's word for meditation. By mindfulness he means you should always remain alert, watchful. You should always remain present. Not a single thing should be done in a sort of sleepy state of mind. You should not move like a somnambulist; you should move with a sharp consciousness.

Buddha used to say, "Not even your breath should be allowed to go in and out without your consciousness." He said to his monks, "Always go on watching your breath coming in, the breath going out. If you move, go on watching your feet moving. If you are talking, be watchful. If you are listening, be watchful. If you are eating, be watchful. Never allow any act to be done without awareness, and then nothing else is needed." This awareness will spread all over your life; it will be a twenty-four-hour thing. There is no need to keep separate hours for meditation. Buddha says meditation cannot be separate from life; it has to spread and mix with life, it has to be one with life.

And the eighth, the last step, is right *samadhi* – when you are totally absorbed into the center of existence.

These seven steps will bring you to it, but still he says: right *samadhi*. Does that mean there is a possibility of a wrong *samadhi* too? Yes, there is a possibility.

If you fall into unconsciousness, if you fall into a coma, that is wrong *samadhi*. It is not right; it should bring you to total awareness, to perfect awareness. You should not fall in a coma, you should not become unconscious.

One can become unconscious. One can go inside so deeply that one can forget the outside. Now look: ordinarily we live outside, we have forgotten the inside. Inside we are unconscious; outside there is a little consciousness. We are out-moving, out-going. Then one day you just stand on your head, you change the whole process: you start forgetting the outside and you start becoming aware inside. A moment comes when you are totally inside and you have forgotten the outside. Buddha says that this is wrong *samadhi*. It is the same man just standing in a reverse posture.

Buddha says right *samadhi* is when, in and out, you are totally aware – not at the cost of the out. In and out, you are aware. Your light of consciousness is burning so bright it fills you with light, it fills your outside also with light. In fact, in right *samadhi* the inner and the outer disappear. There is only light. Right *samadhi* is not inner; right *samadhi* is transcendental to both inner and outer. Right *samadhi* is transcendental to duality, to division.

Now the sutra. This sutra simply says how a sannyasin should be.

> *The Buddha said:*
> *Those who follow the way are like unto warriors who fight single-handed with a multitude of foes. They may all go out of the fort in full armor; but among them are some who are faint-hearted, and some who go halfway and beat a retreat, and some who are killed in the affray, and some who come home victorious.*
> *O monks, if you desire to attain enlightenment, you should steadily walk in your way, with a resolute heart, with courage, and should be fearless in whatever environment you may happen to be, and destroy every evil influence that you may come across; for thus you shall reach the goal.*

These eight steps are the work.

Buddha says there are many types of people: a few are cowards who never go on the way; a few go fully armored but come back as they start feeling difficulties arising; a few go half the way half-heartedly, then return back; a few go a little further but are killed because they could never gather their energy, they could never become integrated, they could be easily destroyed. They were not ready enough to go into the battle – maybe outwardly they were full of armor, maybe outwardly looking very strong, but inwardly hollow, empty. There are only very few who go into the battle, win the battle, and come back home.

That coming back home is what *samadhi* is, and these seven steps before *samadhi* are the battle, the way. Move slowly, otherwise you may be killed.

For example: if a person of false morality goes into the battle he will be killed. You have to be authentically moral. "Authentically moral" means that you have to be moral from within. Those false faces learned from the outside won't help. You will remain hollow inside. And you have to move step-by-step. You cannot jump steps, otherwise those missing gaps will become dangerous.

That's why I have talked about these eight steps, this eightfold path. This sutra is meaningful only if you understand these eight steps. "Coming home" means *samadhi*. That means you have come to the very center of existence.

Let me read it again:

> *Those who follow the way are like unto warriors who fight single-handed with a multitude of foes.*

Foes are many, and you are alone. So you have to be perfectly ready, otherwise you will miss the goal.

> *They may all go out of the fort in full armor; but among them are some who are faint-hearted…*

If you have not lived the right view, right intention, right speech, you will remain faint-hearted. You will remain very weak, a weakling. You will remain impotent.

> *…and some who go halfway and beat a retreat…*

If you have not practiced right morality and right livelihood, this is going to happen: you will go only half way. You will be a runner, an escapist.

> *…and some who are killed in the affray…*

Some who go full-heartedly but are killed. If you have not practiced right effort and right mindfulness, this is going to happen. But there are only a few,

> *...who come home victorious.*

If you have practiced all the seven steps you will come home victorious, you will attain to *samadhi.*

> *...you should steadily walk in your way, with a resolute heart, with courage, and should be fearless in whatever environment you may happen to be, and destroy every evil influence that you may come across; for thus you shall reach the goal.*

Enough for today.

2

PAIN

ACCEPT IT, WELCOME IT, BE WITH IT

Osho,
I have glimpses of how psychological, existential pain is created by the ego. It is homemade, and it can be unmade. But what about physical pain: why is it there? Is it a necessary part of dying? I do not feel I am afraid of death as much as I am afraid of physical pain, senility, old age.

Psychological pain can be dissolved; and only psychological pain can be dissolved. The other pain, the physical pain, is part of life and death; there is no way to dissolve it. But it never creates a problem. Have you ever observed? – the problem is only when you are thinking about it. If you think of old age you become afraid, but old people are not trembling. If you think of illness you become afraid, but when the illness has already happened there is no fear, there is no problem. One accepts it as a fact. The real problem is always psychological. The physical pain is part of life. When you start thinking about it, it is not physical pain at all; it has become psychological. You think about death; there is fear. But when death actually happens there is no fear. Fear is always about something in the future. Fear never exists in the present moment.

If you are going to the front in a war you will be afraid, you will be very apprehensive. You will tremble, you will not be able to sleep, many nightmares will haunt you. But once you are at the front – ask the soldiers – once you are on the front you forget all about it. Bullets may be passing and you can enjoy your lunch; and bombs may be falling and you can play cards.

You can ask Gurudayal. He has been in the war, he has been to the front, he has been a soldier; he knows fear is about the future. Then the problem is not physical because the fear exists in your psychology. When the pain is actual, physical, there is no problem in it.

Reality never comes as a problem; it is only ideas about reality that create the problem.

So the first thing to be understood is, if you can dissolve the psychological pain, there is no problem. Then you start living in the moment. "Psychological" means of the past, of the future – never of the present. Mind never exists in the present. In the present, reality exists, not the mind. Mind exists in the past and the future, and in past and future reality does not exist. In fact, mind and reality never come across each other. They have never seen each other's face. Reality remains unknown to mind, and mind remains unknown to reality.

There is an old fable...

Darkness approached God and said, "Enough is enough! Your sun goes on haunting me, chasing me; I can never rest. Wherever

I go to rest he is there and I have to run away again. And I have not done any wrong to him. This is unjust. I have come to you to get justice."

It was perfectly right; the complaint was true.

And God called the sun and asked the sun, "Why do you go on chasing this poor woman, darkness? What has she done to you?"

The sun said, "I don't know her at all. I have never seen her. Just call her in front of me; only then can I say something. I don't remember ever having done any wrong to her because I don't know her. We are not familiar. Nobody has ever introduced us to each other, we are not even acquainted. I am hearing about this woman, this darkness, for the first time. Call her."

The case remains pending because God could not call darkness before the sun. They cannot exist together, they cannot encounter each other. When darkness is, the sun cannot be; when the sun is, the darkness cannot be.

Exactly the same is the relationship between mind and reality: psychology is the problem, reality is never a problem. You just dissolve your psychological problems – and they are dissolved by dissolving the center of them all, the ego. Once you don't think yourself separate from existence, problems simply evaporate – as dewdrops disappear in the morning when the sun rises, not even leaving a trace behind. They simply disappear.

Physical pain will remain, but again I will insist that it has never been a problem to anybody. If your leg is broken, it is broken. It is not a problem. The problem is only in imagination: "If my leg is broken, then what am I going to do? How am I to avoid, or how am I to behave and live my life so my leg is never broken?" Now, if you become afraid about such things you cannot live because your legs can be broken, your neck can be broken, your eyes can go blind. Anything is possible, millions of things are possible. If you become obsessed with all these problems which are possible... I am not saying they are not possible. They are all possible. Whatsoever has happened to any human being, ever, can happen to you. Cancer can happen, TB can happen, death can happen; everything is possible. Man is vulnerable. You can just go outside on the road and you can be hit by a car.

I am not saying don't go outside on the road. You can sit in a room and the roof can fall. There is no way to save yourself totally and perfectly. You can be lying down on your bed, but do you know ninety-seven percent of people die on a bed? That is the most dangerous place. Avoid it as much as you can; never go to bed. Ninety-seven percent of people die in bed. Even traveling by airplane is not so dangerous; it is more dangerous to be in bed. And remember, more people die in the night – so, remain trembling. Then it is up to you. Then you will not be able to live at all.

Psychological problems are the only problems. You can become paranoid, you can become split, you can become paralyzed because of fear – but this is nothing to do with reality.

You see a blind man walking on the road perfectly well; blindness in itself is not the problem. You can see beggars – their legs broken, their hands gone, and still laughing, still gossiping with each other, still talking about women, making remarks, singing a tune. Just watch life: life is never a problem. Man has tremendous capacity to adjust to the fact, but man has no capacity to adjust to the future. Once you try to protect yourself and secure yourself in the future, then you will be in a turmoil, in a chaos. You will start falling apart. Then there are millions of problems – problems and problems and problems. You cannot even commit suicide because the poison may not be the right poison. In India you cannot rely on anything. They may have mixed something in it; it may not be poison at all. You may take it and you will lie down and you will wait and wait and wait – and death is not coming. Then everything creates a problem.

Mulla Nasruddin was going to commit suicide. He came across an astrologer on the street, and the astrologer said, "Mulla, wait. Let me see your hand."

He said, "What do I have to do now with astrology? I am going to commit suicide. So there is no point; now there is no future."

The astrologer said, "Wait. Let me see whether you can succeed or not."

Future remains. You may not succeed, you may be caught by the police, or you may misfire. There is no way to be certain about the future – not even about death, not even about suicide. What to say about life? Life is such a complex phenomenon, how can you be certain? Everything is possible and nothing is certain. If you become afraid, this is just your psychology. Something has to be done to your mind.

And if you understand me rightly, meditation is nothing but an effort to look at reality without the mind because that is the only way to look at reality. If the mind is there it distorts, it corrupts. Drop the mind and see reality – direct, immediate, face-to-face. And there is no problem. Reality has never created any problem for anybody. I am here, you are also here – I don't see a single problem. If I fall ill, I fall ill. What is there to be worried about? Why make a fuss about it? If I die, I die.

A problem needs space; in the present moment there is no space. Things only happen, there is no time to think about it. You can think about the past because there is distance; you can think about the future, there is distance. In fact, future and past are created just to give us space so that we can worry. And the more space you have, the more worry.

Now in India they are much more worried because they think, "Next life. And... And..." ad infinitum: "What is going to happen in the next life?" A person is doing something and thinks not only about the consequences that are going to happen here now, he thinks, "What karma am I going to gather for my future life?" Now he will become even more worried; he has more space. How is he going to fill that space? – he will fill it with more and more problems. Worry is a way to fill the empty space of the future.

The questioner says, "I have glimpses of how psychological, existential pain is created by ego. It is homemade, and it can be unmade." Just understanding it intellectually won't help; you have to do it. Do it, and then the next question will disappear. Do it, and then you will find there is not any problem left.

"But what about physical pain?" Now this is how problems arise. Intellectually you have understood one thing, but that doesn't make any sense. The next question immediately brings your reality to the surface: you have not understood.

It is as if a blind man goes on groping with his stick; he finds his path by it. And then we say, "Your eyes can be cured, but then you will have to drop your walking stick. It is not needed." The blind man will say, "I can understand that my eyes can be cured, but how can I walk without my stick?"

Now, intellectually he has understood that eyes can be cured, but existentially, experientially, he has not understood it – otherwise the next question wouldn't arise.

Sometimes people come to me and they ask one question, and I say, "Go on, ask the next two" – because one question may not show the reality. People may be just showing their intellectual understanding. But with the next question they are bound to be caught. They are bound to be because with the next question, immediately they will miss.

The first part of the question is perfect, but you have got the point only through the mind. It is not yet chewed well, it is not yet digested. It has not become blood, bones, marrow. It is not yet part of your existence. Otherwise you can never ask, "What about the physical pain?" The very question is psychological. Physical pain is not a problem – when it is there, it is there; when it is not there, it is not there. A problem arises when something is not there and you want it to be there, or when something is there and you don't want it to be there. A problem is always psychological. "Why is it there?" Now, this is all psychological. Who is to say why it is there? There is nobody to answer it. Only explanations can be given, but those are not really answers. Explanations are simple.

It is very simple: pain is there because pleasure is there. Pleasure cannot exist without pain. If you want a life absolutely painless, then you will have to live a life absolutely pleasureless. They come together in one package. They are not two things really; they are one thing – not different, not separate, and cannot be separated. That's what man has been doing through the centuries: separating, to somehow have all the pleasures of the world and not have any pain; but this is not possible. The more pleasures you have, the more pain also. The bigger the peak, the deeper will be the valley by the side. You want no valleys and you want big peaks. Then the peaks cannot exist; they can exist only with valleys. The valley is nothing but a situation in which a peak becomes possible. The peak and the valley are joined together.

You want pleasure and you don't want pain. For example: you

love a woman or you love a man, and when the woman is with you, you are happy. Now, you would like to be happy whenever she is with you, but when she goes away you don't want the pain. If you are really happy with a woman when she is with you, how can you avoid the pain of separation when she is gone and she is no longer there? You will miss her, you will feel the absence. The absence will become pain. The presence was becoming pleasure, so absence is bound to become pain. If you really want that you should not have any pain, then you should start avoiding all pleasure. Then when the woman is there don't feel happy; just remain sad, just remain unhappy – so that when she goes, there is no problem.

If somebody greets you, you feel happy; then when somebody insults you, you will feel unhappy. This trick has been tried. This has been one of the most basic tricks that all of the so-called religious people have tried: if you want to avoid pain, avoid pleasure. But then what is the point? If you want to avoid death, avoid life – but then what is the point of it all? You will be dead. Before death, you will be dead. If you want to be perfectly secure, enter into your grave and lie down there. You will be perfectly secure. Don't breathe because if you breathe there is danger. There are all sorts of infections, particularly in Pune. Never breathe in Pune; you breathe infections. A million diseases exist all around you; how can you breathe? The air is polluted, there is danger, so don't breathe, don't move – just don't live. Commit suicide; then there will be no pain.

But then why are you searching for pleasure? You want no pain and all pleasure. You demand something impossible: you want that two plus two should not be four. You want them to become five, or three, or anything, but never four. But they are four. Whatsoever you do, howsoever you deceive yourself and others, they will remain four.

Pain and pleasure go together like night and day, like birth and death, like love and hate. In a better world, with a more developed language, we will not use words like *hate* and *love*, *anger*, *compassion*, *day*, *night*. We will make some words which will carry both together: *lovehate* – one word; *daynight* – one word, not two; *birthdeath* – one word, not two; *painpleasure* – one word, not two. The language creates an illusion.

In language pain is separate, pleasure is separate. If you want to look in the dictionary for *pain*, you have to look for *pain*; *pleasure* will be separate. If you want to look for *pleasure*, then you have to look for *pleasure*. But in reality pain and pleasure are together, just as your right and left hands are together, just as two wings of a bird are together. The dictionary creates a great illusion; language is a very great source of illusions. It says "love," and when it says "love" you never think about hate. You completely forget about hate, but love cannot exist without hate. That's why you love someone and you hate the same person.

Many disciples come to me very disturbed because they say, "We love you, but we hate you also." This creates a great uneasiness in them. Never be uneasy about it. If you love me, you will hate me too. There will be moments when the hate part will be on top of you; there will be moments when the love part will be on top of you. Don't be uneasy about it; it is natural and human.

You would like a world where coldness exists without anything like heat, or heat exists without anything like cold. Just think about it; it is absurd because heat and cold are together. It depends on what you call them.

You can put water in two buckets: in one, hot water, boiling, and in the other, cold, ice-cold water. Just put both your hands in them and just feel. Are there two sensations? Or just one spectrum? On one extreme is cold, on the other extreme is hot. Then let them settle. By and by you will see that you are coming closer and closer; the hot is becoming less hot, and the cold is becoming less cold. After a few hours you will say, "They are both the same now." Or you can try with one bucket of water: put one hand near heat and one hand near ice. Make one hand cold and one hot, and dip both hands in one bucket of water and feel what it is. One hand will say it is cold, one hand will say it is hot, but it is the same water. It is relative. Something may look like pleasure to you, and the same thing may look like pain to somebody else.

For example: you are making love to a woman; you think it is very pleasurable. Ask a buddha; he will be simply horrified: "What are you doing? Have you gone mad?" Maybe that's why people make love in private – otherwise others will laugh and ridicule. All the movements of lovemaking will look very absurd. They will look ridiculous. In a passionate state of mind, you are almost drunk.

When you are angry you do something; in that moment it gives you pleasure, otherwise you wouldn't do it. Anger gives tremendous pleasure, power, the feeling of power. But when anger is gone you start feeling repentance, remorse. You start feeling that it was not good. Now it is painful; when it was there you felt power and you felt pleasure. Now you look again in a less insane state; in a less feverish state you look again. You are more cool and collected now; now it looks painful. The same thing can be pleasurable, the same thing can be painful – it depends. And the same thing can be pleasurable to you and for somebody else can be painful – that too depends. Pleasure and pain go together.

What I am saying, what my suggestion is for you to do is: there are two ways, and only two ways to get out of it. One is, start becoming more and more insensitive. That's what old religions have been teaching – become insensitive. When you are dull, insensitive, unintelligent – a crust, a hard crust surrounds your being. You will neither feel pain nor will you feel pleasure. That's what is happening to Jaina monks and other monks – they try to become insensitive. By and by, you can become insensitive. Then nothing feels pleasurable, nothing feels painful. You come to a state of stupor, stupidity; you become very aloof. You are almost dead; your eyes lose fire, your being loses all energy. You are just dead stuff, a stagnant thing, and you will start stinking of death. This is one way – simple, easy, cheap. I don't suggest it. It is life-negative. It is violent; it is violence against yourself. It is self-torture.

Try it, it is simple. You can go to Varanasi and you can see people, sannyasins, lying on a bed of thorns – and you will be amazed. But what have they learned? They have not learned anything – just that if you go on lying on hard things your body becomes dead, it doesn't feel. But just to avoid pain they are avoiding life itself. It is as if you wanted to be healthy and you wanted to drop the disease; just to drop the disease you killed yourself because the disease was too painful. But now you don't exist at all.

What I suggest is a very life-affirmative, life-loving way. My suggestion is: when there is pain, go deeply into it, don't avoid it. Let it be so, be open to it, become as sensitive as possible. Let the pain and its arrow penetrate you to your very core. Suffer it. When the pleasure comes, let that too move you to your innermost core. Dance it. When there is pain be with pain, and when there is pleasure be with pleasure. Become so totally sensitive that each moment of pain and pleasure is a great adventure.

I would like to tell you one thing: that if you can do this, you will understand that pain too is beautiful. It is as beautiful as pleasure. It also brings a sharpness to your being; it also brings awareness to your being – sometimes even more than pleasure. Pleasure dulls. That's why people who live just in indulgence will be found to be shallow. You will not see any depth in them. They have not known pain at all; they have lived only on the surface, moving from one pleasure to another. The playboys don't know what pain is.

Pain makes you very alert, and pain makes you very compassionate, and pain makes you sensitive to others' pains too. Pain makes you immense, huge, big. The heart grows because of pain. And it is beautiful, it has its own beauty. I am not saying seek pain; I am only saying whenever it is there, enjoy that too. It is a gift of existence and there must be a hidden treasure in it. Enjoy that too; don't reject. Accept it, welcome it, be with it. In the beginning it will be difficult, arduous, but by and by you will learn the taste of it. The taste has to be learned; it is just like other tastes. If you start drinking alcohol, in the beginning the taste is just bad and bitter.

Mulla Nasruddin is a drunkard. One day his wife went to the pub, and he was drinking there with his friends. The wife was in a really bad mood; she had tried every way and he wouldn't listen. Today she wanted to shock him. And of course he was a little puzzled; she had never come to the pub: "Is she going to create a scene here? Home, it is okay. Home is the place where scenes are created and enacted, but in the pub?"

She came and just sat by his side and said, "Mulla, I have also decided to drink, from today. He was a little more puzzled. But then he poured a glass for her. She tasted and it was so bitter, and she just could not believe it. She said, "It is so bitter, Mulla."

Mulla said, "Look! And you have always been thinking that

I am enjoying. It is a great *sadhana*; it is not easy."

When you start anything new you have to learn the taste. And of course the taste of pain is bitter. But once you have learned it, it gives you such sharpness and brilliance. It shakes all dust, all stupor and sleepiness away from you. It makes you so fully mindful that nothing else can make you so mindful. In pain you can be more meditative than in pleasure. Pleasure is more distracting. Pleasure engulfs you. In pleasure you abandon consciousness. Pleasure tends to make you unconscious; pleasure is a sort of oblivion, a forgetfulness. Pain is a remembrance: you cannot forget pain.

Have you not observed? Whenever you are in pain you remember God, never when you are happy and in pleasure. Who bothers? In fact, when you are in pleasure you forget yourself, you forget God, you forget everything – things are going so well. But in pain, you remember God.

So pain can become a very creative energy; it can become a remembrance of godliness. It can become prayerfulness, it can become meditation, it can become awareness.

What do I teach? I teach when pain is there, use it as awareness, as meditation, as a sharpening of the soul. And when pleasure is there, then use it as a drowning, as a forgetfulness. Both are ways to reach to godliness. One is to remember yourself totally, and one is to forget yourself totally. Pain and pleasure can both be used, but to use them you have to be very, very intelligent. What I am teaching is not the stupid person's way; what I am teaching is the intelligent, the wise man's way. Whatsoever existence gives you, try to find a way to use it in such a way that it becomes a creative growth situation for you.

The second question:

Osho,
After today's lecture, I felt as if levitating and flying. I
walked along the road in front of the ashram gate,
approached a flowering bush, and looked at it,
suddenly having the sensation of being one with

nature and floating like driftwood in the river. All of a sudden I realized that the driftwood had stepped into a heap of dog shit. Do you happen to see any symbolic significance to this?

The significance is there, but not symbolic; it is very real. You need not go into symbology because it is not a dream, it happened when you were perfectly awake. The reality is saying something to you.

Listening to me you can feel that you are levitating, but you cannot levitate. The feeling is not the thing, not the real thing. Listening to me you can feel very happy, but that happiness is like a reflection. It is my happiness reflected in your mirror, it is not your happiness. You are bound to land somewhere in dog shit.

One should not depend on anybody else. You need your happiness. Listening to me you can become engulfed, you can be overwhelmed, but the farther you go from me that music will start disappearing from you. It was not yours in the first place.

It is as if I am sitting here and in my light your darkness disappears. Then you go away; the farther away you go, the darkness starts surrounding you again.

It is as the Sufis say…

Two travelers were going into a forest. One had a lamp, a lantern of his own, the other had none. But the other was not even aware of the fact. They both walked in light because one had the lantern, so the other also had the light on the path. Then came the moment where they had to depart; their paths were going in separate directions. And when the man with the lantern went on his path, suddenly the other traveler recognized, realized, that there was immense darkness all around.

You can walk with me to a certain extent. The disciple can walk with the master to a certain extent, but then the paths separate. Then you have to go on your own way. Suddenly you will find you are in darkness.

So while you are with a master, don't just enjoy his bliss. Enjoy, but learn also how to create your own bliss and your own light.

Those moments with a master have to be enjoyed tremendously. Good, but just enjoyment is not enough. You have to learn the secret of how to create your own light so when the master departs, or you have to go on your own way and paths are separate, you are not lost in darkness. Otherwise this will happen again and again.

I heard one day that Mulla Nasruddin had been caught by the police, so I went to see him in the jail. I asked him, "Mulla, how do you happen to be here? What happened?"

He said, "Housebreaking, and my fault too."

I asked him, "And how was that?"

He said, "I spent three months getting acquainted with the dog, and then I went and stepped on the cat."

You have to be fully aware. In Zen they say the art of meditation is almost the art of being a thief. You have to be so aware that you can walk into somebody else's house where you may never have been before; not only can you enter, you can remove things without making any noise; not only that, but without any light in the dark night. You have to be like a thief: very aware, very conscious.

What happened to this questioner? – he was floating, he was no longer in this world, he had moved into another world. A vision had dawned on him; he was in a dream, he was not aware, he was drunk. Hence he stepped in dog shit.

This is very, very meaningful; remember it. Otherwise there are many ways to land in wrong places. Unless you are tremendously aware, many times you will come nearer to home and again you will miss the door.

The third question:

Osho,
Are you also the poor man's guru?

Certainly. Whenever you give me an opportunity to contradict myself I never lose it. I contain contradictions. I am vast. I never feel uneasy about contradictions; I love them.

Yes, I am the poor man's guru. But if you understand me there is no contradiction. My definition of a rich man and my definition of a poor man have to be understood well.

Jesus says, "Blessed are the poor because theirs is the kingdom of God." And mind you, he does not say theirs will be the kingdom of God; he says theirs *is* the kingdom of God. Let me repeat it: he says, "Blessed are the poor because theirs is the kingdom of God." But who are the poor in Jesus' definition? – the same people I call rich.

I call a man rich who has become absolutely frustrated with the world, who has known all that it can give, and has come to know that all of it is illusory. He has become aware of his inner poverty. "No richness of the world can fulfill my hungry heart; nothing that I can possess can ever be a contentment to me. My poverty remains untouched by my riches." I call this man a rich man because he has come to see the futility of all riches; but he is also the poor man, the really poor because he has understood his inner poverty. He is "the poor in spirit."

Now let me confuse you a little more.

There are two types of rich men: one, the first type, who has riches; and the other, who has no riches but still is a rich man – because he has the desire to be rich. The first has riches, the second has no riches, but both are rich men – because both move for more and for more and for more. You may have ten rupees and you desire a hundred rupees. Somebody has ten million rupees and he is desiring a hundred million rupees. What is the difference? – the proportion is the same. Both are moving toward riches.

So there are rich people with riches and there are rich people with no riches at all. A beggar can also be rich if he is still moving into desire.

Then there are two types of poor people: a poor person who has no riches, and a poor person who has all the riches in the world. If the poor person has understood that there is no meaning in riches, and the person who has all the riches has also understood that there is no meaning in riches, then both are poor in spirit. The basic thing to realize is that whatsoever is outside is not going to fulfill you. Whether you are rich or poor does not matter.

That's why I said that if a poor man wants to be religious he will have to have more intelligence than the rich man – because he will have to substitute by his intelligence what is lacking in riches. He will have to have a great vision, visualization power. If you have a beautiful woman, it is very easy to understand that no contentment comes just by having a beautiful woman by your side. It is very easy to understand it; great intelligence is not needed. But if you don't have a woman and you live in a desert alone, and dream – and dreams come, and you fantasize about women – now, to understand that just by getting a woman you cannot be satisfied is difficult, very difficult. When you have riches by your side it is very simple to understand. Not much intelligence is needed to see that nothing has happened to your inner world. But when you don't have anything, not even something to eat, no house to give you shelter, it is very difficult to see that houses, food, money, are all meaningless. It is very difficult for a poor man to understand that money is meaningless. For a rich man, it is very simple.

That's why I say if a rich man does not become religious he must be extraordinarily stupid, and if a poor man becomes religious he must be extraordinarily intelligent. When you have, it is very simple to see the arithmetic that nothing has happened; but when you don't have, then just to visualize and imagine that even by having it nothing is going to happen, is very difficult. A lurking doubt will remain inside – maybe there is something in it. The whole world is running after it. "Are they all fools? Am I alone the wise man? Then why is the whole world running after riches, money, power, prestige?" It is very difficult. When you live in a palace you know that life does not happen just by living in a palace. But when you live on the road, you live in a slum, it is very difficult to understand that just by living in a palace nothing happens. That's why I told you I am a rich man's guru. But only for the rich man who has understood that he is not rich is there the possibility of opening into the religious dimension. When he has understood his inner poverty, only then. So whosoever understands that he is poor, and he has nothing, and this world cannot give you anything, is capable of making contact with a master. There is no other way.

Sometimes it seems very hard. Listening to me, sometimes you become very much disturbed. The moment I say that I am only a rich man's guru, of course you become disturbed. You are not rich; then am I not your guru? But you misunderstood me. You could not get the point of it.

Many times it is happening: I say something, you hear something else.

Three little old ladies, loving but deaf, met at the supermarket.

"Beautiful day," said one.

"No, it is Thursday," said the other.

"I'm thirsty too," said the third. "Let us have a cup of tea."

This is how things transpire between me and you. I say something, you hear something, and then you go on questioning and I go on answering...

Two guys talking: one said, "I got married because I was tired of going to the laundromat, eating in restaurants, and wearing socks with holes."

The other guy said, "That's funny. I got divorced for the same reason."

When I say a poor man cannot be religious, it hurts – and particularly in a country like India, which is poor. It hurts very much, and more so because India thinks it is a religious country, and I say a poor man cannot be religious. The country is poor and has pretensions of being rich. It hurts very deeply, it wounds the ego. But try to understand.

There is a hierarchy, and unless you have fulfilled the lower needs first, the higher needs don't arise. In life you follow the rule very arithmetically: a boy has to go to the primary school, then to the middle school, then to the high school, then to a college, then to a university. There is a hierarchy. If somebody says, "I want to enter the university directly," you won't allow. You will say, "First you have to fulfill a few requirements."

God is the ultimate truth, and now everybody thinks he should be able to approach directly and that there should be no requirement. This is absolute nonsense. To me, your physical needs have to be fulfilled first. Your body has to be in a deep contentment, a well-being. When the body is perfectly well, healthy, has a pleasure of its own, is like a beautifully humming car – no disturbance, no noise... I am not talking about Indian cars.

They say that when the manufacturer of Ambassador cars died, when Birla died, the man who received him at the gate of heaven was very angry and said, "We have received many complaints about your car, this Ambassador: that except for the horn, the whole mechanism makes a noise."

When the car is really beautifully humming and the mechanism has a rhythm to it, there is well-being. When your body is humming in a musical, harmonious way, when everything fits together, when there is nothing wrong and you are simply happy with the body, suddenly there is an upsurge of energy. You start seeking aesthetic objects: art, music, poetry, painting. Suddenly you become interested in Picasso, Michelangelo, Mozart. Suddenly your taste starts growing for something beautiful.

When your mind is also humming, when your mind is also in well-being – the music is there, the poetry is there, the beauty is there, and you are satisfied. Again another jump, another quantum leap, and you start asking about truth, you ask about God. You ask the ultimate question only in an ultimate state of well-being, not before it. Then the search starts. Now it is very difficult; it is as difficult as in this story...

Myron Cohen tells about the lady who was asked, "Sadie, if you found a million dollars in the street, what would you do with it?"

"That depends," answered Sadie. "If I found it belonged to somebody very poor, I would give it back."

Now, one million dollars! And the lady says, "If I found it belonged to somebody very poor, then I would give it back. It depends; otherwise I am going to keep it. If it belongs to a rich man what is the point of giving it back?" But one million dollars belonging to somebody very poor? Look at the absurdity of it.

I have never come across a man whose lower needs are not fulfilled who can really inquire into the truth of God – not possible. I feel sorry to say so, but truth is truth, and it has to be said even if it hurts. I cannot do anything; it is so. Then his desire remains hanging around – his unfulfilled layer. He may talk about prayer, he may talk about love, but he will mean sex. If his sex is unfulfilled, his talk about love is not going to be about love; it will be about unfulfilled sex. He may use the word *love*; that is irrelevant, that doesn't make any difference. But if you go deeper into his love and his talk about love, you will find sexuality hidden there.

It is impossible to jump to higher needs when the lower are not fulfilled. India was, one day in the past, a religious country – in the days of Buddha and Mahavira. It was religious because it was the richest country in the world. It was thought to be as a golden bird – most fabulous, most rich, luxurious. It has known its days: it was young, full of energy and vigor. It was at its peak. Nobody can remain at the peak forever. It goes on changing. In those days India was religious because it was rich. Then the richness was gone; India became poorer and poorer.

There is a logic in it. Whenever a country is very rich it starts becoming religious; when it starts becoming religious it becomes poor. When it becomes poor it is difficult to be religious. This is the mechanism, this is the dialectic. Why does it happen?

Now look at America: America is now the most affluent country in the world, but the young generation is going against technology. The young generation talks about love, prayer, meditation. But if you go against technology, and if you burn Cadillacs, Rolls Royces, and you start living like mendicants, you become hippies and yippies and you drop out of the society, now what will happen? If it happens on a larger scale, America will become the poorest country in the world. Now look at the dialectics of it: America is interested in religion, America is interested in meditation, America is interested in God because it is rich. Now, once you become interested in God you say, "What is there in riches? Nothing. A poor man's life is beautiful: I would like to be a vagabond like Buddha, I would like to be a wanderer. I don't want to continue with this mechanical society. I don't want to be part of a consumer society anymore." Then you drop out; then bigger portions of the society drop out.

And you are the future – because the young generation will have to decide. The older generation will disappear soon. And when the new generation has to decide, it knows no technology. You will fall from your riches; you will become poor. When you become poor, then you will go on carrying that religion which happened when you were rich, as a hangover. Just see it: when you were rich, religion was true because you were trying to reach a higher peak. Now you have fallen from the riches, and you have fallen because of religion. Now you will carry a hangover of religion for centuries. You will go on talking about meditation but it will not mean anything.

That's why in India the hangover has continued. India has known a golden peak. When it knew the golden peak, Buddha and Mahavira and Neminatha and all intelligent people dropped out of the society. They became mendicants, wanderers, *bhikkhus*; they started begging. They said, "This is all nonsense. These great palaces and these great riches are all useless." And they were right: I am not saying they were wrong; I am simply telling you how the mechanism functions, how the wheel moves. They were right; they had to say this, there is no way to avoid it. But when they said it, millions were convinced. Buddha had thousands of disciples, and they all came from rich families. They were either from royal families, or they were from very rich families. Of course, a few poor people also came. But in fact, at the time nobody was poor.

Now in America there are poor people, but if you look at them from the Indian standard, they are very rich. Even a poor person can have a car in America. Even your chauffeur can come in his car. Now, in India, just to think that a driver has his own car – nobody will believe it. "Then why does he drive somebody else's car? It is impossible."

I used to stay in Indore at a rich man's family. He had gone for the first time to Switzerland, and the guide who was traveling with him to show him places invited him to his house. He had a beautiful house in the hills. This rich man was telling me – he had travelled to the West for the first time – he was telling me, "I could not believe, I was amazed because the guide had nine rooms – just a wife and husband. And each room with attached bathroom." In his house where I used to stay, he had only two rooms with attached bathrooms, and he is one of the richest men of Indore. One was for me and one was for himself; attached bathrooms are a luxury. He could not believe it, and he could not understand why the man was functioning as a guide. He had his own car, he had his own house, he had a beautiful garden – so why was he working as a guide? This rich man felt poor in comparison to that poor man.

India was rich, even the poor men were rich. Millions of people were converted by Buddha and Mahavira, and they all left their riches. Just think of the point: if millions of people suddenly turn into beggars, only a very rich society can afford them. Otherwise, how will you afford it? Who will give them food? Who will give them shelter? They were all sheltered, they were all getting good food, they were getting good clothes. In fact Buddha had to make rules that they should not receive more than this, otherwise people were given so many things that it would become difficult for the beggar to carry all that load. So, one should not receive more than this – a limited amount. If you received more, then immediately you had to give something. Your possessions should be of a limited number. There were millions of *bhikkhus*, and Buddha had to make rules for them not to possess more. It was a rich country; religion flowered. When religion flowered, the country became poor because of its very flowering. When the country became poor, the religion continued as a hangover. Now India is not a religious country; religion is just a hangover from the past. If you look at the past, you can think, "Yes, one time it must have been a religious country." But if you look at the future, it is going to be a communist country, sooner or later. It is one of the most materialist countries in the world now.

Now, let me tell you another thing: when a country becomes poor it becomes materialist; when it becomes materialist it does not bother about religion at all – or, at the most pays lip service. Then it starts becoming rich; materialism makes you rich. When you again become rich, one day you become religious. This way the wheel goes on moving.

Religion is always for the rich. And a hangover religion is very dangerous: it does not allow you to be really materialist, and you are materialist. It does not give you freedom to be really materialist. I am not against materialism because I know that only at the highest peak of materialism does religion happen.

Karl Marx had predicted that the richest country of the world would become communist. But he failed; his prediction was wrong. It was wrong because he never understood the real dialectics of society; he only understood the economic structure. If he was right, then America should have been communist, not China, not Russia. Both are poor countries, the poorest. Karl Marx was wrong.

What I am saying is truer: a rich country can never become communist; only a poor country becomes communist. A rich country becomes religious, not communist. A poor country becomes communist – but this is how it is. I am not saying it should not be so; I am not saying anything about what should be and what should not be. I am simply saying what is; this is the mechanism. Now if Russia really becomes rich someday, it will lose contact with its communism. That's why there is a conflict between China and Russia: Russia is richer than China. China is really a poor man's country, and only the poor man can be materialist. Now to China, Russia seems to be bourgeois. They don't want to have anything to do with Russia, it is already a bourgeois country. Sooner or later when Russia becomes richer... That is bound to happen: when you become materialist, technological, scientific, you become rich. When you become rich, suddenly religion starts flowering.

In Russia, you will be surprised to know that there are secret societies now gathering together somewhere in private, praying, meditating – because now it is illegal. You cannot pray in public, you cannot talk about meditation in public. But there are societies, and people even risk their lives just to be together and talk about Jesus and Buddha. But they are all secret societies.

The last question:

Osho,
For the record, two days ago, for reasons clearly spiritual, you admitted to speaking only a modest five thousand words per day. From a purely scientific viewpoint, this statement would seem to contain certain inaccuracies. The actual figure – and this any transcriber, editor or tape operator will independently

verify – is approximately three times the amount, counting both the morning discourse and the evening darshan. This means that one hundred and five thousand words are spoken each week, and a handsome total of five million five hundred thousand words are given to us in one year. In three short years a chain of such words would indeed girdle the earth.
Is this a record for an enlightened voice?
We feel the master needs the opportunity to verify or refute such extravagant claims.

They are not extravagant, and I absolutely agree with you. But, a master always has his ways to escape; you cannot catch him so easily. He can always bring some esoteric thing into it.

Yes, fifteen thousand words are spoken, but remember, I am not saying I am speaking. Fifteen thousand words per day are spoken: five thousand from the body, five thousand from the mind, five thousand from me.

Let me tell you one anecdote:

A jaguar persuaded a cat to teach him how to pounce. After a few successful experiments with bugs and insects, the jaguar, his appetite whetted, decided to try out this new technique on the cat itself. The cat, however, jumped out of danger like a flash, and the jaguar landed in a heap.

"That is not fair!" whined the jaguar. "You did not teach me that trick."

"A smart teacher," the cat reminded him, "never teaches a pupil all his tricks."

Remember that.

And you are right: my mathematics is poor. It has always been so. So whenever it comes to mathematics I will always agree with you. But metaphysics has its own ways to get out of any entanglement. That's why I can so easily contradict myself. I speak only five thousand words a day.

Enough for today.

3

REMEMBER THE MIDDLE

AND YOU WILL ALWAYS BE RIGHT

One night a monk was reciting a sutra bequeathed by Kashyapabuddha. His tone was so mournful and his voice so fainting, as if he were going out of existence. The Buddha asked the monk, "What was your occupation before you became a homeless monk?"

Said the monk, "I was very fond of playing the guitar."

The Buddha said, "How did you find it when the strings were too loose?"

Said the monk, "No sound is possible."

"How when the strings were too tight?"

"They crack."

"How when they were neither too tight nor too loose?"

"Every note sounds in its proper tone."

The Buddha then said to the monk: "Religious discipline is also like unto playing the guitar. When the mind is properly adjusted and quietly applied, the way is attainable; but when you are too fervently bent on it, your body grows tired; and when your body is tired, your spirit becomes weary; when your spirit is weary, your discipline will relax; and with the relaxation of discipline there follows many an evil. Therefore, be calm and pure, and the way will be gained."

Man's whole misery consists in his being off-center. There is a maladjustment between the hub and the wheel. There is a maladjustment between you and reality, and that maladjustment manifests itself in a thousand and one ways. The farther away you are from reality, the more miserable. Hell is the farthest point from reality. The closer you are to reality, the closer you are to heaven. When there is no maladjustment between you and reality, you are heaven itself.

It is not a question of going anywhere, it is a question of how to get in tune with reality again. It is a rediscovery – because in the mother's womb each child is centered in reality. In the mother's womb each child is profoundly blissful. Of course he is unaware of it – not knowing anything about it. He's so one with his bliss that there is no knower left behind. Blissfulness is his being, and there is no distinction between the knower and the known. So of course the child is not aware that he is blissful. You become aware only when you have lost something.

Mulla Nasruddin was saying to his son one day, "You don't know what happiness is until you get married – and then it is too late."

It is so. It is very difficult to know something without losing it because when you have not lost it you are so totally one with it. There is no distance: the observer and the observed are one, the known and the knower are one. Every child is in a profoundly blissful state.

Psychologists also agree with this. They say that the whole search of religion is nothing but a way to again find the womb of the mother. They use it as a criticism of religion, but to me it is not criticism at all. It is simply true. Yes, the search for religion is again a search for the womb. The search for religion is again a search to make this whole existence a womb.

The child is in absolute tune with the mother. The child is never out of tune with the mother. The child does not know that he is separate from the mother. If the mother is healthy, the child is healthy; if the mother is ill, the child is ill; if the mother is sad, the child is sad; if the mother is happy, the child is happy; if the mother is dancing, the child is dancing; if the mother is sitting silently, the child is silent. The child has no boundaries of his own yet. This is the purest bliss, but it has to be lost.

The child is born, and suddenly he is thrown off-center. Suddenly he is uprooted from the earth, from the mother. He loses his moorings and he does not know who he is. There was no need to know it when he was with her. There was no need to know – he was all, and there was no need to know, there was no distinction. There was no "you," so there was no question of "I." The reality was undivided. It was *advait*, pure *advait*, pure nonduality.

But once the child is born – the umbilical cord is cut and he starts breathing on his own – suddenly his whole being becomes a quest to know "Who am I?" It is natural. Now he starts becoming aware of his boundaries: his body, his needs. Sometimes he is happy, sometimes unhappy, sometimes he is fulfilled, sometimes not fulfilled; sometimes he is hungry and crying and there is no sign of his mother anywhere; sometimes he is on the mother's breast, again enjoying oneness with her. But now there are many moods and many climates, and he will start, by and by, to feel the separation. A divorce has happened, the marriage is broken.

He was absolutely married to the mother; now he will always be separate. He has to find out who he is. And the whole life one goes on trying to find out who one is. This is the most fundamental question.

First the child becomes aware of "mine," then of "me," then of "you," then of "I." This is how it proceeds. This is precisely the procedure, exactly in this order. First he becomes aware of "mine." Watch it because this is your construction, the structure of the ego. First the child becomes aware of "mine" – this toy is mine, this mother is mine. He starts possessing. The possessor enters first: possessiveness is very basic. Hence all the religions say to become nonpossessive because with possession starts hell. Watch small children: very jealous, possessive, each child trying to snatch everything from everybody else and trying to protect his own toys. You will see that children are very violent, almost indifferent to others' needs. If a child is playing with his toy and another child comes you can see an Adolf Hitler, a Genghis Khan, a Nadirshah. He will cling to his toy; he is ready to hit, he is ready to fight. It is a question of territory, a question of domination. Possessiveness enters first; that is the basic poison. The child starts saying, "This is mine."

Now look – nothing can be "mine" in reality, in truth. We come empty-handed, we go empty-handed. This whole business of "mine" and "thine" is just a dream. But once the child says, "This is mine," now he is entering into a maladjustment with reality. So you will find that the more you have this idea of "mine," the more you will be miserable, the more you will suffer. Everything: "This house is mine; this woman is mine; this man is mine," and everywhere you immediately claim and possess, and misery enters.

Two persons are in love. If it is just a beginning, the "mine" has not started because if "mine" has not started, the mind has not started. Once the "mine" starts, the ego is on the way. The ego is the crystallized "mine." And once the "mine" starts, love is lost. Love is beautiful only when there is no "mine." But it enters immediately because that has become our very structure. That is our foundation in this world. We are wrongly based.

I have heard...

A six-year-old boy was playing with the girl next door who was five.

"Want to wrestle?" he asked.

She said, "I can't wrestle. I am a girl."

He continued, "Want to play ball?"

She replied, "I can't play ball. I am a girl."

Finally he said, "Okay, wanna play house?"

She said, "All right. I will be the father."

From the very beginning, who dominates whom? Who possesses whom? Hence all the religions – Eastern, Western – all the religions that have existed on earth emphasize nonpossessiveness, nonattachment, because that will take the very earth from beneath your feet. If you become nonpossessive the ego cannot exist. If you become aware of this basic flaw of your being, this claim for "mine," you will be surprised that all your misery can be dropped by dropping this single word. This is not just a word, it is your whole style of life. The wrong style of life is based on "mine"; the right style of life knows no "mine," no "thine."

Once we say "mine" we are making ourselves separate from the whole. Now this separation will grow, and each step will take you farther away.

I have heard...

A small child was sitting with the family. The father and mother were quarreling, as usual. Then the father became almost mad. Afraid he might hit the woman, or that he might do something wrong, he ran out of the house.

The small child was watching. He said, "Will daddy be coming back?"

The mother said, "Yes, within fifteen minutes he will be back."

The child said, "Oh nuts! I was thinking to have his dessert."

Once the "mine" enters, you are a competitor with everybody. Once the "mine" enters, your life will now be a life of competition, struggle, conflict, violence, aggression.

The next step of "mine" is "me." When you have something to claim as mine, suddenly through that claim arises the idea "Now I am the center of my possessions." The possessions become your territory, and through those possessions arises a new idea of "me."

Once you are settled with "me," you can see clearly that you have a boundary, and those who are outside the boundary are "you." The other becomes clear; now things start falling apart.

The universe is one, it is a unity. Nothing is divided. Everything is connected with everything else. It is a tremendous connectedness. You are connected with the earth, you are connected with the trees, you are connected with the stars. Stars are connected with you, stars are connected with the trees, with the rivers, with the mountains. Everything is interconnected. Nothing is separate; nothing can be separate. Separation is not possible.

Each moment you are breathing – you breathe in, you breathe out –there is a continuous bridge with existence. You eat, existence enters you; you defecate, it becomes manure – the apple on the tree will become part of your body tomorrow, and some part of your body will become manure, will become food for the tree. It is a continuous give and take. Not for a single moment does it stop. When it stops, you are dead.

What is death? – separation is death. To be in unity is to be alive, to be out of unity is to be dead. So the more you think, "I am separate," the less sensitive you will be, more dead, dragging, dull. The more you feel you are connected, the more this whole existence is part of you and you are part of this whole existence. Once you understand that we are members of each other, then suddenly the vision changes. Then these trees are not alien; they are continuously preparing food for you. And then you are not alien to them because you are continuously preparing food for them. When you breathe in, you take oxygen in; when you breathe out, you give carbon dioxide. The trees breathe in carbon dioxide and breathe out oxygen – there is a continuous communion. We are in tune. The reality is a unity but with the idea of "me–you," we are falling out of the reality. And once a wrong conception settles inside, your whole vision becomes upside down.

I have heard...

The young New Yorker was in Texas for the very first time. Seeing a herd of buffalo, he asked his host what they were.

"They are just wild pigs," said his host. "Everything in Texas is big."

A little later the visitor saw a flight of eagles and asked what they were.

"They are just sparrows," said his host. "Everything is big in Texas."

Later that night the visitor went looking for the toilet and fell into the swimming pool. "For Pete's sake," he cried. "Nobody pull the flush!"

Once you have a wrong conception of things, then that conception will distort everything. If "everything is big in Texas," then the swimming pool must be a toilet. It is natural – one wrong conception leads to another wrong conception, and one small wrong conception leads to a bigger wrong conception. If you go on settling with this, one day you simply don't know what reality is. You are simply clouded by your own conceptions.

"Me," then "you," and then as a reflection arises "I." "I" is the subtlest, the most crystallized form of possessiveness. Once you have uttered "I," you have committed sacrilege. Once you have said "I," you are broken completely from existence. Not really broken, otherwise you would die; but in your ideas you are completely broken from reality. Now you will be in a continuous fight with reality. You will be fighting your own roots, you will be fighting with yourself.

That's why Buddha says, be like driftwood. You can be a piece of driftwood only if you have dropped the idea of "I." Otherwise you cannot be driftwood. Struggle will persist. That's why it becomes so difficult when you come to meditate. If I say to just sit silently, you cannot do that – such a simple thing. One would think it is the simplest thing; there should be no need to teach it. One should simply sit and be. But you cannot sit because the "I" cannot allow you a moment of relaxation. Once a moment of relaxation is allowed, you will be able to see reality. Once reality is known, the "I" will have to be dropped. Then it cannot persist. So the "I" never even allows you a holiday. Even if you go to the hills, to the summer resorts, the "I" never allows you a holiday even there. You take your radio, you take your TV set, you take all your problems and you remain occupied. There, at a hill station, you had gone to relax, but you continue your whole pattern in the same way. You don't relax.

The "I" cannot relax. It exists through tensions. It will create new tensions, it will create new worries, it will constantly manufacture new problems, it won't allow you any rest. Even a minute's rest and the whole house of the "I" starts toppling down – because the reality is so beautiful and the "I" is so ugly. One continues to fight his way unnecessarily. You are fighting for things which are going to happen of their own accord. You are unnecessarily fighting. You are desiring things which are going to be yours if you don't desire. In fact, by desiring you will lose them.

That's why Buddha says, "Float with the stream. Let it take you to the ocean."

Mine, me, you, I – this is the trap. And this trap creates misery, neurosis, madness.

Now the problem is: the child has to go through it because he does not know who he is and he needs some sort of identity – maybe a false identity, but it is better than no identity. He needs some identity. He needs to know exactly who he is, so a false center is created. The "I" is not your real center. It is a false center – utilitarian, make-believe, just manufactured by you. It has nothing to do with your real center. Your real center is the center of all. Your real self is the self of all. At the center, the whole of existence is one – just as at the source of light, the sun, all rays are one. The farther away they go, the farther away they are from each other.

Your real center is not only your center, it is the center of the whole. But we have created small centers of our own, homemade, manufactured by ourselves. There is a need because the child is born without any boundary, with no idea of who he is. It is a survival necessity. How will he survive? He has to be given a name, he has to be given an idea of who he is. Of course this idea comes from the outside: somebody says you are beautiful, somebody says you are intelligent, somebody says you are so vital. You gather the things that people say. Out of all that people say about you, you gather a certain image. You never look into yourself, at who you are. This image is going to be false because nobody else can know who you are, and nobody else can say who you are. Your inner reality is not available to anybody else except you. Your inner reality is impenetrable to anybody else except you. Only you can be there.

The day you realize that your identity is false, put together – you have collected opinions from people...

Sometime just think, just sit silently and think who you are. Many ideas will arise. Just go on watching from where they come and you will be able to find the source. Something comes from your mother – much; about eighty to ninety percent. Something comes from your father, something comes from your school-teachers, something comes from your friends, something from the society. Just watch: you will be able to tell from where it comes. Nothing comes from you, not even one percent comes from you. What type of identity is this in which you have not contributed at all? And you are the only one who could have contributed, in fact the whole hundred percent.

The day you understand this, religion becomes important. The day you understand this, you start seeking for some technique, some method to enter into your being and know exactly, really, existentially, who you are. No more collections of images from the outside, no more asking others to mirror your reality – but to face it directly, immediately; to enter into your nature, to feel it there. What is the need to ask anybody? And whom are you asking? They are as ignorant about themselves as you are about yourself. They don't know themselves; how can they know you? Just see how things are functioning, how things go on functioning, how things go on happening: one falsity leads to another falsity. You are almost swindled, duped. You are conned, and those who have swindled you may not have done it knowingly. They may have been swindled by others. Your father, your mother, your teachers, have been duped by others – their fathers, their mothers, their teachers. And they have duped you in turn. Are you going to do the same to your children too?

In a better world, where people are more intelligent, more aware, they will teach the child, "This idea of your identity is false. It is needed, we are giving it to you, but it is only for the time being, before you yourself discover who you are. It is not going to be your reality. And the sooner you find out who you are, the better. The sooner you can drop this idea, the better – because from that very moment you will really be born, and you will be really real, authentic. You will become an individual."

The ideas that we gather from others give us a personality, and the knowledge that we come to know from within gives us individuality. Personality is false, individuality is real. Personality is borrowed; reality, individuality, your authenticity, can never be borrowed. Nobody can say who you are.

Your body can be seen by others. They can say whether your body is beautiful or not, and that too depends – because no criterion for beauty exists. That depends on the idea of the person, on what he thinks is beautiful. Two persons never agree. It is almost like "like" and "dislike." You may fall in love with a woman and you may think she is the most beautiful woman in the world – and your friends may laugh at you. I'm not saying they are right, I'm not saying you are right. I'm simply saying there is simply no criterion. You may think the woman is horrible and your friend is mad, but there is no criterion. There is no objective way to know who is beautiful, what is beautiful. It depends on your mind, your conditioning.

I have overheard...

A male elephant was watching a female elephant wiggle by. Said he, almost charmed, "Wow! A perfect 250 by 210 by 400."

For an elephant, of course, those are the proportions of beauty – not for a man. And as you are laughing about the proportions, elephants laugh about your ideas of beauty.

In fact even a single individual's idea of beauty goes on changing. In childhood you have different ideas of beauty, in youth different ideas, in old age different ideas. And then it depends on your necessity, your need.

I have heard...

There was an advertisement in a farmer's magazine. The farmer had advertised that he wanted to meet a woman nearabout thirty years of age. He himself was forty-one. Object: marriage. But one condition had to be fulfilled: the woman had to have a tractor, and she had to send a picture of the tractor.

It depends on your need, on your ideas, on your philosophy, religion, conditioning, culture. Somebody can say something about your body; that too is not objective. Somebody can say something about your mind – a teacher can say you are very intelligent – but that too depends because there is no way to decide who is intelligent. The very idea of an intelligence quotient, measuring the intelligence, has failed. Psychologists were thinking that they would be able to measure intelligence, but it has failed. Now it is out of date. It does not mean much.

Who is intelligent? A child who is efficient in mathematics, or a child who is very efficient in painting? Who is intelligent? A child who can compose poetry, or a child who can make an engine or a mechanism? Who is intelligent? There is simply no way to say. Of course, ordinarily the mathematician, the mechanic, the technologist will be thought intelligent because he has more utility. A painting does not have much utility. A poem has no survival value: you cannot merchandise it. In the marketplace nobody will bother about it. But if you can create a gadget, a mechanical device, many people will be interested in it. But how to decide?

In a different society – for example in ancient China three thousand years ago, a man who could compose poetry was thought to be more intelligent than a man who could devise a machine because the society existed on different principles. Lao Tzu had said that machines are not needed; Lao Tzu had said that machines are a way to cheat nature, to exploit nature. They are aggressive, man does not need any mechanical things. Poetry, painting, sculpture, music, is more valuable. So a child who was a born musician was thought to be more intelligent than a mathematician – because what will you do with a mathematician? Of what use is it? But in the modern world the mathematician is more useful, has more utility, has more market value.

But this is not going to be so for long. Sooner or later, even within this century, a few countries will come to such affluence that again they will need music, poetry, sculpture. People would like to listen to great music, would like to see dance, would like to enter into the realms of beauty, would like to go into deeper tune with reality. Who will bother about a mathematician, a technologist, an engineer? Sooner or later this is going to change. It depends on the needs of the society.

People can say something about your body, something about your mind, but that too is not of any value. Who can say anything about your soul? – not even your mother who has given birth to you, not even your father.

When Buddha became enlightened he went back home. His father was very angry, naturally so. It is very difficult to satisfy a father because whatsoever you do will go against his ambitions. It is very difficult to satisfy a father: if you don't have any personality, if you don't have any individuality, if you don't have any unique intelligence, you are dull. You may be obedient, but then the father is not satisfied because of your dullness, stupidity. You are obedient, okay; but what is the point of your being obedient? You have nothing to give. If you are intelligent, unique, have something to give, then you cannot be obedient. Intelligence is always rebellious. Only dull and stupid people are obedient.

In the world today there is so much rebellion only because there has been an explosion of intelligence. Each generation is more intelligent than the previous one, hence more rebellion, more disobedience, more chaos in the world. You can watch it in your children. Just observe your children impartially: were you so intelligent when you were a child? Now look at children: they are so intelligent. You may not see it because it hurts. You may not see it, you may deny it, but just watch – and it has to be so. It is natural that consciousness goes on evolving. So when a child is intelligent, he's rebellious, and the father is not satisfied. When the child is obedient but he is not intelligent, then too he is not satisfied. It is difficult to satisfy a father.

Even Buddha could not satisfy his father. Buddha's father must have thought that he had become a hippie. Maybe the term was not there, so he must have thought it in some other terms, but that's exactly what he was saying to Buddha when he came. He was very angry, annoyed, and he said, "What have you done? You are a king's son, and you are moving like a beggar? Drop all this nonsense and come back home. I am your father. Though you have pained me, and you have been a pain in my neck, still my heart is that of a father: I can forgive you. My doors are still open. You can come."

Buddha laughed. He said, "You don't know me at all. I have entered into a great kingdom." The father, of course, became more furious.

He said, "Stop all this. I know you well. I have given you birth."

Buddha said, "There you are mistaken, there you err. You have given birth to my body, but not to me; and you don't know me at all. Even as I am standing in front of you, you are not seeing me. You are so full of your idea that you are the father and I am your son. That idea is functioning like a barrier. Just look at me. The son that has left your house has not come back. That person is gone, that person is dead. I am a totally new being. I come with a new identity, I come with a new realization, I come as awareness. I had gone as unconsciousness. I had gone as Gautam Siddhartha, your son. Now I come as Buddha, as enlightened – just enlightened. I had gone with a false identity, now I come with a real realization of who I am. Look at me."

In fact, there is no way for anybody else to see your reality. You have to go into it yourself. It cannot be done by servants, you cannot pay somebody to do it for you.

A great Sufi saint was called by Caliph Omar to pray in his court. He came, but he said, "I cannot do it. There are a few things you have to do for yourself. You have to breathe for yourself; nobody else can do it. You have to make love to your woman yourself; nobody else can do it for you. You have to pray for yourself; I cannot do it. Sorry." He said, "I can pray, but that will be prayer for myself. It will not be for you."

He had brought a great truth home. There are things which nobody can do for you. At least one thing can never be done by anybody else – that is, to give you the answer to who you are. No, you have to go; you have to dig deep into your own being. Layers and layers of identity, false identity, have to be broken.

There is fear when one enters into oneself because chaos comes in. Somehow you have managed with your false identity. You have settled with it. You know your name is this or that; you have certain credentials, certificates, degrees, universities, colleges, prestige, money, heritage. You have certain ways to define yourself. You have a certain definition, howsoever workable – but it works. Going in means dropping this workable definition. There will be chaos.

Before you can come to your center you will have to pass

through a very chaotic state. That's why there is fear. Nobody wants to go in. People go on teaching "know thyself"; we listen, but we never listen. We never bother about it. There is a very certain idea in the mind that chaos will be let loose and you will be lost in it, you will be engulfed in it. Because of the fear of that chaos, we go on clinging to anything from the outside. But this is wasting your life.

The day you become courageous enough to enter into your being you have become a sannyasin. Sannyas means now you are taking your life into your own hands. Now you are trying to live the life that is yours, authentically. Now you are no longer playing roles. Now you will not allow anybody else to write the story of your life. Now you are ready to unfold that which you have always carried like a seed within you. Chaos is the problem; so when people become religious they begin to find some way to avoid the chaos. That has to be understood before we can enter into this sutra.

A certain identity is there. For example you are rich, you have a lot of money – that is your identity. When a person starts thinking, "How to know myself?" and when he comes to listen to the truths always explained by the sages – that "mine," "me," "you," "I," have to be dropped – he thinks, "Okay, so I will drop all my riches and I will become poor." He drops one identity – the identity of being rich – but he has moved to the other extreme. To avoid one wrong he has moved to its opposite wrong. This is a fundamental thing: if you move against a wrong too much, you will again enter into another wrong. One wrong opposed by another thing cannot be corrected; the opposite is also wrong. Just in the middle, somewhere, is truth.

When you are rich you have an identity. You drop that, you become poor, you become a beggar; now you have another identity. The first one was borrowed from the society, the second one is also borrowed from the society. Now everybody will say that you have renounced the world, you are a great sannyasin, you have dropped out of the world, you are simply great. You were great because you had money, now you are great because you have renounced the money, but the identity is coming from the outside. First you were rich, now you are poor; now poverty is your richness. You were egoistic, you became humble; but now humbleness is your ego.

One can move from one disease to another disease very easily, just like a pendulum can swing from one extreme to another extreme.

Buddha says extremes are what wrong is. To be an extremist is to be in the wrong. Be in the middle, be balanced – *samyak* – and that's where right is. Just be in the middle, don't move from one polarity to another. That's what people are doing. Somebody is rushing after women, then one day he decides it is futile; he starts running away from women. But running continues. First he was chasing, now he's afraid some woman may be chasing him. That's how it happens: if you chase a woman, she runs. If you start running from her, she starts chasing you. Life is very mysterious, but the running continues. It is a game. Only one can be the chaser and one has to be the chased. Either you are the chaser or the woman becomes the chaser, but the game continues.

Buddha says, "Stop in the middle."

This sutra is part of a very famous story in Buddha's life. The story is about a prince named Srona.

Srona was a very rich prince, and he lived the life of a super-Epicurean: eat, drink, be merry. He had lived as deeply in indulgence as possible. He had never known anything about discipline, he had never heard anything about awareness. Women, wine – that was all, that was his whole life, confined to two words: women and wine. The whole day he was drunk, and the whole night he was indulging in sexuality. He was a maniac. But, by and by, the extreme started tiring him. By and by, he became alert to what he was doing to his life. When you indulge too much, one day or other, if you are a little intelligent, you start feeling the whole futility of it.

One day, when Buddha was passing through his town, Srona heard about Buddha. He had been thinking for many days, "There must be another way of life, and there must be more to life than the way I am living it." Hearing that Buddha had come, he went to see him. He was an extremist. Seeing Buddha – his silence, his grace, his peace – he was touched. His heart was overwhelmed. He bowed down to Buddha and he said, "Give me sannyas this very moment!"

Buddha said, "Wait. Don't be in such a hurry."

"But," he said, "I cannot wait. I don't know what waiting is. When I want to do something, I want to do something. And enough is enough. I have lived the life of a debauch, and I have been simply wasting myself. It has been suicidal. Now I cannot go back home. Accept me."

Even Buddha's disciples said, "Why don't you accept him? You never say no to anybody. Why are you hesitating?" Ananda said, "Why are you hesitating? He is great prince, well known, and he is ready. He is ready to surrender totally."

Buddha said, "I am hesitating because I am afraid this may be just another extreme. This man has been just indulgent. Now he may renounce and just move to another extreme – and renunciation is in the middle."

But Srona persisted; he wouldn't go. He was sitting there from the morning till the evening. He was a man of that type. The more Buddha said no, the more he became insistent. Next morning, Buddha accepted him as a disciple. This sutra is about Srona.

The story says that when Srona became a *bhikkhu*, a monk, immediately he turned to the other extreme – the extreme that Buddha was afraid of, was apprehensive about. *Bhikkhus*, Buddha's *bhikkus*, his monks, used to take one meal every day; Srona would take only two meals every week. When the *bhikkhus* would walk, move from one town to another, then they would walk on the road. But this Srona would never walk on the path. He would walk in the forest, would get hurt. His feet would start bleeding; there were wounds. Buddha's *bhikkhus* were very tranquil people, silent people because the whole teaching is to remain in the middle. They were never indulgent and they were never ascetic, but this Srona became a great ascetic. When everybody would be sitting under the trees, he would stand in the hot sun. He had a beautiful body, he was a beautiful young man. He became dark, black, and within a few months it was impossible to recognize him. When people from his capital would come they would be surprised he had changed so much. He had become lean and thin, his eyes had lost luster, his face had lost all grace; he had started becoming ugly. And he was always ill because the body has a limit of tolerance to certain things. But he was not worried; in fact he was enjoying it. All the monks started feeling that he was some great soul. Everybody started feeling that he was superior to them. Now a new ego was arising in Srona.

This sutra is about Srona.

> *One night a monk was reciting a sutra bequeathed by Kashyapabuddha. His tone was so mournful and his voice so fainting, as if he were going out of existence.*

Of course he must have become very sad, he must have become very low and depressed, he must have lost all joy. He was torturing himself. He must have been a little masochistic. He was destroying himself and enjoying the violence. He must have become very serious, a long face; he must have become very deeply ill – all well-being disappeared. He was not a flowering. In fact, the tree was dying.

He was reciting a sutra given by Kashyapabuddha. When you recite a sutra you have to recite it in joy, otherwise it is meaningless. When you pray, if you cannot pray joyfully, it is meaningless. Don't waste your time because your prayer never reaches unless it rides on the horse of joy. Unless you can celebrate, your prayer is never heard. Only through celebration does it reach because existence understands only one language, and that is celebration – no other language. It does not understand English, it does not understand Sanskrit, it does not understand Arabic; it understands only one language: the language of flowers, the language of clouds, the language of peacocks, the language of the cuckoos, the language of joy, the language of greenery, of rivers rushing to the ocean, glaciers gliding down from the mountains. It knows dance, it knows what singing is. Words are not meaningful, only music. It understands sounds, it does not understand words.

Language is man-created; joy is from existence, from God. So whenever you meditate, you pray, you recite a sutra, or you recite the Koran, do it in joy. Otherwise don't do it. There is no need because it is just useless. You are wasting your time. And you may be bugging him, and he may get annoyed, and you may repent later on. At least don't bug him.

I have heard about a Sufi mystic, Hassan. He passed by a

mosque, and a man was reciting the Koran. His voice was so horrible, and he was doing it in such a terrible way, and he was so sad and so serious – as if all his laughter had dried up. His voice sounded like a ghost voice.

Hassan said, "What are you doing?"

He said, "For God's sake, I am reciting the Koran."

Hassan said, "For God's sake, stop!"

Unless you do it in joy, please don't do it. For God's sake, never do it. It is better to be an atheist and not to believe in God than to do something in sadness, depression, than to do something ugly and call it prayer.

But you can do only that which you are. You cannot manage joy suddenly. Unless it is bubbling, unless it is welling up in your being, unless it runs like sap, you cannot manage it. It is not a question of managing your face because God is not looking at your face; God is looking at your heart, so you cannot deceive. Unless joy is in your being, it will not reach; your prayer will never be heard.

That's why I insist that if you can dance and sing, that will do. There is no need to actually verbalize your prayer; let it be exhibited in dance, let it be exhibited in singing. There is no need. You can play guitar or you can play on the flute – that will do. You are using something universal.

> *His tone was so mournful and his voice so fainting, as if he were going out of existence. The Buddha asked the monk, "What was your occupation before you became a homeless monk?"*
> *Said the monk, "I was very fond of playing the guitar."*
> *The Buddha said, "How did you find it when the strings were too loose?"*
> *Said the monk, "No sound is possible."*

When the strings are too loose, sound is not possible...

> *"How when the strings were too tight?"*
> *"They crack."*
> *"How when they were neither too tight nor too loose?"*

> *"Every note sounds in its proper tone."*
> *The Buddha then said to the monk: "Religious discipline is also like unto playing the guitar. When the mind is properly adjusted and quietly applied, the way is attainable…"*

In fact, when the mind is just in the middle, neither too loose nor too tight: balanced, tranquil, still, neither moving left nor right; when the pendulum of the mind has stopped just in the middle – time disappears, the clock stops. In that very moment the way is attainable. In fact, the way is attained. This is the *way*: to be in the middle is the way. You are missing the way because you are not in the middle – and the way is in the middle. In life's situations, in every situation, one has to be alert not to go to the extreme. Otherwise, sometimes the strings are too loose and the music does not arise, and sometimes they are too tight and they crack and instead of music they create just noise. Music is possible only when things are just in the middle. There is a point when the strings are neither tight nor loose.

You must have seen it: whenever Indian musicians play, first they try to bring their instruments to the middle. The drummer will drum his tabla and will feel whether it is in the middle or not; otherwise he will tighten something or loosen something. The veena player will tighten or loosen his strings.

It happened once:

A viceroy was invited by a nawab of Lucknow, and to welcome him he had asked his best musicians to play something for the viceroy. Of course, as it is done traditionally, the musicians started tightening and loosening their instruments. The nawab asked the viceroy, "What type of music do you like most?"

Just to be polite, the viceroy said, "Exactly this music that is going on" – just to be polite! He could not understand what was going on. And then, just to be polite, the nawab ordered the musicians to continue. For three hours they simply continued.

There is a point when the strings are neither loose nor tight – and only a master knows it. It is easy to play on a guitar; it is difficult to bring the guitar to that tuning where music is born, and naturally born, effortlessly born. A man becomes a master or a maestro when he can tune his instrument. Playing is not so difficult; tuning is more difficult – because for tuning you have to learn what the exact middle is. You have to be very alert, very sensitive. Your ear has to be very, very sensitive. Only then can you fix where the middle is.

And Buddha says:

> *Religious discipline is also like unto playing the guitar. When the mind is properly adjusted and quietly applied, the way is attainable; but when you are too fervently bent on it, your body grows tired; and when your body is tired, your spirit becomes weary; when your spirit is weary, your discipline will relax; and with the relaxation of discipline there follows many an evil. Therefore, be calm and pure, and the way will be gained.*

You have to remember it in every life situation. This sutra is of tremendous import because mind tends to move to the polar opposite. If you move to the polar opposite you have again missed the middle, and you are as far away from the middle as you were before. Somebody is an egoist – he becomes a humble man.

The real man of awareness is neither an egoist nor humble. He does not know the language of humility and ego. Humbleness is also the opposite of ego. It is not really opposite; it is the same language. When you say somebody is a humble person, what do you mean? You say that he is not an egoist – that means that from the peak of ego he has moved into the valley of humbleness. But if you come across a buddha, you cannot say he is humble, you cannot say he is an egoist. He simply is. He has not dropped from the peak to the valley. He has just come onto plain ground. That is one of the most difficult things to understand.

A Jesus is not humble in the sense that other saints are humble. A Jesus is not an egoist in the sense that people are egoists. He simply does not know what ego and what humbleness are: he has dropped out of that duality. He simply is, and he responds out of his isness. Sometimes he will look very egoistic to you; that is your interpretation. Sometimes he will look very humble to you; that too is your interpretation.

For example: Christians will talk about those stories in which Jesus looks very humble, that he touched and washed the feet of his disciples – so humble. But they avoid a few other things in which he doesn't look so humble. He chased the moneylenders out of the temple with a whip in his hand. Somehow they avoid that story because there he was not humble at all. He was in a rage. He was a rebel, a revolutionary. In fact, he's neither humble nor egoistic.

The same is true about all those who have attained. Krishna was working as a charioteer for Arjuna: that is his humbleness. Hindus talk about it very much "What humbleness." Anti-Hindus will not talk about it. They will say, "What egoism." He says to Arjuna, "Forget all religions and come to my feet" What egoism! What more can you ask? "This is the peak of egoism." But in fact he is neither. If the situation demands, he can become a driver to his own disciple. He can take the horses to the river, give them a bath, wash them, massage them – the horses of his disciple. And then in another moment he can say to Arjuna, "Forget all I said. Drop all religions, drop all your ideologies. Come to my feet." Now, this is very paradoxical.

But a real man of realization is neither humble nor egoistic. Whatsoever the situation, he responds totally.

Remember, Buddha says whenever you are in the middle, you are on the way. Whenever you are leaning toward the right and left, you are going astray.

"Keeping in the middle" is what he means by being calm because whenever you lean to the left or to the right, you become excited. So never be a rightist and never be a leftist. Just be in the middle and you will be nowhere, and you will be nobody – because in the middle all excitement is lost. One is simply calm.

That's what he means by "being pure." When you lean to the left, the left corrupts you. When you lean to the right, the right corrupts you. When you don't lean, when you are simply in the middle, nothing corrupts you. You become incorruptible. You are pure. *Therefore, be calm and pure, and the way will be gained.*

I told you that a child learns "mine," "me," "you," "I." Now you can move to the opposite and you can say, "Nothing is mine." You can say that there is no ego in you, and you don't possess anything – "me" exists not, and you are also a divine form, a form of the formless. But if it is just moving to the other extreme then nothing is gained. If it is an understanding from the middle, then something is gained. But from the middle you will not say, "I don't possess anything" – remember it. This is possible only if you still think that something can be possessed. One day you think you can possess, another day you deny and you say, "I don't possess anything. I renounce." But in your renunciation also there is possession. How can you renounce the world if you don't possess it?

A real man of understanding never renounces anything. He simply understands, "Nothing is there to possess, so how can I renounce?"

It is said about a Japanese emperor that he renounced his kingdom and went to a Zen master. He bowed down at his feet and said in tremendous humbleness, "I have renounced the kingdom."

The Zen master said, "Then it is better that you go and possess it again, claim it again. It is better that you go."

The emperor was very disturbed. He said, "What do you mean? I have really renounced it."

The master said, "If you have really renounced it, then how can you say that you have renounced it? Real renunciation is simple understanding that nothing belongs to you. There is nothing to renounce."

Renunciation is possible only if, in the first place, you accept that possession is possible. Nonattachment is possible only if, in the first place, you accept that attachment is possible. A real man of understanding comes to know that attachment is not possible. Attachment is false, possession is false: it is not possible. It is impossible to possess. Then what is the point of renouncing? What is the point of becoming nonattached? Attachment simply disappears. If attachment disappears and there is nothing left behind, not even nonattachment – the idea of nonattachment – then you are pure and calm. If attachment disappears but now it is replaced with nonattachment, you have moved to the other extreme. When violence disappears, it is not that there is nonviolence in you. What is the point of nonviolence? Violence has disappeared, and nonviolence with it. The dualities go together. Now suddenly you are left alone, pure. If you get into one, you get into the other too.

"Well, young man, I understand you want to become my son-in-law," said the father to his daughter's boyfriend, Mulla Nasruddin.

"No sir, not exactly," replied Nasruddin. "But if I marry your daughter, I don't see how I can get out of it."

The man had asked, "Well, young man, I understand you want to become my son-in-law"; and said Nasruddin, "No sir, not exactly. But if I marry your daughter I don't see how I can get out of it."

If you marry someone's daughter you become a son-in-law too, at the same time. It is not possible to choose one out of the two; they go together. In fact to call them two is not right. They are one phenomenon just looked at from two sides.

When you become violent, nonviolence comes in. When you become nonviolent, violence waits behind. They go together. All dualities go together. When sex disappears, celibacy disappears too – remember it. If you start claiming that you have become a celibate then sexuality still exists, and any day it can explode. You are sitting on a volcano. When sex has gone, what is the meaning of celibacy? Then it is simply meaningless, the word is meaningless. *Celibacy* can carry a meaning only in reference to sex.

Buddha says when both dualities are gone, you are simply in the middle – silent, calm, pure. The way is attained. The way is the middle way.

Finally, to make you remember it always, let me condense the whole thing into one sentence: whenever you are tired, frustrated, finished with something, remain alert – the mind will tend to go to the opposite.

When the strings are too loose, the mind will tend to make them too tight – and there, again you miss. And when the mind is too tight, the strings are too tight, one day you will get tired of that too because the music will not be coming out of it. Then the mind will tend again to make them too loose.

This is how life goes: one life after another, you go on moving from one pole to another. You become a volleyball kicked from this side to that, kicked from that side to this. If you want to get out of this game, this game of samsara, this game of the world, then be in the middle. Whenever a moment comes to decide, be very alert: never go to the other extreme. Remember to remain in the middle.

If you can learn to remain in the middle you have learned all that is there to learn, and all that is worth learning. Buddha's way is called *majjhim nikai*, "the middle way." He is one of the most penetrating seekers of truth. He has made something very profound, discovered something which you can use. It is not a ritual, it is not a prayer. It is something to do with your awareness. His whole field of work is awareness.

So remain in the middle. If you have been eating too much, don't start fasting. That is too simple. That's how people go on. I know many people: the first two or three months they will fast and diet, and then they will rush into food. Then they will become obsessed, for two or three months they will eat too much. Again, whatsoever the fast has done to their bodies is undone. Again they are ready to fast. This way they go on – volleyballs kicked from here to there.

Right food, right quantity, eaten with awareness, is enough. You need not eat too much, you need not fast.

Remember the middle and you will always be right.

Enough for today.

4

MIND IS A SOUL DISTURBED

AND SOUL IS MIND SILENCED

The first question:

Osho,
How to become integrated?

Integration has nothing to do with "becoming." In fact, all efforts to become bring disintegration. Integration is already there at the deepest core of your being; it has not to be brought in. At your very center you are integrated, otherwise you could not exist at all. How can you exist without a center? The bullock-cart moves, the wheel moves because there is an unmoving center on which the wheel moves. It moves on the hub. If the cart is moving, the hub is there – you may know it, you may not know it.

You are alive, you are breathing, you are conscious; life is moving, so there must be a hub to the wheel of life. You may not be aware, but it is there. Without it, you cannot be.

So the first thing, and very fundamental: becoming is not the issue. You are. You have just to go in and see it. It is a discovery, not an achievement. You have been carrying it all along, but you have become too attached to the periphery, and your back is to the center. You have become too outgoing, so you cannot look in.

Create a little insight. The word *insight* is beautiful – it means: sight in, to look in, to see in. Eyes open outward, hands spread outward, legs move away from you. Sit silently; relax the periphery, close your eyes and just go in. Not with effort – just relax, as if one is drowning and one cannot do anything. We go on doing even when we are drowning.

If you can simply allow it to happen, it will come to surface. Out of the clouds you will see the center arising.

There are two modes of life: one is the action mode, you do something; the other is the reception mode, you simply receive. The action mode is outgoing. If you want more money you cannot just sit. It is not going to come that way. You will have to struggle for it, compete, and you will have to use all sorts of ways and means: legal, illegal, right, wrong. Money is not going to come just by sitting. If you want to become powerful, if you want to become a politician, you will have to do something about it. It is not going to come on its own.

There is an action mode. The action mode is the outgoing mode. And there is an inaction mode too: you don't do anything, you simply allow it to happen. We have forgotten that language. That forgotten language has to be learned again.

Integration does not have to be brought in – it is already there. We have forgotten how to look at it, we have forgotten how to understand it. Move from the action mode more and more to the receptive, passive mode.

I'm not saying to leave the world of action – because that will make you lopsided again. You are lopsided right now. You have only one mode to your life and that is action, doing something. There are people who cannot think of sitting silently; it is impossible. They cannot allow themselves a moment's relaxation. They are only interested in action.

I have heard...

Mulla Nasruddin's wife was standing near the window; it was a beautiful sunset and the birds were flying back to their nests. It was really a wonderful evening, and she told Nasruddin, "Look! Come here. See what a beautiful sunset!"

Nasruddin, never looking away from his newspaper, said "Now what is he doing, this sun?"

If something is being done, then he is interested. If it is just a sunset, then what is the point of looking at it?

You are interested only in action – if something is happening. This has become too fixed. It has to be relaxed a little: you have to go for a few moments, for a few hours, sometimes for a few days, totally to the other mode of life, just sitting and allowing things to happen. When you look at a sunset you are not expected to do anything. You simply look. When you look at a flower, what are you supposed to do? You simply look.

In fact there is no effort, even of looking at the flower. It is effortless. Your eyes are open, the flower is there, a moment of deep communion comes when the looked-at and the looker both disappear. Then there is beauty, then there is benediction. Then suddenly you are not the observer and the flower is not the observed because to observe there must still be some action. Now you are there and the flower is there, and somehow you overlap each other's boundaries. The flower enters into you, you enter into the flower, and there is a sudden revelation. Call it beauty, call it truth, call it godliness.

These rare moments have to be allowed more and more. I cannot say they have to be cultivated, I cannot say you have to train for those moments, I cannot say that you have to do something – because again that will be using the language of the action mode, and will be very deeply misinterpreted. No, I can simply say to allow these moments more and more. Sometimes simply don't do anything. Relax on the lawn and look at the sky. Sometimes close the eyes and just look at your inner world – thoughts moving, floating; desires arising, going. Look at the colorful dreamworld that goes on within you. Just look. Don't say, "I want to stop these thoughts" – again you have moved into the action mode. Don't say, "I am meditating. Go! All thoughts, go away from me" – because if you start saying that, you have started doing something.

As if you are not: this is one of the most ancient meditations still used in some monasteries of Tibet. The meditation is based on the truth that I am saying to you. They teach that sometimes you can simply disappear. Sitting in the garden, just start feeling that you are disappearing. Just see how the world will look when you have gone from the world, when you are no longer here, when you have become absolutely transparent. Just try for a single second not to be. In your own home, be as if you are not.

Just think, one day you will not be. One day you will be gone, you will be dead; the radio will still continue, the wife will still prepare the breakfast, the children will still be getting ready for school. Think that today you are gone, you just are not. Become a ghost. Just sitting in your chair, simply disappear, simply think, "I have no more reality; I am not." And just see how the house continues. There will be tremendous peace and silence. Everything will continue as it is. Without you, everything will continue as it is. Nothing will be missed. Then what is the point of always remaining occupied, doing something, doing something, obsessed with action? What is the point? You will be gone, and whatsoever you have done will disappear – as if you had signed your name on the sands and the wind comes, and the signature disappears. Everything is finished as if you had never existed.

It is really a beautiful meditation. You can try it many times in twenty-four hours, just half a second will do. For half a second, simply stop; you are not and the world continues. When you become more and more alert to the fact that without you the world continues perfectly well, then you will be able to learn another part of your being which has been neglected for long, for lives – and that is the receptive mode. You simply allow, you become a door; things go on happening without you.

This is what Buddha means when he says become like driftwood. Float in the stream like timber, and wherever the stream goes let it take you; don't make any effort. The whole Buddhist approach belongs to the receptive mode. That's why you see Buddha sitting under a tree. All his images are of sitting – sitting and doing nothing. He's simply sitting there; he's not doing anything.

You don't have that type of image of Jesus. He still goes on following the action mode. That's where Christianity has missed the deepest possibility. Christianity became active: the Christian missionary goes on serving the poor, goes to the hospital, does this and that, and his whole effort is to do something good. Yes, very good – but he remains in the action mode, and reality can only be known in the receptive mode. So a Christian missionary will be a good man, a very good man, but not a saint in the Eastern sense.

Now even in the East a person who goes on doing things is worshipped as a mahatma – because the East is poor, ill. There are thousands of lepers, blind people, uneducated people; they need education, they need medicine, they need service, they need a thousand and one things. Suddenly the active person has become important. So Gandhi is a mahatma, Vinoba is a saint, and Mother Theresa of Calcutta has become very important. But nobody looks at whether they have attained to the receptive mode or not.

Now if Buddha comes, nobody is going to pay respect to him because he will not be running a school or a hospital. He will again be sitting under a *bodhi* tree, just sitting silently. Not that nothing is done by him – tremendous vibes are created by his being, but they are very subtle. He transforms the whole world by sitting under his *bodhi* tree, but to look at those vibrations you will have to be attuned, you will have to grow. To recognize a buddha is to be already on the path. To recognize a Mother Theresa is very easy. There is nothing much in it. Anybody can see that she is doing good work.

To do good work is one thing, and to be good is totally another. I'm not saying don't do good works. I am saying: let good works come out of your being good.

First attain to the receptive mode, first attain to the passive, first attain to the nonactive. And when your inner being flowers and you have come to know the integration inside – which is always there, the center is always there – when you have recognized that center, suddenly death disappears for you. Suddenly all worries disappear because you are no longer a body now, and no longer a mind.

Then compassion arises, love arises, prayerfulness arises. You become a showering, a blessing to the world. Now nobody can say what will happen to such a man – whether he will go and become a revolutionary like Jesus and chase the moneylenders from the temple, or whether he will go and serve the poor, or whether he will just continue sitting under the *bodhi* tree and spreading his fragrance. Or perhaps he will become a Meera and dance and sing the glory of God. Nobody knows; it is unpredictable.

You ask me, "How to become integrated?" My whole effort here is to make you aware that nothing is needed, nothing more is needed. You have it already there, existing inside you. But you have to make approaches, doors, ways to discover it. You have to dig for it; the treasure is there.

So it is not a question of how to become integrated. "How to know that I am already integrated?" is the right question.

The question comes from Nisagar, and I can understand why it comes from her. She has been related to Gurdjieff work in the West. Gurdjieff had a very strange idea – meaningful, but still strange. He used to say to his disciples, "The soul does not exist, the center does not exist. It has to be created; man is not born with a soul" – a very strange theory. But I can understand what he was emphasizing: man is not born with a soul, he has to crystallize his soul by effort. Hence Gurdjieff's whole system is called "the work." It is work and work and work. It is effort – again the action mode.

In fact, in the West it is very difficult to teach people the nonaction mode. So he was teaching techniques, methods of becoming integrated. He would say, "There is no soul already there." Not that there is no soul, and not that he was not aware of it, but it was a device. People had become very lethargic about the soul. They thought, "It is already there – so why worry, why bother? It is there. Any day we can find it, so let us in the meanwhile find other things which are not already there. Meanwhile, let us find beautiful women, more wine, more money, more power – things which are not there.

So let us seek these. And the day we are fed up with all this, at any moment, we will close our eyes and we will go in, and the soul will be there. It is never lost; you cannot lose it and you cannot gain it. It is already there." So people have become very lethargic.

You can see it in the East. The whole East has become so lousy and lethargic. The soul is there and everybody knows it, everybody has heard it. God is within the heart, he is already there, so why create any fuss about him? People seek that which is not there.

Gurdjieff became aware of this fact: that the theory that the soul is already there had made people very lethargic, very uninterested in the soul – very uninterested, absolutely uninterested in the inner world. The mind is interested only in that which gives a challenge, which is an adventure. So Gurdjieff, to fit with the Western mind, started saying that the soul is not there: "Don't sit patiently, do something – because when people die, not all survive. Only those who have integrated their centers will survive. Others will simply disappear like vegetables, so it is for you choose. You are taking a risk," Gurdjieff said. "If you do something – and doing means arduous doing, hard work, a whole life devoted – only then will you be able to survive death. Otherwise you are going to be discarded. You will be thrown in the junkyard. God is not going to choose you unless you are integrated. You have to earn it. Only very few will be saved after death, not all."

This is a very strange theory, never propounded before, never in the whole history of humanity. There have been people who say, "There is no soul." We know them; they are atheists. They have always been there. There are people who say, "There is soul, and it cannot be destroyed. Even death cannot destroy it." We have heard about them; they have always been there. But Gurdjieff is saying something absolutely new, something which had never been said before. He is saying that the soul is possible; it is not actual. It is simply possible. You may attain to it, you may not attain to it. You may miss it. There is more possibility that you will miss it because the way you are living, you are not earning it. Gurdjieff said, "Man is like a seed. It is not necessary that the seed will become a tree. It is not necessary; the seed may not find the right soil. Even if the right soil is found, there may be no rains. Or even if there are rains, animals may come and destroy the plant. There are a thousand and one difficulties. The seed is not necessarily going to be a tree. If one thousand and one protections are taken, only then is the seed going to become a tree. You are not a soul; you are just a possibility. A thousand and one efforts have to be made; only then will you become a soul. Only rarely: in one million, one person becomes a soul. All others simply vegetate, die, and disappear."

I say it is a strange theory because it is not true. And I say it is very meaningful because something like this is needed – at least in the West it is needed. Otherwise, nobody bothers about the soul. But all the techniques that Gurdjieff was using are basically the same techniques that we have used in the East for discovering the soul. He simply changed the words. He called it "creating the soul," "integrating the soul," "crystallizing the center." But those techniques are the same.

You are already integrated. Not on the periphery – on the periphery there is much turmoil. You are fragmented on the periphery. Move inward, and the deeper you go the more you will find that you are integrated. There comes a point at the very innermost shrine of your being where you suddenly find you are a unity, absolute unity. So it is a question of discovering. How to discover it?

I would like to give Nisagar a technique. It is a very simple technique, but in the beginning it looks very hard. If you try, you will find it is simple. If you don't try and only think about it, it will look very hard. The technique is: only do that which you enjoy. If you don't enjoy, don't do it. Try it – because enjoyment comes only from your center. If you are doing something and you enjoy it, you start getting reconnected with the center. If you do something which you don't enjoy, you are disconnected from the center. Joy arises from the center, and from nowhere else. So let it be a criterion, and be a fanatic about it.

You are walking on the road; suddenly you recognize that you are not enjoying the walk. Stop. Finished – this is not to be done.

I used to do it in my university days, and people thought that I was crazy. Suddenly I would stop, and then I would remain in that spot for half an hour, an hour, unless I started enjoying walking again. My professors were so afraid that when there were examinations they would put me in a car and take me to the university hall. They would leave me at the door and wait there. Had I reached to my desk or not? If I was taking my bath and suddenly I realized that I was not enjoying it, I would stop. What is the point then? If I was eating and I recognized suddenly that I was not enjoying, then I would stop.

I had joined the mathematics class in my high school. The first day, I went in and the teacher was just introducing the subject. In the middle I stood up and tried to walk out. He said, "Where are you going without asking? I won't allow you in again." I said, "I'm not coming back again; don't be worried. That's why I am not asking. Finished – I am not enjoying it. I will find some other subject which I can enjoy because if I cannot enjoy it, I am not going to do it. It is torture, it is violence."

By and by, it became a key. I suddenly recognized that whenever you are enjoying something you are centered. Enjoyment is just the sound of being centered. Enjoyment is just the humming sound of being centered. Whenever you are not enjoying something, you are off-center. Then don't force it, there is no need. If people think you crazy, let them think you crazy. Within a few days you will, by your own experience, find how you were missing yourself. You were doing a thousand and one things which you never enjoyed, and you were doing them because you were taught to. You were just fulfilling your duties.

People have destroyed even such a beautiful thing as love. You come home and you kiss your wife because it has to be so, it has to be done. Now, a beautiful thing like a kiss, a flowerlike thing, has been destroyed. By and by, without enjoying it, you will go on kissing your wife; you will forget the joy of kissing another human being. You shake hands with anybody you meet – cold, with no meaning in it, with no message in it, no warmth flowing. It is just dead hands shaking each other and saying "Hello." Then you start, by and by, learning this dead gesture, this cold gesture. You become frozen, you become an ice-cube. And then you say, "How to enter the center?"

The center is available when you are warm, when you are flowing, melting, in love, in joy, in dance, in delight. It is up to you. Just go on doing only those things which you really love to do and you enjoy. If you don't enjoy, stop. Find something else that you will enjoy. There is bound to be something that you will enjoy. I have never come across a person who cannot enjoy anything. There are persons who may not enjoy one thing, then another, then another, but life is vast. Don't remain engaged; become floating. Let there be more streaming of energy. Let it flow, let it meet with other energies that surround you. Soon you will be able to see that the problem was not how to become integrated, the problem was that you have forgotten how to flow. In a flowing energy you are suddenly integrated. It happens sometimes accidentally too, but the reason is the same.

Sometimes you fall in love with a woman or a man, and suddenly you feel integrated, suddenly you feel you are one for the first time. Your eyes have a glow, your face has a radiance, and your intellect is no longer dull. Something starts burning bright in your being; a song arises, your walk has a quality of dance in it now. You are a totally different being.

But these are rare moments because we don't learn the secret. The secret is that there be something that you have started to enjoy. That's the whole secret. A painter may be hungry and painting, and still you can see that his face is so contented. A poet may be poor, but when he is singing his song he is the richest man in the world. Nobody is richer than him. What is the secret of it? The secret is that he is enjoying this moment. Whenever you enjoy something, you are in tune with yourself and you are in tune with the universe – because your center is the center of all.

So let this small insight be a climate for you: do only that which you enjoy, otherwise stop. You are reading a newspaper and halfway through it you suddenly recognize that you are not enjoying it – then there is no necessity. Then why are you reading? Stop it here and now. If you are talking to somebody and in the middle you recognize that you are not enjoying it, you have just said half a sentence, stop then and there. You are not enjoying, you are not obliged to continue. In the beginning it will look a little weird. But my sannyasins are weird, so I don't think there is any problem. You can practice it.

Nisagar is old, but I can see a childlike quality in her. She can also do it. And I hope she will do it. Within a few days many contacts will be made with the center, and then you will understand what I mean when I go on repeating again and again that that which you are seeking is already in you. It is not in the future. It has nothing to do with the future. It is already herenow, it is already the case.

The second question:

> *Osho,*
> *Why is it that by giving a name or a theory to an uncomfortable, confusing or painful place, I feel better?*

The human ego always feels humiliated when it comes across a fact that it cannot explain. Whenever the human ego comes across a fact that it cannot name, and it has to recognize its ignorance, it feels very offended. That's why people go on labeling things. They are no longer interested in things themselves; they are more interested in labeling.

If they see a flower they don't see the beauty of it, they don't smell the fragrance of it, they don't look at the message of it. They simply start looking as to what species the flower belongs, what its name is. The flower really has no name. If you ask the flower, it cannot say any name to you. It has no identity card, it has no passport, it has no identity. It is simply there, and all names are given by man. And man is really continuously giving names, since the days of Adam.

There is a story in the Bible that God created things and he told Adam, "You name it and that will be its name " – a beautiful story. So he started naming things. God created the rose, and Adam looked at it and he called it a "rose." Not that he knew it was a rose – nobody knew, not even God. God had told Adam to say a name, and whatsoever he said would be the name. And the names that he gave to things have remained, but they were just accidental. It was a very crazy way to name things, but that was the only way – because things don't have any name. And man has named many things very wrongly.

When God created woman he asked Adam; that was the last

thing Adam named. He called her "Hava," or "Eva," or "Eve," or "Havva." These were the different pronunciations of what he called her: "Hava," or "Habba," or "Eve." "Hava" means life; he called the woman his life. But down through the centuries man has suffered very much; and many times he tried to change the name, but it was too late. Since then this has been a continuous effort: all that scientists go on doing is just naming things.

And you ask, "Why do you name it?" It is the same old technique; it is just a crazy way. They discover a new star; why do they name it? Why do they call it Pluto, or Neptune, or anything? Who decides? They go on naming things, just anything that comes to the mind. Now even on the moon they have decided on names. Wherever man reaches, the first thing he does is to decide on labels. Man has an obsession. The moment you see somebody you ask, "What is your name? What is your religion? What is your country?" Are these things in any way helpful to know this man who is standing in front of you? What difference does it make? How does it make any difference whether he is called Robert, or Rama or Rahim? It makes no difference. But it is easier – if the man is called Rahim you know he is a Mohammedan. If you are a Hindu, now there is a conflict. Now you can avoid this man: "This is not worth it, it is dangerous." Now you can remain alert: "This is a Mohammedan." He must be carrying a knife, and he may kill you. Or if he is Rama, you are very happy: "So he is a Hindu – and not only a Hindu, but he must be religious; his name is Rama." You are very happy. Suddenly there is no barrier: you would like to talk to this man, you will come a little closer. You are ready to expose yourself to him.

Naming, knowing who is who, helps you to become a little more certain about the uncertain reality. But the reality remains uncertain.

Once it happened...

I was traveling and there was only one other passenger in my compartment. He asked me what my name was. I told him a name. Then after a few minutes I said, "Sorry, that was not my name." I told him another name. Now he became very suspicious. I was the same man, but he became very suspicious. When the conductor came, he told him that he wanted to change compartments. "What type of man is this? Just a few minutes ago he said 'This is my name,' and then he himself says 'I am sorry.' Is he crazy? It is dangerous to sleep with this man in the night."

When he was leaving I said, "Sorry, the first name was right."

He simply escaped without saying anything.

Names, labels, categories: the mind feels very happy. If you can explain – maybe your explanation is absurd, foolish – just the explanation makes you feel happy. People go to outlandish lengths, exotic explanations because nobody wants to recognize the simple fact that they don't know. If somebody asks, "What is your name?" and you say, "I don't know because when I came, I came without a name," if somebody asks to what country you belong and you say, "I don't know because the earth is one" – then that man will feel uncomfortable, uneasy. Any explanation will do.

People have a very great desire to remain knowledgeable because knowledge is security and knowledge is power. That's why each century invents its own nonsense – because there are millions of problems which can never be solved. Who knows who made the world? But there are foolish people who want to know. Only foolish people want to know who made the world. The question is foolish, it is foolish because the question will lead into an infinite regress. If you say, "God made the world," then the question arises, "Who made God?" And you go on and on; it cannot be ended. There is no way to end it.

But there are people who are ready to supply you with answers. You ask and they are ready. They manufacture answers. Three hundred religions exist on the earth, and three hundred religions have at least three thousand metaphysical theories, and each theory is against the other, and there is no way to decide who is right – because all are wrong. You cannot decide because all are just imagination.

I was reading...

In a ladies' Turkish bath, one woman was standing out because of the length of her breasts. She had very, very long breasts, almost incredible.

"Oh dear, what happened to your breasts?" she was asked by a friend.

"Well," she tried to explain, "my husband is such a baby, he likes to sleep sucking my breasts."

"Well, so does mine," said the friend, still not understanding.

"The problem is," continued the first woman, "my husband and I sleep in two different rooms."

Now everything is explained, now there is no problem. If you look at your metaphysical theories you will find such explanations. They are all stupid, but they satisfy a certain urge. They help a certain uneasiness. They help you relax – "God created the world?" Okay, so you know the answer; so you are in the know, you are not ignorant. Then you would like to know what God looks like. Then somebody, some painter, some sculptor, will make an image.

A small boy was painting something and the mother asked, "You seem to be so interested. What are you doing? You have been there for hours."

The boy said, "I am trying to draw the face of God."

The mother laughed. She said, "Nobody knows how God looks."

The child said, "Wait. When I have finished, everybody will know."

That's what has been done. Temples, images, paintings – nobody knows how God looks. It is everybody's guess, so you can give four faces to God, one thousand hands to God – it is up to you. Your God is your creation, but once you have made it, it is very difficult. If somebody says that it is just imagination, a guess, you will be angry. You will start fighting. That's why religions have been fighting with each other. Why does so much fight go on? Whether God had three faces or four, what difference does it make? But no, it is a great problem, and the problem is psychological.

If you say to the person who has always believed that God has three faces that he has four, you are disturbing. You are disturbing his knowledge. He is not worried about God – who is worried about God? But he is worried about it. He has settled himself, he was feeling secure in his knowledge, he was feeling that he was in the know. Now here you come and you say, "No, God has four faces." Now you create an anxiety in him, again the same anxiety that was there before he had decided. That's why one religion does not want to listen to another religion's ideas – because it creates anxiety. It creates a great turmoil, it creates a great chaos.

People want to remain fixed in their ideas; nobody should disturb them. But this is not knowledge, this is belief. Belief means you cannot recognize the fact that you don't know. You are not courageous enough to recognize that you are ignorant. Cowards carry many beliefs with them so there is no need to recognize the fact of ignorance. But ignorance is more beautiful than false knowledge; at least it is true, authentic. If a person says, "I don't know," to me, he is the beginning of a religious consciousness. He is at the door. If the person who says, "I know," gets disturbed if you say anything against him and is worried and starts protecting and defending himself, then it seems that his knowledge is just a security measure. He has just created a make-believe around him. He had been living in his dream, and you come and you disturb the dream.

You cannot disturb a man of knowing because a man of knowing knows that the ultimate cannot be known. You can have a taste of it, but you can never formulate it. The ultimate remains a mystery; mystery is its very nature. There is no way to dissolve the mystery. He knows his ignorance, he knows the ultimate mystery. And the ultimate mystery and the seeker's ignorance meet with each other, and there is a great communion.

When the person of knowledge goes to truth, he never listens to truth – because truth is also disturbing. He has his belief; the truth has to follow his belief, the truth has to come in the form of his belief. Only then can he recognize it.

It is said about Tulsidas, a great Hindu poet – I will not call him a great Hindu saint, but he was really a great poet…

He was taken to a temple of Krishna in Mathura. He was a follower of Rama. A person took him to this beautiful temple, and Krishna's statue was there with a flute on his lips. But Tulsidas would not bow down. The friends asked, "Why? Why don't you bow down?"

He said, "I cannot. I can bow down only to Rama. If," he said to Krishna's statue, "if you want me to bow down to you, then you will have to become Rama. Change your form, and rather than the flute take a bow, as Rama carries a bow."

The story says that Krishna transformed his form. He became Rama with a bow on his shoulder. And then Tulsidas bowed down.

The story must be fiction, but it is very symbolic: a person who has a belief would always like to force truth to come according to his belief, according to his channel. But truth never comes according to you. So half the story seems to be true and the other half seems to be fiction. It seems to be true that Tulsidas said that he would not bow down unless Krishna took the form of Rama because he was a devotee of Rama's. Up to this point the story seems to be true. But Krishna taking the form of Rama? Truth following your belief? That means truth has to bow to you first, and then you will bow down to truth. That is ugly. Even to conceive it is horrible. No, truth is not there to fulfill anybody's expectations.

Beliefs become barriers, but beliefs help. They help you to dissolve anxiety.

The questioner asks, "Why is it that by giving a name or a theory to an uncomfortable, confusing, or painful place, I feel better?" – because you become knowledgeable. Then the problem is dissolved. There is no mystery. You know, but this knowledge is very dangerous. Don't do it any more.

Remain uncomfortable. It is better to remain uncomfortable. If you feel uneasiness, remain with your uneasiness, but don't just try to find an explanation. Don't invent any explanations. Remain uneasy; accept that as natural, and soon you will come to a point where you will start loving the mystery of things. Then the uneasiness will disappear and you will not become knowledgeable. You will not become a pundit, a scholar – because the scholar is in a worse place. Even sinners have reached to truth, but nobody has ever heard of a scholar – because the scholar is in a worse place. Even sinners have reached to truth, but nobody has ever heard of any pundit reaching to truth. It is impossible; it does not happen. The more you know, the farther away you are from truth because the more corrupted you become with your knowledge. The more innocent you are, and the more your eyes are not filled by any theory and are simply there like open windows ready to absorb truth, the better it is.

Be innocent, not knowledgeable. Be ignorant. It is better because in your ignorance you accept the mystery of life. Life cannot be explained. All explanations are very tiny, small, rigid, and life is so vast, so immense, it cannot be contained in any explanation, neither Christian, nor Hindu, nor Mohammedan, nor Jaina, nor Buddhist. All attempts to explain have failed, all religions have failed.

So don't choose convenience, choose truth. The truth is that truth is a mystery. Don't name it, and don't feel good just by naming it. Your name explains nothing; it simply protects you from truth. You become closed to truth, you are defending yourself against truth. And what type of defense is this? – it is destructive. Don't be defensive; be vulnerable. If truth makes you uncomfortable, let it be so. That is the price one has to pay for truth.

The third question:

> *Osho,*
> *I know I am a woman, but at times I display traits that seem to be very masculine. Are there such things as innately female or male characteristics?*

Listen to the question. "I know I am a woman" – that too has become knowledge: "I know." Can't it be said simply that you are a woman? Has it to go through knowledge? It is as if somebody says, "I think fire is hot." Can't you say simply, "Fire is hot?" Does it have to go through your thinking first? You say, "I think that fire is hot." Fire is simply hot; your thinking is not needed. Either you are a woman or a man. What is the point of saying, "I know I am a woman?" Why does everything have to go through the door of knowledge? Why can't facts simply be facts?

Even the question shows – everything shows your mind; even the formulation of the question shows it.

I have heard...

When asked by the marriage counselor what seemed to be the

problem in their marriage, the husband replied, "I don't have a problem. But old what's-her-name..." and he stopped and pointed to his wife, "she does not think I pay enough attention to her."

"What's-her-name" he says. He does not even know the name of his wife. The very formulation shows the problem.

"I know I am a woman" Please stop knowing, start feeling. Feel you are a woman. Feeling is from a different center; it is from the heart. Knowing is from a different center; it is from the head. Knowing is dead, feeling is alive.

People come to me and they say, "I think I have fallen in love." Can't you simply fall in love? Has the head to interfere everywhere? Has the head to always be between you and your relationships, in any relationship, in every relationship? Can't you put your head aside a little?

There is a famous dictum of a Western philosopher, Rene Descartes: *cogito ergo sum* – I think, therefore I am. This is absurd: I think, therefore I am? It shows that thinking is primary and being is secondary – I think, therefore I am.

Thinking is secondary. Being is first. First you are, then you think. If you are not, then who is going to think? Thinking cannot exist in a vacuum. If somebody says, "I am, therefore I think," it is right. But to say "I think, therefore I am" is simply absurd. But still there is a meaning to it: Descartes is the father of Western philosophy, and the whole Western mind has been influenced by two persons – Aristotle and Descartes. So in the West everything goes through thinking; even being goes through thinking. Even being is not a simple fact; you have to think about it first, then you are – as if it is a logical conclusion. It is existential, it is not logical.

So first stop thinking that you are a man or woman. Just know it. Knowing is direct. Somebody else can be in doubt, but you should not be in doubt. Somebody else can think about whether you are a man or a woman – and if you live in hippie style, sometimes it can be very difficult.

When I give sannyas to somebody and I cannot decide, I have to ask Mukta, "Mukta, what do you think?" Now she has learned; whenever she feels that I will be in doubt, she silently whispers, "She is a woman."

Two hippies entered a hotel, and the hotel manager said, "You cannot come in because we follow particular rules. Anybody who enters here has to wear a tie."

So the one said, "Okay." He went out. Fifteen minutes later he came with a tie, and the manager said, "Okay, you can enter, but what about the other?"

He said, "He is my wife. Don't you even allow women to come into the hotel without ties?"

If others are in doubt as to whether you are a he or a she, it is okay. But you yourself? Then the doubt has entered very deep and has become a disease. Drop that.

But the question is very significant: "I know I am a woman, but at times I display traits that seem to be very masculine. Are there such things as innately female or male characteristics?" Each individual is both because each individual is born out of both, a mother and a father. A part of you comes from your father, a part of you comes from your mother, so you cannot be absolutely a man or absolutely a woman. In fact, everybody is unisex: the difference is only of degrees, quantity. A man is more man than woman, that's all; a woman is more woman than man, that's all. The difference is of degree. That's why there is the possibility of a change of sex. If hormones can be injected and your inner balance can be changed, a man can become a woman, a woman can become a man. By the end of this century, people will be changing sex in large numbers because it is natural. One gets fed up with being a man, always a man, always a man; one gets fed up with being a woman, and one wants to change places. By the end of this century, changing sex will become a very common thing. And it is good. A person can have three or four lives in one life: for a few years you remain a woman, then you become a man, and then you become a woman again. It can be done now. It is scientifically feasible and better processes will be available soon. It can be done because each is both.

If you are a man, then the conscious part of your brain is man and the unconscious part is woman. If you are a woman, then the conscious part is a woman and the unconscious part is a man. And many times there are reversals also.

For example, as a man becomes older, he starts becoming more feminine, and when women become older they start becoming more masculine. Old women start growing mustaches, their voices become more like a male's, they become more quarrelsome, fighting, angry, irritated. As a man becomes old he becomes more docile, more obedient, more henpecked.

Mulla Nasruddin's wife was telling her kids, of which there were fifteen, "From this month, every month I am going to give an award to the most obedient child."

They all said, "This is unjust."

She said, "Why?"

They all said, "Papa will always win the award."

By and by the man becomes docile, and by and by the woman becomes more dominating. And there are changes every day also. If a woman becomes very angry, she loses her conscious part and the unconscious becomes very predominant. An angry woman is more dangerous than an angry man. An enraged woman is more dangerous than an enraged man because the woman's unconscious part is very fresh. It is rarely used, so when it is used she can become very dangerous. If a woman loves you, she loves you tremendously; if she hates you, then she hates you tremendously.

When a man is loving, his love is very deep, deeper than a woman's because his unconscious part is unused. In love, man goes very deep, deeper than woman because for a woman to love is very ordinary. It is her usual way; she is loving. But for a man to fall in love is very difficult. It is not his usual way, it rarely happens. But when it happens then his love is so deep that no woman can compete with him.

This is my observation: if a woman loves – and all women love – love is just natural. It is part of the feminine mind. Ordinarily a man never loves so much. Ordinarily love is just one of the many things that they do, one of the many things, and may not even be the most important. Sometimes business is more important, and love is just a recreation, just a relaxation from business, secondary to business. If they have to choose, they will choose business.

A Jew was caught red-handed with a gun in his hand.

He was going to kill a man: the man was making love to his wife. The magistrate asked, "Your gun was loaded, then why didn't you really kill him? Were you simply pretending or something?"

The man said, "When I took my gun and I was just about to kill him, this man asked, 'How much will you take for the gun?' Now, how can you kill a man who is talking business?"

A Jew is a Jew: how can you kill a man when he is talking business? Then you forget all about the wife, that he was making love to your wife, when business comes.

There are people for whom politics is more important than love – money, respectability, morality; a thousand things are there for a man. But a woman loves. She loves totally – that is her one thing. It is not one thing in many. When a man loves, he loves for a few minutes in a day. When a woman loves, she loves for twenty-four hours. This is natural. But if sometimes a man loves, then no woman can be compared to him because then his inner woman erupts. Then there arises a Majnu, or a Farhad; a great lover is born. Have you seen this fact that Majnu and Farhad and this type of man has existed, but no woman has existed in the stories to compare to them? Why? Nobody has loved so madly, no woman has loved so madly as Majnu, no woman has loved so madly as Farhad, because when a man really goes into love, then he is no longer a man. Then his inner unconscious explodes and takes total possession of him.

When a woman becomes angry, aggressive, she can be very dangerous. Never provoke a woman. If you provoke a man he will follow some rules and regulations of fight and war; a woman does not follow these. She simply will jump upon you and tear you, bite you, kill you – she will not follow any rules. She does not know them. Her man is not trained at all; when he explodes, he simply explodes.

Both of these are together in you. What does the seeker have to do, what does a disciple have to do? He has to become aware of both, and he has to drop being identified with either. A true seeker has to drop identities. He has to learn that he is neither a man nor a woman; he is the witness. Then you go beyond biology. Only then do you go beyond body – because man and woman exist in the body. At the most, their reflections exist in the mind. But the soul is neither man nor woman. You have to go beyond both. So watch, and remain distant, aloof. Remain aware. When the woman is there functioning, watch; when the man is there functioning, watch – but remain alert that you are neither.

That's why real awareness always leads you beyond sex, and celibacy happens on its own accord. To be in sex you have either to be identified with the male or identified with the female. A real celibate is one who has gone beyond, who is neither.

But I am not talking about repression. I am not saying that you should repress. I am not saying that you should repress your woman or repress your man. I am against all repression. I am saying express your womanhood, express your manhood, but remain alert because if you repress then it will come in some way or other.

Let me tell you one anecdote:

The three priests, dressed in slacks and T-shirts, were about to tee off when the golf hustler interrupted and asked if he could make up the foursome. "Okay," said the eldest priest. "But we must tell you, we are not good golfers."

Of course, the hustler swore he was a poor player too. "And how about a bet to make it more interesting?" One of the priests protested that they never bet, but to please him they made a rather steep wager. Naturally the golf hustler won and the priests paid up.

When they all returned to the locker rooms, the hustler was shocked to see their habits and offered to return the money.

"No, we made a bet and we stick to it. It will teach us a lesson," said the eldest priest.

"Well," said the man, "I still feel funny hustling priests. Is there anything I can do?"

"Do you have parents?" asked the priest.

"Yes, I do."

"Well bring them to me and I will marry them."

Repression is like that: you want to say "bastard," but you go roundabout.

And repression can create a change, but not a real change. You will move from one extreme to the other. Only awareness can take you beyond the duality.

Let me tell you one more anecdote.

On a long train ride in the hot afternoon, one of the passengers kept repeating aloud, "God, I am thirsty! God, I am thirsty! God, I am thirsty!" Annoyed by such mantric repetitions, the traveler sitting in front of him brought the thirsty man a large bottle of cold soda at the coming station. With eyes beaming in gratitude, the thirsty man stood up, grabbed the bottle, and drank it at once. For a split moment he seemed happy, satisfied, content. Then he sat down again and started repeating aloud, "God, I was thirsty! God, I was thirsty! God, I was so thirsty!"

But the mantra continues. You can move from one extreme to the other; the change will be just on the surface. Deep down you will remain the same, and the change has to happen in depth. Only awareness goes into depth. Repression is just whitewashing; it does not change your roots, it is not radical.

Osho,
I am confused about the difference between surrender and following my inner light. It seems that when I want to surrender, I am afraid to be responsible for myself, and when I want to follow my inner light, I'm afraid of what you will ask of me in surrender.

You have to be absolutely clear about it. If you already have the inner light there is no need for any surrender because surrender is only going to help you to bring the inner light. If you have it already, then forget all about surrender. But you don't have it. Just to avoid surrender you imagine that you have it.

If you have it, you have it. Then the question of surrender does not arise. You don't have it; you only have inner darkness, no inner light, so when you go in you find darkness. Then you start thinking of surrender. When you start thinking of surrender then you become afraid because the ego comes in. It is not the inner light that is hindering you, inner light never hinders anybody.

Let me say it in this way: if you surrender, it is a help to the inner light; if there is inner light, it is a help to surrender because inner light and surrender are two aspects of the same coin.

If you have inner light, then there is no fear in surrendering because fear comes only because of the ego. The inner light is already a surrendering phenomenon; you are already surrendered.

So if you have the inner light, first I say there is no need to surrender. Second, I say that if you have the inner light, then there will be no problem in surrender. If you don't have the inner light, then there is trouble. Then you need surrender in the first place, and you will avoid surrender in the second place. Let me tell you one very beautiful story. Meditate over it.

One day, an atheist was walking along a cliff when he slipped and fell over the edge. As he plunged downward he managed to grab the branch of a small tree that was growing from a crevice in the rock. Hanging there, swaying in the cold wind, he realized how helpless his position was. Far below were jagged boulders and there was no way to climb up. His grip on the branch was weakening every second. "Well," he thought, "only God can save me now. I have never believed in God but I might be wrong. What have I to lose?" So he called out, "God, if you exist, save me, and I will believe in you." There was no answer. He called again, "Please God, I never believed in you, but if you will save me now I will believe in you from now on!"

Suddenly a great voice boomed down from the clouds, "Oh no you won't, I know your kind."

The man was so surprised, he almost lost his grip on the branch. "Please God, you are wrong. I really mean it; I will believe."

"Oh no you won't. That's what they all say."

The man pleaded and argued. Finally God said, "Alright, I will save you. Let go of the branch."

"Let go of the branch!" the man exclaimed. "Do you think I am crazy?"

Think about this.

Even when you have nothing to lose, you are afraid to surrender. Now the man says, "Let go of the branch! Do you think I am crazy?" Hanging on to this branch in the cold wind, and his grip every moment becoming weaker and weaker, and still he is not ready to surrender.

You can be saved only when you surrender. Your surrender shows that you trust; there is no other way to show it. Your prayer is not enough. The man was praying. "Save me!" but he could not show trust. Your prayer is impotent. If there is no trust to back it, then it means nothing. Only your trust shows that your prayer is meaningful, that you really mean it.

If you feel that on your own nothing is happening and you are getting more and more lost in darkness… On your own, if you see that only death is coming closer and closer and your grip is becoming weaker and weaker and you will dissolve into death sooner or later – if you see that, my message is: let go of the branch. If you can let go, immediately, in that very let-go, you are saved because you are saved from yourself.

The problem is not somewhere outside; the problem is your ego. You have to be saved from the ego. The problem is man himself; man has to be saved from man himself. The enemy is not outside, the enemy is within. In surrender you drop that enemy. In that very dropping the inner darkness disappears – not that you surrender and I will do something. Remember, nobody can do anything. When you surrender, in that very surrender something happens and your inner light starts burning, your inner light starts becoming clear. Clouds disappear.

Not that through your surrender I will do something to you. You do something to you through your surrender. I am just an excuse, and this has to be understood.

Don't surrender to me in order not to have any responsibility. Don't surrender to me in greed. Don't surrender to me thinking that now I will do something. Nobody can do anything to you; that is your total freedom, nobody can interfere in it. I am just an excuse. Without me it will be difficult for you to surrender. Otherwise, you can go and you can surrender to the sky; the same will happen. You can go and you can surrender to a Buddha statue and the same will happen. You can go to a mosque where there is no statue and surrender, and the same will happen. These are all excuses. You can use whichever excuse you like best – but surrender you have to do.

In surrender your ego is dropped. Your ego is your ignorance, your ego is your darkness, your ego is your prison.

Enough for today.

5

THE DISCIPLINE OF TRANSCENDENCE

The Buddha said:

When a man makes utensils out of a metal which has been thoroughly cleansed of dross, the utensils will be excellent. You monks, who wish to follow the way, make your own hearts clean from the dirt of evil passions, and your conduct will be unimpeachable.

The Buddha said:

Even if one escapes from the evil creations, it is one's rare fortune to be born a human being. If one be born a man, it is one's rare fortune to be perfect in all the six senses. Even if he be perfect in all the six senses, it is his rare fortune to be born in the time of a buddha. Even if he be born in the time of a buddha, it is his rare fortune to see the enlightened. Even if he be able to see the enlightened, it is his rare fortune to have his heart awakened in faith. Even if he have faith, it is his rare fortune to awaken the heart of intelligence. Even if he awakens the heart of intelligence, it is his rare fortune to realize a spiritual state which is above discipline and attainment.

The Buddha said:
O children of Buddha! You are away from me ever so many thousand miles, but if you remember and think of my precepts, you shall surely gain the fruit of enlightenment. You may, standing by my side, see me always, but if you observe not my precepts, you shall never gain enlightenment.

Consciousness is like a lake: with waves it becomes the mind, without waves it becomes the soul. The difference is only of turmoil. Mind is a soul disturbed, and soul is mind silenced. The mind is just the ill state of affairs, and the soul is the healthy state of affairs. Mind is not something separate from the soul, as waves are not separate from the lake. The lake can be without waves, but the waves cannot be without the lake. The soul can be without the mind, but the mind cannot be without the soul.

When there are great winds and the lake is disturbed, there is turmoil. And the lake loses one quality in that turmoil, and that is the quality of reflection. Then it cannot reflect the real. The real becomes distorted. There may be a full moon in the sky, but now the lake is not capable of reflecting it. The moon will still be reflected, but in a distorted way. It will be reflected in thousands of fragments. It will not be a unity; it will not be collected, integrated. It will not be one. The real is one. But now the lake will reflect many millions of moons; the whole surface of the lake may be filled with silver. Everywhere, moons and moons – but this is not true. The truth is one: when the mind reflects it, it becomes many; when consciousness reflects it, it is one.

Consciousness is neither Hindu nor Mohammedan nor Christian. If you are a Hindu, you are still in the mind, distorted. If you are a Mohammedan, you are still in the mind, distorted. Once the mind has settled and the waves are no longer there, you are simply a consciousness – with no adjective attached to it, with no conditioning attached to it. Then truth is one. In fact, even to say that truth is one is not right because one is meaningful only in the context of many. Truth is so "one" that in the East we have never called it one; we call it nondual – not two.

Why have we chosen a roundabout way in calling it not two? We want to say that it is difficult to speak of it as one because one implies two, three, four. We simply say not two. We don't say what it is, we simply say what it is not. There is no "manyness" in it – that's all. We have to express it *via negativa*, by saying that it is not two. It is so one and it is so alone that only it exists, and nothing else. But that is reflected in consciousness when the mind is no longer there. When I say the mind is no longer there, remember, I am not talking about the mind as a faculty. The mind is not a faculty. It is simply a disturbed state: consciousness waving, shaking, trembling, not at home.

What winds blow on the consciousness and disturb it? Buddha says the name of that wind is passion, desire.

Watch, and you will see the truth of Buddha's saying. It is a fact, it has nothing to do with any theory. Buddha is not interested in abstract systems, he simply says that which is. He's not formulating a philosophy. Always remember, never forget, that he is very experimental, existential. His whole approach is just to say something that you can immediately experience, and your experience will prove that he is right. There is no other way to prove right or wrong. There is no way to argue about it.

Just sometimes sit silently; even if for a single moment desire stops, you will see that all turmoil has disappeared. Sitting silently, not desiring anything; sitting silently, not moving in the future; sitting silently, contented; in that single moment you will be able to understand what Buddha means. Suddenly you will see that there are no waves at all. All the waves have gone. The waves arise only when you desire, when you are discontented with the present and you hope for the future.

Desire is a tension between the present and the future. In that tension, waves arise. Then you are shattered – and consciousness is very fragile. Consciousness is very soft: just a slight desire, just a flicker of desire, and the whole lake is disturbed. Go sometimes: watch, sit by the bank of a lake. See – there are no ripples. Throw a small pebble, a very small pebble, in the biggest of lakes, and the small pebble will start creating ripples, and those ripples will go on spreading to the farthest bank. Just a small pebble creates so much disturbance. Just a slight desire and disturbance comes through the back door.

Desire is disturbance, passion is a fever. In passion you are not yourself. In passion you are beside yourself. In passion you are not centered, you lose your balance. In passion you do things you cannot even imagine that you could have done. Many murderers have confessed in the courts, down through the centuries, that they had not committed the crime. It happened; they were in such rage, they were almost mad. They had not done it deliberately, it had happened. They are not criminals, they are victims of their own rage. You may think they are deceiving, you may think they are now trying to escape from punishment – no, it is not so.

Murder is impossible if you are conscious, if you are silent, if you are centered. It happens only when you are not, when you are so clouded, when there are only waves and waves and the surface of the lake is completely disturbed. Then it happens: all wrong happens only when you are disturbed. Ordinarily, religious people say, "Cultivate character." Buddha says, "Cultivate consciousness." Ordinary religious teachers say, "Do good." Buddha says, "Be silent and good will be done." The good follows silence as your shadow follows you. There is no way to do good unless you are silent. You can do good, but only wrong will happen if you are not silent. That's why the so-called do-gooders go on doing a thousand and one mischiefs in the world. Your so-called do-gooders are the most mischievous people, but they are doing good for your sake, they are doing it for good, and you cannot even escape from them.

Everybody knows that good parents are dangerous parents. A parent that is too good is bound to be a wrong parent because he will encage you. Too much good is destructive. A good mother will destroy you because the mother herself is not centered. Her good is enforced; she is trying to do good. The good is not natural and spontaneous. It is not like a shadow; it is effort, it is violent. Your so-called mahatmas go on crippling people, destroying people, destroying their freedom in many ways. They go on trying to dominate by subtle methods, in subtle ways, but the whole desire is to dominate. And it is very easy to dominate somebody when you are good: he cannot even rebel against you. You can escape against a bad mother, but what to do against a good mother? She's so good that you start feeling bad. Watch it: everybody has passed through that state, and it has to be understood. Otherwise you will never be able to accept yourself.

Whenever there is a child, there is bound to be some conflict between the child and the parents, particularly between the child and the mother in the beginning, and then later on with the father. It is natural – the mother has her own way, her own ideas, her own philosophy of how life should be lived. The child is almost wild; he knows no society, no culture, no religion. He's coming directly from existence; he's as wild as existence. He has nothing but freedom, so there is bound to be some conflict. And the child has to be initiated into the walls of the society. He cannot be left alone – that too is true. So conflict is natural. If the mother is very good then the child is in a difficulty, a very great anguish and anxiety. The anxiety is that the child loves his freedom and knows, intrinsically, that freedom is good. Freedom is an intrinsic value. There is no need to prove that freedom is good. Freedom is good, it is self-evidently good. Everybody is born with that desire. That's why we called the ultimate goal in the East "total freedom," *moksha*: where the intrinsic desire is completely fulfilled and one has no limitations of any sort. One is absolutely free, unconditionally free.

Every child is born with that intrinsic desire to be free, and now everywhere there is bondage. The mother says, "Don't do this, don't do that, sit here, don't go there." And the child feels pulled and pushed from everywhere. Now, if the mother is bad, there is not much difficulty; the child can think that the mother is bad and deep in his heart he can start hating her. Simple, it is arithmetical – she is destroying his freedom and he hates her. Maybe, for political reasons, he cannot express it, so he becomes a diplomat. He knows that she is the rottenest woman in the world, but he goes on paying lip service.

But if the mother is good then the problem arises. Then the child is at a loss to figure it out; the mother is good, and freedom is good: "Now, if Mother is good then I must be wrong, and my freedom must be wrong. If I am good and my freedom is good, then Mother must be wrong." Now, to think that the mother is wrong is impossible – because she is really good, and she goes on caring, loving, and doing a thousand and one things for the child. The mother is really good, the child knows that she is good. So there is only one possibility to decide, and that is: "I must be wrong. My mother is good, I must be wrong."

Once the child starts thinking, "I must be wrong," he starts rejecting himself. I ordinarily never come across a person who accepts himself totally. If you don't accept yourself totally, you will never grow because growth is out of acceptance. If you go on rejecting yourself, you are creating a split. You will be schizophrenic. The part that you reject will hang around your neck like a great burden, a great sorrow, a great anxiety, a tension. You cannot throw it away because it is part of you. It cannot be divided; at the most you can throw it into unconsciousness. You can become unaware of it, you can forget about it, you can believe that it is not there. That's how the unconscious is created.

The unconscious is not a natural thing. The unconscious is the part of your being that you have rejected and you don't even want to face. You don't want to encounter it, you don't want to see that it exists at all. It is there: deep down in your being it goes on manipulating you. It will take many types of revenge because it also needs expression. Now, this is the whole misery of human beings. A good mother can create the idea of a bad child. The child himself starts rejecting himself. This is a division, a split in personality. The child is becoming neurotic because to feel good with oneself should be a natural and easy thing. That's what your religious preachers go on doing, what your priests go on doing: go to the mosque, go to the temple, go to the church, and they are there – thundering, condemnatory, ready to throw you into hell, ready to reward you with heaven if you listen to them, if you follow them. Of course you cannot follow because their demands are impossible, and their demands are impossible because they don't show you the way to be good. They simply say. "Be good."

The way to be good has nothing to do with being good. The way to be good has something to do with centering, with awareness. Being good has nothing to do with your character. A really good person has no character at all; he is characterless. And when I say "characterless," I mean he has no armor, no armature around him. He has no defenses around him, he's simply open. He's as characterless as a flower. He's neither good nor bad. He's simply there – alert, conscious, responsible. If something happens he will respond, but he will respond directly, he will respond from here. He will respond out of the now, he will not respond out of the past. "Character" means you go on carrying the things that you have learned in your past. "Character" means the conscience that has been preached to you and forced upon you. Conscience is a prison for consciousness.

Buddha brought a revolution into the world of religion, the greatest ever. The revolution was that he emphasized consciousness and not conscience. He emphasized awareness and not character. Of course, character comes automatically, but it comes like a shadow. You are not to carry it; it is not a burden then. Have you ever watched? Your shadow goes on following you, and you are not burdened, and you need not take care of it. You need not think about it. Even if you forget completely, it will be there. You cannot lose it.

Buddha says character is real only when you cannot lose it. If you are afraid that you can lose it, then it is conscience and not consciousness.

So the first thing to be understood before we enter into these sutras is that a man becomes blind by passion, by desire. Why does he become blind by passion and desire? – because desire and passion bring two things: first, a discontent with the present. It is the very root of desire. If you are not discontented with the present, desire cannot exist. Desire can come into existence only with discontent.

Just see: if you are sitting here and if you are contented in this moment – and I don't see why you should not be contented in this moment – then there is no desire. And when there is no desire, there is such calm, such quiet, the silence becomes so solid that you can almost touch it. You can taste it, you can hold it in your hands.

Whenever there is contentment there is no desire. When there is no desire you are at home, relaxed. In that relaxed state there is no mind. Mind is the accumulated tensions. Mind is not a faculty, mind is just a bundle of all your desires, all the waves that you go on creating. One passion is lost; before it is lost you get involved in another passion. One desire is finished, and even before it is finished you start planning for another trip in the future.

So you go on rushing into the future and you go on missing the present. And presence is possible only in the present. When you are present there is no mind and this state of no-mind is the goal, the Buddhist goal.

When there is no tension, no thought, no desire, no passion, a great well-being arises in your soul. It wells up; that's what benediction is. You feel tremendously happy, and you feel happy for no reason. You feel tremendously high, but this high has no cause to it. It is not that you have taken some drug, or alcohol; it is not that you have been chanting a mantra – because a mantra also changes your chemistry. The constant repetition of a certain sound brings changes in your body chemistry. It is a drug. A mantra is a drug, a very subtle drug: it creates certain waves in your being. If you go on chanting a certain mantra – om, om, om – by and by, the sound "om" changes your whole body chemistry.

Or you can go on a fast. And look at the absurdity: people who preach fasting are against drugs, but fasting is a chemical change. It is as much a drug as any other drug. When you fast what are you doing? – you are not giving certain chemicals to your body; chemicals which, if not given, will change the inner balance of chemicals. It is the same. Either you take a drug, which changes your inner proportion of chemicals or you stop taking food, which changes your inner balance of chemicals. When people feel high, when Mahatma Gandhi says that he feels very high when he is on a fast, he's not talking about anything different from what Timothy Leary says. Both are saying the same thing, both are talking about chemistry. Though ordinarily we don't see fasting as a drug, it is a drug – it can make you high, it can make you weightless.

Or you can go on chanting. Chanting creates changes in the physical body chemistry. That's why a few sounds have become very important. Down through the centuries many people have tried many mantras. Then a few mantras succeeded and a few failed. Those that have succeeded are the mantras which immediately bring changes to your chemistry. You may call it Transcendental Meditation: it is again a drug. Now, Maharishi Mahesh Yogi is very much against drugs, and TM itself is a subtle drug.

Or, you can change your body chemistry through postures, yoga; you can change your body chemistry through certain types of breathing, but all changes are basically chemical. When you breathe deeply you bring more oxygen to the body, and more oxygen in the body starts changing your chemistry – you start feeling high. When you don't breathe deeply more carbon dioxide collects in the lungs. The proportion changes; you feel dull, you feel low, you feel depressed. Yes, that word is right: you feel very "pressed" by something. It is carbon dioxide that brings depression; you are under a rock.

But these are all changes – physical, chemical. They don't go deeper than that. Buddha says, "Just being aware, just being aware and contented." He does not even preach a certain pattern, a rhythm of breathing. He says let the breathing be natural. He does not preach fasting; he preaches right food, the right quantity of food. He does not preach vigilance in the night. There are many sects, particularly Mohammedans, who stay awake the whole night. That too changes the body chemistry.

Buddha simply says one thing is needed, and that is that you should not move into the future, you should remain present herenow. You should remain contented with the moment. Move with the moment, don't go ahead, don't jump ahead. Let there be no passion. *Passion* means: jumping ahead of yourself. Then you create anxiety, then you create frustration, then you create worry, and then a thousand and one waves arise on the surface of your consciousness. You become a mind. When these waves disappear, you are again a consciousness. Try it sometime.

Gurdjieff used to give a method to his disciples. He used to call it "The Stop Exercise." He taught his disciples to sometimes, suddenly, stop the whole world. By stopping yourself, you can stop the whole world. You are walking on the road; suddenly, with a jerk, you stop. For a half-second you simply remain unmoving.

That sudden nonmoving will also help the mind to stop because the mind takes time. If you stop slowly, slowly, then the mind will not stop; it will get adjusted. If you suddenly stop then there is a shock; the mind stops. In that moment of sudden stopping you will be able to see that the whole world has stopped because all the waves have disappeared.

Try it: just dancing, suddenly stop. Running, suddenly stop. Swimming, suddenly stop. Talking, suddenly stop; and for a single moment be absolutely unmoving, as if you have become a statue. You will see that your mind has stopped – for a split second, of course. Again it takes possession of you, but in that single moment you will see that it is so silent that it will become a glimpse, it will become a great support. You will know that this is how reality is. In that single moment, that which is will reveal itself to you. That's what God is, or truth, or nirvana.

> *The Buddha said:*
> *When a man makes utensils out of a metal which has been thoroughly cleansed of dross, the utensils will be excellent. You monks, who wish to follow the way, make your own hearts clean from the dirt of evil passions, and your conduct will be unimpeachable.*

Cleanse your heart from the dross of passion. And in fact, to do it nothing much is needed. It is not really the case that you have become impure. You are simply disturbed, that's all; that's what impurity is. Whenever you are undisturbed, impurity disappears. Impurity is not something that has entered into your being. It is just on the surface, like waves. So if you want it to happen, it can happen right now. Don't play with explanations. Don't say, "How can it happen right now? I have many karmas to settle first." All nonsense: tricks of the mind to postpone. The mind says, "How can I do it right now? First I have to settle many, many lives' karmas." But do you know how many lives you have been here? – millions of lives. If you really have to settle those karmas, you will again take millions of lives to settle them. And after you have settled them millions of lives will have again passed – and in these lives again you would be doing many karmas.

There is no way to avoid it. If you are alive you will do something or other. You will eat something, karma is created. You will breathe, karma is created. You will walk, karma is created. You will sleep, karma is created. Any action is karma. So this is a vicious circle. For millions of lives you have existed; now to settle those karmas again millions of lives will be needed. And even after that, nothing will be settled because in these millions of lives again you will be doing karmas. Then you cannot get out of this, out of this mess. Then there is no way out.

Buddha says there is a way out. It is not a question of settling the past karmas; it is simply settling the present state of mind, that's all.

It is just herenow. If you understand, the settlement can happen. You have never done anything; you have been simply dreaming. The action or the actor, the doer and the doing – all are dreams.

Buddha says your innermost core is simply empty. It has never done anything. It cannot do. It is a witness, by its very nature.

Watch it. Find out whether what he says is true or not. Try it in your life. You were a child, now you are no longer a child. Then you were a young man, now you are no longer young; now you have become old: the childhood body has gone, the childhood mind has disappeared. Then you had another body in your youth; that has gone. The vigor, the vitality, the youth, the beauty – everything has disappeared. You had a different type of mind – very ambitious, very desirous, very egoistic. Now all that is a story of the past. Now death is coming; you can hear the sound of its coming closer every day. You can feel that every day the distance is becoming smaller and smaller. But watch one thing: you have remained the same. Your innermost core has not changed a little bit, it has not changed at all. When you were a child, it was the same consciousness watching from behind. You were young; it was the same consciousness watching. Then you became old; it is the same consciousness.

It is as if consciousness is a mirror. A child stands before the mirror, the mirror reflects the child; a young man stands before the mirror, the mirror reflects the young man; an old man stands before the mirror, the mirror reflects the old man – but the mirror is neither child, nor young, nor old. When all have gone there is simply a mirror reflecting nothing, just being there.

Your consciousness is a mirror.

This metaphor of the mirror is tremendously meaningful. It will be very helpful on the way if you can understand it. Consciousness is just standing behind, watching. It is a witness. Things come and go, just like a movie. You sit in a movie house; on the screen many things come and go. Sometimes you get identified too. Sometimes you become identified with an actor. Maybe he is beautiful, powerful, has a charm, a grace of personality, is impressive, has some charisma: you get identified, you forget yourself. For a moment you start thinking as if he is you. Sometimes it happens that there is a very sad scene, and you start crying, Your eyes are wet – and there is nothing on the screen: just light and shadow passing. And you know it, but you have forgotten for a moment. If you remember it, you will start laughing at yourself: "What are you doing? Crying? Weeping?" But it happens when you read a novel too. At least there is something on the screen. Reading a novel there is nothing – no screen, no actors, nothing. Just in your own fantasy the novel goes on and on and on. Suddenly sometimes you feel very happy, and sometimes you feel very sad; the climate of the novel starts possessing you.

This is exactly what is happening in life. Life is a great stage, a great drama. It is very complex because you are the actor, and you are the director, and you are the film, and you are the screen, and you are the projector, and you are the audience too. Now you are all layers: one part playing the role of an actor, another part directing, another part functioning as a screen, another part working as a projector. And behind it all is your real reality – the witness who is just watching.

This watcher: once you start feeling its existence, once you start getting settled with it, are more and more in tune with it – then you will see what Buddha means when he says consciousness is a mirror. The mirror is never contaminated; it only appears to be. You can put a heap of dung before a mirror; of course it will reflect it. But still the mirror is not contaminated, it is not polluted. It doesn't become impure because a heap of manure or dung is reflected in it; it remains still pure. Remove the dung and the mirror is there in all its purity. Even when the dung was reflected, the mirror was not contaminated. So whatsoever is impure is really a reflection, it is mirrored. Buddha says if you get cleansed of this dross, the dirt of evil and passions, your conduct will be unimpeachable.

So the emphasis is not on conduct. The emphasis is on the mirrorlike purity of consciousness.

> *The Buddha said:*
> *Even if one escapes from the evil creations, it is one's fortune to be born a human being.*

These are the seven great rare fortunes. Buddha talks of them many times, in many ways. They have to be understood; they are of great import.

First: it is a rare fortune to be born as a human being. Why? Why is it not a rare fortune to be born as a dog? Or as a buffalo? Or as a donkey? Or as a tree? Or as a rock? Why is it a rare blessing to be born as a human being? – because except for human beings, the whole of nature is fast asleep. You also are not awake. Let me repeat: the whole of nature is asleep except for man, and man is also not awake, but just in the middle.

Sometimes it happens in the morning that you go on tossing and turning in the bed. You know that now it is time to get up, and still there is sleep. It is a midway state. You can hear the milkman talking to your wife, you can hear the children rushing and getting ready for school, you can hear the bus stop outside the house to take the children, and still dreaming also continues. You still feel sleepy, the eyes are closed. Sometimes you drift into sleep, sometimes you drift out of it. This is the state of human beings.

Buddha says it is a rare blessing because the whole of nature is very deeply asleep, so deeply asleep that there is not even a dream. It is in a state of *sushupti*. Man has come to the second state: the state of dreaming. At least there is a certain dream. Dream means that you are not fast asleep anymore. You are certainly not awake because when you become awake you become a buddha. You are somewhere in between the animals and a buddha. You are hanging in a limbo.

Buddha says it is a great opportunity, a rare blessing, because if you make a little effort you can become awake. A dog cannot become awake, whatsoever effort he makes. A tree cannot become awake; howsoever hard it tries, it is not possible. If a tree tries hard, it will become a dog. If the dog tries hard, the dog may become a man. But awakening happens only when you are a human being. The way toward godliness goes only from the human being. In the East we think – and the thought has much validity in it – that even *devas*, angels, gods, are not as blessed as a man. Why? – because man stands on the crossroads. Even gods, if they are to become liberated, will have to be born as men.

Animals are fast asleep, man is just on the midway point, and the gods are too much in their dreams. The world of the gods is a dreamworld. That's why they have so many beautiful *apsaras*: it is a dreamworld, a fantasy. They live in a fantasy. Man lives just midway, and there is a possibility that he can move toward more awakened states of being. He can become an awakening.

...it is one's rare fortune to be born as a human being. So don't miss this great opportunity. It is after very great struggle that you are born as human beings; it is simply ridiculous to waste it. For millions of lives you have been moving toward this state. Now that you have come, you may destroy it just by eating, drinking and being merry. You may simply lose the whole opportunity. There are people who, if you tell them to pray or meditate, they will say, "Where is the time? We don't have any time." Then you can see them playing cards in a club, and you ask, "What are you doing?" And they say, "Killing time." The same people. When it is a question of meditating they say, "But there is no time." But when it is a question of drinking, of gambling, of going to a movie, or just sitting glued for hours before the TV, they have enough time. Then you ask them; they say, "We are killing time."

Are you killing time, or is time killing you? Who has ever been able to kill time? Otherwise, with so many people who have been killing time, by this time, time would have died. Nobody has been able to kill time. Time kills everybody. Each moment time brings death. In India we have the same word for both: we call time *kal*; and for death we also have the same name, *kal* because time brings death.

Time is death. Each moment, you are slipping into death.

Each moment, death is coming closer and closer and closer. All clocks are in the service of death. The whole of time is serving death. It is a rare opportunity to be a human being, and it is very easy to lose it. Buddha reminds us. The second thing he says:

> *Even If one be born a man, it is one's rare fortune to be perfect in all the six senses.*

There are people who may be born as men, but are blind, or deaf, or dumb, or mentally retarded. Then too it is impossible: nobody has ever heard of any mentally retarded person becoming a buddha. It has never been heard of, it is not possible. Great intelligence is needed. It is very difficult to become aware if your senses are missing – because for awareness, sensitivity is a must. A man who has eyes and a man who has no eyes are in different states, altogether different states. The man who has eyes is more sensitive because eyes are the most sensitive part of the body. Eighty percent of your sensitivity belongs to the eyes. A man who is blind is only twenty percent as sensitive as a person who has eyes. A man who is blind is enclosed in a subtle darkness, and there is no way to get out of it. He lives surrounded in a very subtle prison. It is very difficult to escape it.

Your outer eyes give you some glimpses, some visions, and you can start thinking about inner eyes too. But a person who has no outer eyes cannot have any conception of what a third eye can be, of what inner eyes can be. One who has never seen anything cannot have any insight. If the "out-sight" is missing, the in-sight will be missing; they exist in a pair. That's why when you see a blind man, great compassion arises in you. Just watching a blind man one feels very, very compassionate. Why? The man is missing so much. He is human, and yet eighty percent of color experience, light, is missing. His whole life is colorless; he does not know what green is. Just think about yourself: if you had never known green, if you had never known a rose, if you had never seen a rainbow, if you had never seen the sunrise and the sunset, if you had never seen the face of a beautiful woman or a man, if you had never seen the beautiful, innocent eyes of a child – if you had never seen the face, the grace of one who has attained – how much you would be missing. You would be more like a rock, less like a human being.

Buddha is not against senses; this sentence will prove it to you. Buddha says sensation, and the lust for sensation is bad, but senses are good. And to be sensitive is an absolute necessity. So become more sensitive.

Let me make it clear to you. If you use your eyes just to reach for lust and you go on looking for lust, then your eyes will become, by and by, dull. Lustful eyes are always dull. Lustful eyes are always ugly. If a man looks at you with lustful eyes you suddenly feel offended – he's trespassing. His eyes function like a knife into the heart. He's not a cultured man, he's not gentlemanly at all.

It happened...

Mulla Nasruddin entered an office – he must have gone for some business. The receptionist was a beautiful woman. He looked at her with such lustful eyes, and then he asked, "Where is the bathroom?"

The woman said, "You go directly to the end of the passage. You will find a room with a sign 'Gentlemen' – and don't let that sign prevent you. Just go in."

When you look at a woman with lustful eyes you are not a gentleman. In fact, you are a little inhuman. When eyes are sensitive, with no lust, they have a depth. When eyes are not sensitive, but only hungering for sensation, they are shallow. You will find them muddy: they will not be transparent. When the eyes are tremendously sensitive, then they have a depth, a transparent depth. You can look into them and you can reach to the very heart of the man. The man becomes available through his eyes, and through the eyes you can see what type of man you are encountering.

Eyes are very indicative. That's why criminals will never look directly into your eyes, they will avoid it. Guilty people will look sideways, they will not look directly because they are not innocent. They know that their eyes can reveal, their eyes can say things which they don't want to say. If you can watch the eyes of a man, you have the very key to his personality.

The same is true about the other senses. Just think of a deaf person who has not heard Wagner, who has not heard Ravi

Shankar, who has not heard the birds singing in the morning – a man for whom cuckoos don't exist, who has not heard somebody singing a love song or a sad song, for whom a flute is just a hollow bamboo. Just think how poor he is.

Buddha says the first blessing is that you are born as a man, the second blessing that you are born with six senses. Now use this opportunity: become more and more sensitive. And how can you become more sensitive? When you don't lust, you become more sensitive. When you lust, your sensitivity is lost; you become shallow. A man who does not lust, by and by gathers so much energy. If a man is without lust, all his senses become clear windows – no smoke, no barriers – and the inner and outer meet through that sensitivity.

> *Even if he be perfect in all the six senses, it is his rare fortune to be born in the time of a buddha.*

Buddha says you may be a human being, you may be born with all senses perfect, but if you are not born in the time of a buddha you will miss the contact with the unknown. You may see the trees, you may see the flowers, you may see the stars, but these are nothing compared to a man of enlightenment because he represents the unknown in the world of the known. He brings a ray of godliness into the darkness of the earth. He's the real flowering of consciousness.

"It is rare," Buddha says, "to be born in the time of a buddha." In fact, it is a great blessing just to occupy the same time, the same space, as a buddha occupies because something of his vital vibrations is bound to touch you. His presence is bound to become a showering of benediction. Even if you never go to him, even if you are against him, even if he passes through your town and you don't have any time to visit him, even then his coolness will bring something to you, something unasked for. He will reach you uninvited. Just think: if Buddha had not been born, the world would not be the same. And Christians have done well to begin their calendar after Christ. It is good: Christ makes a tremendous break with the past. Just his existence – Christ was a buddha – his existence created a totally different history. It is good that Christians date their history as after Christ and before Christ. Before Christ it is nothing; it is all ordinary. After Christ a tremendous phenomenon happened, and humanity started moving at a different altitude.

In India we could not do that because we have encountered so many buddhas. It was difficult for us to do it that way. Otherwise there would be so many calendars, and it would be confusing. But whenever a buddha exists humanity takes a turn, an upward turn. Whenever a buddha enters into history, history is never again the same; the total perspective changes. And when a buddha is present it is very easy if you meditate because his energy is moving. You can simply ride on his wave. When you are doing your meditations alone and a buddha is not present, you are fighting with such great barriers single-handedly; it is almost impossible, improbable, that you will be the conqueror.

With a buddha it is almost like this…

Ramakrishna used to say, "When the wind is blowing in the right direction, you simply leave your boat in the stream and the wind will take it. Just wait for the right direction; then you need not make any effort. You simply sit in the boat, the wind will take it." When a buddha is blowing and the whole existence is in an uprise, then everything is going toward godliness. You can simply join hands, and you can ride on the wave very easily. You can simply leave your boat in the stream, and the stream is already going.

Hence Buddha is right when he says to be born in the time of a buddha is a rare opportunity.

> *Even if he be born in the time of a buddha, it is his rare fortune to see the enlightened.*

But difficulties are there: you may be born in the time of a buddha but you may never go to see him because just the very idea that somebody is enlightened is against your ego. You cannot believe that somebody is enlightened and you are not. It is impossible that somebody has gone ahead of you. You cannot believe it because of your ego, and you will find a thousand and one reasons not to go to a buddha. You will find arguments that he is wrong, that he is a megalomaniac, that he is claiming to be but is not really a buddha – "What is the proof?" People used to go to

Buddha and ask, "What is your proof? Who is your witness?"

Now these are foolish questions. Who can be a witness? Buddhahood happens in such deep aloneness that nobody can be a witness. It is not an act in the world, it is an act out of the world. Who can be a witness? It happens in tremendous aloneness. It happens at the innermost core – nobody can see it. A buddha has to be self-proclaimed; there is no other way. Who will certify that he is a buddha? People used to go to him and they would find a thousand and one ways to prove that whatsoever he was saying did or did not coincide with the old scriptures. It never coincides; it cannot, in the very nature of things because whenever somebody becomes enlightened he brings a different vision into the world, which had never existed before.

Each enlightened person brings a new gift to the world, which had not existed before. So if you look in the Vedas you may not find it; if you look in the Upanishads you may not find what Buddha is saying. It will look a little rebellious, unorthodox. An enlightened person is rebellious, is unorthodox because truth is rebellious and truth is unorthodox. So whenever a buddha comes, people just start looking in their old scriptures to see whether there is a proof, and it never happens.

When Christ came, Jews started looking in their old scriptures, and they never became convinced that he was the messiah for whom they were waiting. They crucified him. Why? – because they could not figure it out.

People believe in scriptures. Scriptures are dead things, and scriptures are made by you, collected by you, interpreted by you. Nobody knows what the scriptures really mean. Nobody can know because the words are there, but the content has to be given by you.

I have heard...

Mulla Nasruddin went to his doctor and said, "I am very worried. A week ago, I came home to find my wife in the arms of another man who talked me into going out for a cup of coffee. The next five nights, exactly the same thing happened."

"My good man," said the doctor, "it is not a doctor you want. It is a solicitor."

"No," insisted the Mulla, "it is a doctor I want. I have just got to know if I am drinking too much coffee."

Now it depends how you take a certain thing, how you interpret it. Interpretation is bound to come from your mind.

Listen to an anecdote…

It was their honeymoon night, and the Jewish bride had put on a sheer nightgown and crawled into bed, only to discover that her Episcopalian husband was about to go to sleep on the couch. It was the month of Lent, when Christians are supposed to drop at least one of their enjoyments.

"George," she called out, "are you not going to make love to me?"

"I can't, honey," he replied, "because it is Lent."

"Why, that's awful!" she exclaimed, bursting into tears. "To whom? and for how long?"

Get it?

Now the passionate mind, the lustful mind, has its own interpretations. Words don't matter much: you project your ideas on the words. If you are looking for something, you will be able to see it. If you are not looking for something, you may not be able to see it. And the natural tendency of the human mind is to first deny that somebody has arrived. It is offensive to the ego. That's why it is very difficult for you.

If somebody comes and says that another man, your neighbor, is a murderer, you immediately believe. You don't bother about any proofs. You say, "I have known him long. I have always thought that he was." If somebody comes and says, "That man is a thief, immoral," this and that, you never bother about any proof. If people bothered about proof there would not be so much gossiping in the world. Who bothers about proof? When somebody is being condemned you immediately believe it because that gives you a feeling that you are better than the other person. But if somebody comes and says, "One man has become a meditator, a great meditator," immediately there is suspicion. You listen to it but you don't want to listen. You say, "It is not possible. I know that man; he is a cheat. How can he meditate? I know him from his very childhood; we were classmates in school. No, he cannot. What is the proof?" you ask. Whenever somebody talks about somebody else being good, you ask for the proof because it hurts your ego: "So, somebody else has become good before me?"

When a buddha walks on the earth he's claiming the impossible, that which only rarely happens. He's saying he has become a buddha, and of course only he can say that. There is no other way to prove it or disprove it. His statement is not provable or disprovable, and your ego feels offended.

Buddha says it is a rare fortune to be born in the time of a buddha, and still rarer a fortune to see the enlightened – to go, to bow, because only if you bow, if you surrender, will you be able to see. It is not a question of physical eyes. Many people saw Buddha walking, passing from one town to another, but they were not the people who had seen him. Only those few rare individuals who became his disciples had seen because it is impossible to see a buddha and not to become a disciple. If you have seen, then you have seen; and then you cannot be the same again. Then your whole life is upside down. Then you are in a chaos, then you are reborn. Then there is going to be a complete collapse of your past, a new birth, and of course all the pain that is always involved in a new birth.

> *Even if he be able to see the enlightened, it is his rare fortune to have his heart awakened in faith.*

You can see, but that is not much. Unless trust arises in you, *...his heart awakened in faith.* Try to understand this word *faith.* It does not mean belief. *Belief* means a dogma, *belief* means believing in a dogma. For example, Christians believe in the Trinity: the Father, the Son, and the Holy Ghost. This is a belief. Or, Hindus believe in the three faces of God; that is a belief.

When you encounter a buddha and you trust the person, then it is faith. Faith is personal; belief is theoretical, conceptual. Faith is like love – you fall in faith as you fall in love. It is not a belief. It is not that Buddha has convinced you about something. No, his being has convinced you about his own being. He has convinced you not to believe in a dogma, he has convinced you that something has happened here in this man. You have become convinced of the fact that here is a man who is transformed, transfigured, who is no longer of this world. It is a conviction, a personal conviction. It is not an argument, it is not theology – it is a love affair.

When people come to me to be initiated into sannyas, I can immediately make the distinction as to whether it is faith or belief. There are two types of people: one person comes and he says, "Whatsoever you say convinces me. Your argument is superb. Your reason appeals to me." Now, this man has come to me as a believer. He has not really come. Someday he can find somebody who can "unconvince" him about me – because there can be better arguments. There is always the possibility because logic is a double-edged sword: it cuts both ways. One argument can be used to destroy the conviction, the same argument can be used to make it. Logic is like a prostitute, or like a lawyer. It can go with anybody, with whosoever pays.

It happened...

In a coffeehouse there was great discussion. One philosopher said in the coffeehouse one day, "If you will give me Aristotle's system of logic, I will force my enemy to a conclusion. Give me the syllogism and that's all I ask."

Another philosopher said, "If you give me the Socratic system of interrogation I will run my adversary into a corner and defeat him immediately. That's all I ask."

Mulla Nasruddin, hearing all this said, "My brother, if you give me a little ready cash, I will always gain my point. I will always draw my adversary to a conclusion because a little ready cash is a wonderful clearer of the intellect."

Logic is not very fundamental; it is superficial. If somebody comes and he says that he believes in what I say, then it is not faith. But there are a few rare people who say, "We don't know what you are saying, we don't even understand much. We enjoy what you say, but that is not the point. We have fallen in love with you." A faith has arisen. Now, nobody can destroy this faith because it is illogical.

You cannot destroy faith because it is not based on logic. Anything based on logic can be destroyed: if you can pull the logic it will collapse. It has a cause; pull the cause away and the effect will disappear. But a faith is uncaused. It is just like falling in love. If you go to Majnu and prove to him that Laila is not the most beautiful woman in the world, and logically you go on proving it, he will say, "Don't unnecessarily puzzle yourself. Nobody can prove it."

It actually happened that the king of Majnu's town called him. He had become very sympathetic toward him. Majnu had been going in the streets in the nights, crying and weeping, and screaming. He would just call, "Laila, Laila." The king became very compassionate. He called him and he said, "You are a fool. I have seen your Laila; she is an ordinary girl. In fact because you were crying so much I thought she must be very beautiful, so I myself became interested. But when I saw her I simply laughed. You are a fool and I have much compassion for your foolishness. You are a good young man; don't waste your life."

He called twelve beautiful women from his harem and he said, "Choose any one." They were the best, the most precious of his kingdom. Majnu looked and he said, "Nothing compared to Laila." And he said to the king, "Sir, if you really want to see Laila, you will need my eyes. Majnu's eyes will be needed. There is no way to see Laila and her beauty except through Majnu's eyes."

A disciple is a Majnu. He is a madman, he has fallen in love. Buddha says: *...his heart awakened in faith*. The presence of Buddha is his appeal. The grace that surrounds Buddha has touched his heart. It is not Buddha's logic, it is not Buddha's philosophy. Even if Buddha remained silent it would not make much difference; the disciple would be convinced all the same. Even if Buddha started contradicting himself it would not make any difference. That's why you see that I go on contradicting. Those who come through intellect by and by disappear. My contradiction helps me to throw the weeds out of my garden. Those who have come through love don't bother. They say, "Okay, you enjoy contradicting yourself, but we love you. You cannot deceive us." They say, "You can go on contradicting, but you cannot force us to run away from you."

Those who come through belief, sooner or later will have to go because truth is paradoxical. Only theories are nonparadoxical. Truth has all the contradictions of life in it. Truth is very illogical, very irrational.

> *Even if he have faith, it is his rare fortune to awaken the heart of intelligence.*

And then Buddha says, "But this is not the end. When your heart is full of love, and full of faith and trust, this is not the end. This is just the beginning." Now you have to help your intelligence to rise and take possession of you. Faith is the door: you should enter through it, but you should not remain at the door. Otherwise, you never enter into the palace. Finally, you have to come to your own experience. It is good to believe, it is good to trust in a buddha, it is good to have faith, but that is not enough – because your faith in Buddha is still not your experience. What has happened to Buddha must happen to you too. Then the second step happens: your own intelligence arises. Now it is not only love toward Buddha; now by your own experience you have become a witness. It is not only unfounded faith. In the beginning faith is unfounded, but in the end it becomes absolutely founded. The foundation is not supplied by logic, the foundation is supplied by your experience. When it has become your own experience, you don't say, "I trust in Buddha." You know it is right, it is true.

Somebody asked Sri Aurobindo, "Do you believe in God?" and he said, "No." The man was puzzled. He had come from Germany, he was a professor. He had come just to listen to this great man. He was simply shocked that this man said, "No." And he was in search of God. He said, "Have I heard you rightly, sir? You say no?"

Aurobindo repeated, "Yes," he said, "absolutely not because there is no question of belief. I know God is. There is no question of belief. You ask, 'Do you believe in God?' I don't believe, I know."

Belief is a poor substitute for knowledge.

So Buddha says first trust. Trust means simply that you have come across a man who is away from you, far away from you. You have come across a man who has shown you your own future, your destiny. It is as if a seed has come to a tree, and the seed has become aware that the tree is possible. And the tree says, "Once I was also a seed just like you." Now trust arises in the seed. If he had never seen the tree, he would never have dreamed about it. How can a seed dream about a tree? He has never seen one. That's why to be born in the time of a buddha is a great blessing – because there exists a tree, and your seed can start dreaming. When the first impact of the tree falls on the seed, he trusts. His own future becomes full of possibilities now. It is not going to be just a repetition of the past, it will be something new. He is thrilled. That thrill is faith. He's thrilled to the very roots. Now, for the first time, he knows there is meaning; now, for the first time, he knows there is destiny. Something is going to happen: "I'm not just an accident. I'm carrying a great message. It has to be translated, it has to be decoded. I have to become a tree and bloom, and spread my fragrance to the winds."

Seeing a buddha, you have seen your own possible buddhahood – that's what faith is. But it is not enough: then you have to work hard to make it real. The seed has to fall into the earth, die into the earth, be born as a sprout. And a thousand and one difficulties have to be crossed: winds are there, thunder is there, animals are there, and the new sprout is very fragile, very weak, with infinite potentiality to become strong. But right now it is not strong; it will need somebody's help, it will need a gardener. That is the meaning of a master.

When you choose a master, you choose a gardener. You say, "Protect me until I have become strong enough to go my own way." But faith is just the door. *Even if he have faith, it is his rare fortune to awaken the heart of intelligence.*

And the last:

> *Even if he awakens the heart of intelligence, it is his rare fortune to realize a spiritual state which is above discipline and attainment.*

The whole goal of discipline is to come to a point where discipline can be dropped. The whole goal of religious practice, *sadhana,* is to come to a moment when all *sadhana* can be dropped and you can be simply spontaneous. Then you have flowered.

For example, if you have to practice meditation, and one day you stop your meditation and the mind jumps back, then this is not a great state. A moment should be desired, longed for, when you can even drop your meditation. But nothing differs; it remains the same. Whether you do meditation or you don't do, you remain meditative. Meditation has become your innermost part, part of your being, no longer something imposed from the outside. Not that you have to force yourself to be good; not that you have to repress your temptations to be bad, no. Now there is no temptation, no enforcement. One has gone beyond discipline. This is what Buddha calls "the discipline of transcendence." This is the seventh fortune, the last, the ultimate.

To be born as a human being is just the beginning, and then you have to come to this point where all discipline can be dropped. Then you have become a god, then you have become as spontaneous as nature. Then there is no tension, then you don't have any character, then you are as innocent as a child. Your awareness is perfect now, your awareness is enough now. Nothing else is needed.

> *The Buddha said:*
> *O children of Buddha! You are away from me ever so many thousands of miles, but if you remember and think of my precepts, you shall surely gain the fruit of enlightenment. You may, standing by my side, see me always, but if you observe not my precepts, you shall never gain enlightenment.*

Buddha says to never stop anywhere unless you have attained to the seventh – the state of a disciplined no-discipline, the state of effortlessness, the state of tao, *dhamma*, the state which Kabir calls *sahaj*, spontaneous. But you have to work hard for it.

So Buddha says, "You can remain with me, and if you don't follow what I am saying, if you don't bring it to your heart, to your intelligence, to your being, then you are thousands of miles away from me. But you may be thousands of miles away from me and if you are following what I have said, you are close to me, and your enlightenment is absolutely certain, assured, promised."

To be close to a buddha, there is only one way to follow his footprints. To be close to a buddha means: become more and more aware, become more and more alert. Bring a little buddhahood to yourself.

The goal is that you also have to become a buddha. Only then will you be able to understand exactly what the meaning and significance and the grandeur of being awakened is.

This consciousness exists within you right now, this very moment. You may not be able to see it. I can see it: it is there like a mirror, and you get identified with all that reflects in the mirror. Drop your identifications: start seeing that you are not the body; start seeing that you are not the mind; start seeing that you are not the emotions, not the thoughts. Start seeing that you are not pleasure and pain. Start seeing neither old nor young; start seeing neither success nor failure. Remember always that you are the witness. By and by, this mirrorlike quality will explode into your being.

The day you recognize that you are a mirror, you are free. You are freedom. This is what *moksha* or nirvana is all about.

Enough for today.

6

BUDDHAHOOD

AWAKEN FROM YOUR SO-CALLED AWAKENED STATE

The first question:

Osho,
Why do I ask so many foolish questions?

Because there are no wise questions, and there cannot be. A wise question exists not. Questioning as such is foolish. I am not condemning it, I am not saying don't ask, but remember, the questioning mind is a confused mind, and out of the confusion comes the question. Whatsoever answer is given to it will enter into the confused mind again. That answer will be distorted; the confused mind will start playing on it and will create many more questions out of it. It is a vicious spiral.

No answer is going to help unless you understand that questioning in itself is futile, unless the understanding grows deep that questioning is meaningless. There is nobody to answer your question. Existence is there without any explanations – and it is absolutely silent. You go on asking, it does not respond. By and by you will understand that questions are meaningless; then they disappear.

The day questions disappear is a great day. On that very day the answer becomes available. The answer never comes through questioning, it comes when the questioning has disappeared. In fact, to say it comes is not right: when the questioning has disappeared you suddenly find that you are the answer, your very being is the answer. That is what you had been seeking and seeking for.

All questions are foolish, they have to be; and all answers are lies. They have to be because you cannot answer a foolish question with truth. There will be no meeting between them. You ask a question, the master goes on answering it in the hope that, by and by, your questioning will disappear. That's the difference between a master and a teacher.

A teacher believes that he can answer your question. He is also a fool, just like you. The master knows there is no answer, but he goes on answering you in the hope that by and by you will start looking deeper, your understanding will grow, and one day suddenly your questions will disappear. You will look inside and you will not find any questions. That very moment you become the answer: you are the answer.

Meanwhile, continue to question; it is an unburdening process. Only by questioning will you come to see that questions are futile. One has to say whatsoever is.

I have heard...

A man rushed into a church, a Catholic church, went into the confessional booth and said, "Father, I have made love to a woman since the morning up to now, twenty-five times!"

Even the Father was surprised. He had listened to many confessions, his whole life had been just listening to confessions, but this was something new – twenty-five times since the morning?

He asked, "Are you married?"

The man said, "Yes, Father, to the same woman." So the Father relaxed and he said, "There is no problem; it is your wife, you can make love."

He said, "I know. And moreover, I'm not a Christian, nor am I a Catholic: I am a Jew. But I had to tell somebody!"

If something is burdening you, overburdening you, you have to tell somebody. You can ask me; let the questions be foolish.

So when I say that all questions are foolish, I am not saying to stop asking. Otherwise, old Paritosh would be in trouble – he has to bring the questions. You continue asking.

By not asking you will not be able to understand that questions are foolish. But by asking, and by my constant answering and yet not answering them – this is the whole process of awareness.

You ask the question; when you ask a question you think it is very serious, you ask a question and you think it is very profound, and then I answer it and I answer it with a joke. The whole profundity, the seriousness is gone; you start laughing. There is a great possibility that you will start laughing at your question, at the ridiculousness of it.

Life is there to be lived. Life has no question mark; it is a mystery, there is no explanation. And it is good that there is none. It would be a great misfortune if there were an explanation. If there were an answer that could satisfy you, just think how flat things would become, how boring, how monotonous. Because no answer can answer your questions, life remains an adventure, it remains a constant search.

Searching, one day you come to a point where you understand that you are wasting your energies in searching. The same energies can be put to celebration: you can enjoy.

These are two approaches toward life: the approach of the questioner, the seeker, the thinker, the philosopher – and the approach of the religious person, the mystic, the poet, the painter, the man of the heart. When a thinker enters into garden, he starts asking questions:

"Why are trees green? Why are roses red?" When a poet enters, he starts singing a song about the red roses and the green trees. When a painter comes, he paints. When a mystic comes, he simply stands there in tremendous awe. His breathing stops, time stops. It is so ecstatic the question does not arise at all.

The philosopher goes on asking. The artist goes on painting, creating the same beauty again and again. The mystic does neither, neither does he ask nor does he create the flower. He is simply there, standing in deep meditation, enjoying. The mystic knows the way of joy.

Learn the way of joy, learn the way of dance. At least learn the way of poetry, and unlearn the ways of the thinker, unlearn the ways that create questions in you.

But it will happen by and by.

You will have to ask many questions.

A convict sits in his cell awaiting a murder trial. In walks a well-dressed lawyer.

The lawyer says, "I am the very best. You have nothing to worry about. I am going to prove that you are completely insane, or were in Europe at the time of the murder. Also, the witnesses are paid off and my uncle is the judge for your case. Meanwhile, try to escape."

There is no answer to any question, there is nobody to answer them. They have never been answered, they cannot be answered by the very nature of things. Meanwhile go on asking because if you don't ask you will not move from the state where you are; and one should be moving.

That is one of the great secrets of life, that life is a movement. If you are stuck somewhere you lose contact with life. Then you are fogged and clouded; then you are lost, and you don't know who are, and where you are going, and what is happening. You miss all the clues.

Go on moving. Wherever you are, one thing has to be remembered: don't get stuck. If your questioning helps you to move, good. A little movement from wherever you are is good. From that place you have to find another place because you are in contact with life only when you are dynamic, moving. Life is a flux, life is a flow. Whenever you are stagnant you lose contact.

In the English language there is a beautiful word: *affluence*. It has lost its original meaning. It has nothing to do with richness, it has nothing to do with luxuries, technological gadgets, a big palace and a big car and a great bank balance. It has nothing to do with these; you may be a millionaire and you may not be affluent.

Affluence means one who is in the flow, one who is flowing. To be with the flow is to be affluent. The original meaning of the word is to be in the flow, moving, flowing, not stuck. If you are flowing, moving with life, you are rich – and that is the only richness there is. All other richness is a false substitute.

So if your questions help you to move – I am not saying they will help you to find the answer because there is none – but if your questioning helps you to move just a step further, good. It is time you should be moving.

Branihan was driving down the road. By the way the car weaved in and out of traffic, you could tell that Branihan was pickled to the gills.

"Where do you think you are going?" asked the motorcycle cop who finally stopped him.

"I'm coming home – hic – from a New Year's Eve party."

"Are you kidding?" asked the cop. "New Year's was three weeks ago!"

"I know," said Branihan. "That's why I figure I better be getting home."

You have been away from your home long enough. You should be getting home by now.

Anything that moves is good. A question, if real, helps you to move. Again, let me repeat: it is not going to help you to find the answer because there is none. But an authentic question that arises from your being is meaningful to you. It may be foolish to me, but is relevant to you. It may be irrelevant in the ultimate understanding of things, but if it is relevant to you let it be foolish, let it be absurd. Ask it – and my answer will just give you a push; you will be moving.

Keep moving. One thing has to be remembered: keep moving. Then you will be alive. That's why a question is more important than a belief. I say all questions are foolish, but beliefs are nothing compared to them. Beliefs are absolutely stupid. Questions are only foolish. To be a fool can be fun, but to be stupid is ugly, to be idiotic is to be ill.

Beliefs are idiotic. Somebody says. "I am a Hindu," somebody says, "I am a Christian," somebody says, "I am a Jaina," somebody says. "I am a Buddhist" – these are idiots because belief means they have come to the answer. A questioner is at least moving. He has not come to the answer, he thinks he can come by questioning; that is why he is foolish. But still, he has not come to the answer. The man of belief who says "I am a Christian" has arrived: he thinks he has found the answer. Now, he is absolutely an idiot. He is stuck, his flow is completely gone. That's why you never see so-called religious people joyous. You will never see them streaming with life, flowering.

The word *flower* too must come from *flow*. I don't know exactly whether it comes from *flow* or not, but it should come. Etymologically, linguistically, it may not. I don't bother, I don't care a little bit. But it should come. *Flower – flow*. Look at a flower; that's what flow is. The whole tree has come to a peak of its flowering. From the roots to the flower there is a continuous flow of life, energy, sap. And in the flower the tree has bloomed, that flow has come to sing a song. There is a dance, the tree has bloomed.

When all your questions disappear, not giving you any belief – all beliefs gone, all questions gone – then all stupidity, all foolishness will be gone. Then there is a flowering, a blooming, and that blooming is the answer. That answers all the questions. Suddenly you are in the know. There is no knowledge, but you are in the know. Suddenly you are at home. Then you are not struggling with life and inquiring about what it is. Now you know, from your deepest core of being, what it is. You have become it, you have allowed it to flow through you. Now you are no longer separate from it.

The English word *religion* is beautiful: it means to be together, to be married, to be tied together, to be in union. It means exactly what the Sanskrit word *yoga* means – to be one. When your small flow is one with the flow of the whole, you are religious. When your small river falls into the great Ganges, and you start flowing with the Ganges and you lose your boundaries, you are religious.

Religion is as beautiful a word as *yoga*. It means you have now come to an ultimate marriage with the whole. Right now when you are stuck you are in a state of divorce, or separation at least. You are moving like a small stream; not even moving – you have become a pool, stagnant, dying, stinking. Get out of it.

If your questions help you to move, go on asking. It is better to be questioning than to be believing because a believer has stopped asking questions. His movement has stopped.

What do you mean when you say "I am a Christian," or "I am a Hindu," or "I am a Mohammedan"? What do you mean? – you mean, "Now there is no questioning in me. I'm tired of questioning; I have started believing." Then your whole life has shrunk. Then you are no longer expanding, then you are no longer exploring, then you are no longer inquiring.

To be a Mohammedan, to be a Hindu, to be a Christian, is worse than to be a questioner and an agnostic. It is better to be an agnostic and go on questioning because if you go on questioning, and if you are courageous enough to go on questioning to the very end, one day it comes: you remain and the question disappears. Not that a belief is given to you. The question simply disappears and a trust arises, a trust in life. Not trust in the Bible, not trust in the Vedas, not trust in the Koran, but a trust in life from where all Vedas and all Korans and all Bibles come and disappear. That trust is the answer.

Become a flow. Go on using anything that helps. Go on questioning. I am not going to give you any answers, I am not a teacher. That's why many times you feel a little worried. You start thinking, "Why does he go on avoiding?" If you watch, I never answer your question directly, I answer something else. I just push you onward. I answer you in such a way that you can ask many more questions. This pushing of your energy toward the ultimate will bring a climax where the questioning mind explodes. And when the question is not, and the belief is not, suddenly mind itself has disappeared. In that state of no-mind you are at home. You have come home.

The second question:

Osho,
Sometimes I think you live in a dreamworld.

From your standpoint that can be said – because whatsoever you think is real I think is unreal. So, naturally, whatsoever I think is real looks unreal to you. But there is one advantage in which I am and you are not, and that advantage is: I have lived in your reality, in your so-called reality. I know both; you know only one.

I was where you are, so I know your reality, and I know my reality now. I am in a better situation to judge who is real and who is unreal. You know only your state, you don't know my state. So wait a little rather than judging it. Come to my state also; then you are totally free to judge.

But whosoever has come to this state has never said that your world is real. Your world is maya: unreal, illusory. To judge, you need to know both. Only then can you compare; you cannot compare by knowing only one. How will you compare?

In the night when you fall asleep you start dreaming. In dreams, dreams look real – because in dreaming you lose all contact with the world, with the world that you have known when you were awake. Now there is no comparison; you cannot compare. For example: if you see a stone, a rock, in your dream, you cannot compare with the real rock that you have seen when you were awake because both rocks are never together. So of course the dream rock also looks real. How to judge it as unreal? There is nothing except it to judge by, there is no criterion. When you wake in the morning, then you realize that it was unreal. But again your judgment is not right because now the dream rock is missing. Now you have the real rock, the so-called real rock, and the dream rock is missing. Again your judgment is not right: only one is there and the other is missing. How can you judge unless you have both together, in front of you?

There is another awakening – that's what we call buddhahood, the ultimate awakening – when you not only awake from your dreams, but you awaken from your so-called awakened state too. Then they both are available and then you can see that both are dreams.

A few dreams are seen with closed eyes, a few dreams are seen with opened eyes, but both are dreams. And when you have awakened and there is no sleep left in you, when no part of your being is unconscious – you are absolutely conscious and your whole being is full of light, luminous – only then do you know what reality is. Right now you are asleep; all that you know is dream.

But I can understand the question. From where you are it will almost seem that I am dreaming. I talk about love; you also know love. But listening to me you become aware that I am talking about something else which is not possible. How can love be nonpossessive? How can love be pure sharing without any self, without any motivation? How can love be unconditional? You listen to me, you listen to my words, but you cannot feel the reality of those words because you know a love which is conditional, you know a love which is always motivated, you know a love which is always based on selfish desires. You know a love which is a trick to dominate and possess; you know a love which is really violent, aggressive.

So when you compare your love with my love, your love looks real to you and my love looks utopian, like fantasy. That's why the world has never trusted buddhas – because they talk about something which has nothing to do with your experience. It is so beyond, it is so transcendental, it is so far out, that you cannot compre hend it. It is incomprehensible. You cannot figure out what it is. In sheer desperation you cling to your reality and you say, "Forget all about it. These people are either mystics or mad: poets of the unknown, dreamers, eccentric, crazy. Forget all about them."

But you also cannot forget, that is the problem, because whenever you come close to a buddha he hits something deep in your heart. Your mind may go on saying that he is a dreamer, but somewhere your heart starts feeling what he is saying. Its fragrance approaches, reaches the heart. What he is singing is heard somewhere, on some level of your being. Maybe it is not very conscious, maybe it is just like groping in the dark, but you have heard. And when you watch a buddha, and if you are fortunate enough to be close to him – if you are blessed enough to become a disciple, to become an initiate – then by and by his reality will become more real than your own reality. That is the meaning of surrender.

Many times you ask me, "What is the meaning of surrender?"

The word is so big that there are many meanings. This is one of the deepest meanings: when you come to a man and you feel that he has gone beyond. Of course, you can only feel; you don't have any conceptual possibility, any mental system to comprehend it. You can only feel. It is very, very dark, but you can feel that it is very alive too. You can feel that something has happened. Your mind wants to deny it, your ego wants to deny it, but your heart starts feeling hypnotized as if a great magnet is pulling you toward some unknown center.

Surrender means falling in love with someone who is almost unreal to you, and yet has an appeal. You surrender your reality; you say, "Okay, my reality is a dream and your reality is real. Now I'm ready. Take me to your reality."

What is your reality, really? Really, what is your reality? What is it except misery? What is it except a few tiny glimpses of happiness, very fleeting? You cannot catch hold and they are gone, and again there is misery. What is your reality except an experience in hell?

I was reading…

A man arrived in hell and was given a guided tour by the Devil.

"You may choose to spend eternity in one of these three rooms," he said.

In the first room people were standing up to their necks in hot water. The water was boiling and evaporating. The man shuddered and closed the door.

In the next room people were up to their necks in icy cold water, and they were shivering. This did not appeal to the man either.

With a smile, the Devil opened the last door. The man was amazed and relieved, as the people were walking around in one foot of cow manure, drinking coffee and chatting pleasantly.

The man said, "This is for me," and began socializing.

A few minutes later one of the assistant devils came and called, "Coffee break is over. Back on your heads!"

So all happiness you know is just a coffee break, and again on your heads!

Just momentary allurements – months and years of misery, and then there comes a small moment. Again you desire that moment and you are ready to suffer again. And even that moment has nothing much in it. If you look into it you will find it hollow inside. Has what you call pleasure really anything substantial in it? Or is it just a hope so that you can carry on somehow in this hell? Without hope it would be too difficult. If there were no hope, how would you live? Even one day would be difficult; even to get out of the bed in the morning would be difficult. For what? The question will arise, "Why? Why get up again, and why go the office again and to the same rotten routine, and the same boss, and the same wife, and the same kids? For what? Enough is enough." You will simply relax and die in your bed. What is the point in getting out of it? There is only the hope that that which has not happened may happen today: "Maybe the opportunity has now come for that which has not happened yet. One should be up and take the opportunity as it comes."

It never comes really. All pleasure is in waiting, in hoping. All pleasure is in the future, in desire; it is never a reality. And you call it real?

My bliss is not in hope. I am not hoping for anything, I have abandoned all hope. In fact, the day I abandoned all hope, reality happened to me. Through hope you don't allow reality to happen. The day you drop desiring, a great bliss descends on you. It was always there, but because of your desiring you were missing it. You were so constantly occupied with desire that you were not available to it, you were closed. Once desiring disappears you are open, you become available.

I have known your reality. I have lived in that misery as long as you have lived in it – for millennia, for many lives. Certainly it is difficult to believe in my bliss, in my truth, and the question arises: "This man may be dreaming."

But one thing I would like to say to you: even if this is a dream, even if it appears like a dream, it is better than your reality. Try it. You have nothing to lose – but still you are so afraid of losing it. Maybe you are so afraid of losing it so that you can go on thinking that you have something. The fear that you may lose it keeps you feeling that you have something to lose. But have you looked in your pocket? There is nothing. In fact, there is a big hole. Your pocket holds nothing, but afraid that you may come across the truth, you never look in your pocket.

Once I was traveling with Mulla Nasruddin. The conductor came and Nasruddin looked into this pocket and that, and the diary, and in the bag and the suitcase. He searched everything, even my suitcase! Then he started looking in my pockets. I said, "Nasruddin, wait! What are you doing?"

He said, "My ticket is lost."

"It cannot be in my pocket or in my suitcase. Have you gone mad?" I was watching, and I told him, "I see that you don't look in your right-side pocket."

He said, "I cannot."

I said, "Why?"

He said, "If it is not there, then finished! Then it is nowhere! So first let me search for it everywhere. That is the last thing because that means I don't have the ticket!"

You don't look in because you are afraid; maybe there is nothing.

Cooperman sold strawberries off his truck out in the suburbs. He knocked on the door of a house: "Wanna buy some strawberries?"

"Come around back," answered the pretty young blonde.

Cooperman walked to the rear, rang the bell and the woman opened the door. To Cooperman's shock she stood there stark naked, with not a stitch of clothes on. Cooperman started to cry. "What is the matter?" asked the blonde.

"Today my wife ran away with my best friend," explained Cooperman. "I lost three thousand dollars on the stock market. And now you are gonna screw me out of my strawberries too!"

Now, only strawberries – but he is crying, afraid that now they are also gone.

What have you got with you? – not even strawberries. And you are so afraid, so apprehensive, so continuously trembling. There is nothing to lose! Try my reality too; you will not be a loser. I say it with such certainty because I know both realities. Your reality is just make-believe; my reality is real.

You are in reality only when you are real. When your awareness is real you live in reality; when your awareness is faulty you live in the unreal. You create it every day, but you don't seem to be aware.

What happens when you fall asleep? Why do dreams come when you are asleep? – your consciousness is lower, very much lower; it almost disappears. Then dreams bubble up. Are you drunk? You take alcohol, and again you are in a dreamworld. Or you take acid, you take LSD or something like that; your consciousness is lowered, you are again in a dreamworld.

That's why it happens that LSD may not give you the same experience as it gave to your friend. Somebody may move into heaven, and somebody may move into hell – because it depends on your mind what type of dream you can create. LSD or any drug can only lower your consciousness. It simply removes all barriers, it simply helps you to move in a private world – the world of the dream. And of course when you are on a drug trip things are tremendously beautiful, very psychedelic, very colorful.

But it depends. If you are a poet and you have lived with trees and flowers and birds you will have a very beautiful world opening up. But if you are a butcher then beware; then you will have the world of the butcher – a nightmare.

That's why different people going into drug trips come back with different experiences. Some say it was paradise, and some say it was hell. It depends on you.

You create the dream. The drug is not the dream-creating thing, the drug simply lowers your consciousness, which does not allow dreaming. Sleep is needed for dreams. The more aware you are, the less possibility there is of dreaming. When you are perfectly aware, dreams disappear. Then you don't create a dream, then you are simply face to face with that which is.

When you are real you live in a real world. What do I mean when I say "when you are real"? – I mean when you are aware. That's what Buddha's message is.

The third question:

Osho,
Does education lead to meditation? Please explain education and religion.

Ordinarily that which is called education is almost against meditation. It should not be so, but it is so. The original meaning of the word *education* is not against meditation. The original meaning is to draw out. To educate means to draw out: whatsoever is hidden in the individual has to be drawn out. The individual has to flower; that is the original meaning of education.

That is what meditation is too. You have to flower in your own being. You don't know what you are going to be, you don't know what flowers will come to you, what will be their color and what will be their perfume – you don't know. Move into the unknown. Simply trust life-energy: it has given birth to you, it is your foundation, it is your being. Trust it, know that you are a child of this universe, and this universe, if it has given birth to you, will take care too.

When you trust yourself, you trust the whole universe also. And this universe is beautiful. Just see – so many flowers are born in this universe, how can you mistrust it? Such tremendous beauty is all around, how can you mistrust it? Such grandeur, such grace, from a small dust particle to the stars such symmetry, such harmony – how can you mistrust it?

Basho has said, "If flowers are born out of this universe, then I trust it." Right? That is enough logic, a great argument: "If this universe can give birth to so many beautiful flowers – if a rose is possible, I trust it. If a lotus is possible, I trust it."

Education is a trust in yourself and in existence – allowing whatsoever is hidden in your unfolding; bringing whatsoever is in, out. But that is not true of the so-called education that goes on in the world. Rather than bringing out, it forces things in. It simply pours in information. Again that word *information* is wrong; it should not be used. It is "*out-formation.*" *Information* means: formation inside you. Something should grow in you – then it is information. But nobody is bothered about you. The society is bothered about its own ideas, ideologies, prejudices, technology; they go on forcing you. Your head is used as a hollow place, so they have to provide the furniture. Ordinarily education, or whatsoever is available in the name of education, is nothing but stuffing your mind with knowledge – because knowledge has some utility. Nobody is bothered about you, nobody is bothered about your destiny. They need more doctors, they need more engineers, they need more generals, they need more technicians, plumbers, electricians. Because they need them, they force you to become a plumber, or they force you to become a doctor, or they force you to become an engineer.

I am not saying there is something wrong with being an engineer or a doctor, but there is certainly something wrong if it is forced from the outside. If somebody flowers into a doctor, then you will see a great healing happening around him. Then he will be a born healer, he will really be a physician, his touch will be golden. He is born to be that.

But when it is forced from the outside and one takes it as a profession because one has to live and one has to learn and earn one's living, one is taken over. Then one is crippled and crushed under the weight. One simply goes on dragging and dragging, and one day dies. There has never been a moment of celebration in that life. Of course, he will leave a lot of money for his children to become doctors in their own turn, to go to university, to the same university where he was destroyed. And his children will do the same to their children, and this is how things go on being transferred from one generation to another. No, I don't call this education. It is crime. It is really a miracle that in spite of this education sometimes a buddha flowers in the world.

It is a miracle. It is simply unbelievable how somebody can escape from it. Education is a methodology to kill you, it is arranged in such a way. And small children are caught in the mechanism of it, not knowing where they are going, not knowing what is being made of them. By the time they become aware, they are completely corrupted, destroyed. By the time they can think about what to do with their lives, they are almost incapable of moving in any other direction.

By the time you are twenty-five or thirty, half of life is gone. Now to change seems to be too risky. You have become a doctor, your practice is going well; suddenly one day you realize that this is not the thing you were meant to be, this is not for you. But now what to do? So go on pretending that you are a doctor. And if the doctor is not happy in being a doctor, he is not going to help any patient. He may drug the patient, he may give medicine, but he is not going to really be a healing force as when a doctor is really a doctor, a born doctor. Everybody is a born something; you may miss it, you may not even know it. Somebody is a born poet – and you cannot make a poet, there is no way to manufacture poets. Somebody is a born painter; you cannot manufacture painters.

But things are very wrongly placed: the painter is working as a doctor, the doctor is working as a painter. The politician is there: maybe he could have been a good plumber, but he has become a prime minister or a president. And the person who could have been a prime minister is a plumber.

This is why there is so much chaos in the world: everybody is wrongly placed, nobody is exactly where he should be. Right education will exactly be a path to meditation. Wrong education is a barrier to meditation because wrong education teaches you things which don't fit with you. And unless something fits with you and you fit with it, you can never be healthy and whole. You will suffer.

So ordinarily, when an educated person becomes interested in meditation, he has to unlearn whatsoever he has learned. He has to go back to his childhood again and start from there, from the *ABC*s. That's why my insistence is for certain meditations in which you can again become a child.

When you dance you are more like a child than like a grown-up person. That's why you don't see dignitaries coming to me and to my meditations. Somebody is a commissioner, a tax collector – he cannot come because he cannot dance. He is a commissioner, or he is a governor – how can he dance with ordinary people?

But if you cannot dance, you may be a governor, but you are dead. If you cannot sing like a child you are a burden on the earth. It is better if you commit suicide. At least you will vacate some space for somebody else to grow and flower. You are not going to flower, that is certain.

Men who have some respectability become very stuck because they cannot do anything, they cannot risk their respectability. They are afraid. They are not happy, they don't know what bliss is, they don't exactly know what being alive means – but they are respectable. So they cling to their respectability, and then die. They never live; they die before they ever start living. There are many people who die before they have ever lived.

My meditations are to bring you back to your childhood – when you were not respectable, when you could do crazy things, when you were innocent, uncorrupted by the society, when you had not learned any tricks of the world, when you were other-worldly, unworldly. I would like you to go back to that point; from there, start again. And this is your life – respectability or money are booby prizes, they are not real prizes. Don't be deceived by them.

You cannot eat respectability, and you cannot eat money, and you cannot eat prestige. They are just games: meaningless, stupid, mediocre. If you are intelligent enough you will understand that you have to live your life and you are not to bother about other things. All other considerations are meaningless. It is your life; you have to live it authentically, lovingly, with great passion and with great compassion, with great energy. You have to become a tidal wave of bliss. Whatsoever is needed to do for it, do.

Unlearning will be needed. Unlearning means that you stop those wrong routes, you stop moving in those wrong ways that the society has forced you, persuaded you, seduced you to go in. Take charge of your own life, become your own master.

That is the meaning of sannyas. That's why I call sannyasins "swami" and the word *swami* means one who has become a master of his own life. It has nothing to do with orthodox swamis; they are not masters of their own lives. They are again on the same train with the same society – with the same stupid power, prestige, politics.

A real sannyasin is one who does not care about others' opinions, who has decided to live his life as he wants to live it. I don't mean for you to be irresponsible. When you start living your life responsibly, you not only care about yourself, you care about others also, but in a totally different way.

Now you will take every care that you don't interfere in anybody else's life. This is what responsibility is; you don't allow anybody to interfere in your life, and naturally you will not interfere in anybody's life. You don't want anybody to guide your life, you don't want your life to be a guided tour. A guided tour is not a tour at all; you want to explore on your own. You want to move in the forest without any map so that you can also be a discoverer, so that you can also come to some fresh spots for the first time.

If you carry a map you always come to the spot where many have come before. It is never new, it is never original, it is never virgin. It is already contaminated, corrupted. Many have moved on it: a map even exists.

When I was a child, in the temple that my parents used to visit, I was surprised: there were maps of heaven and hell and *moksha*. One day I told my father, "If maps exist about *moksha*, then I am not interested in it."

He said, "Why?"

I said, "If maps exist, then it is already rotten. Many people have reached there, even mapmakers have reached there. Everything is measured and they know every spot, named and labeled. This seems to be just an extension of the same old world; it is nothing new. I would like to move in a world which has no map. I would like to be an explorer." That day I stopped going into the temple.

My father asked me, "Why don't you come now?"

I said, "Remove those maps. I cannot tolerate those maps there; they are very offensive. Just think about it: even *moksha* is measured? Then is there nothing immeasurable."

All the buddhas have said that truth is immeasurable; all the buddhas have said that truth is not only unknown, it is unknowable. It is an uncharted sea: you take your small boat and you go into the uncharted sea. Take the adventure; it is risky, it is dangerous, but in risk and danger the soul flowers, becomes integrated.

To me, if education is right, it will be just a part of meditation. Meditation will be the last point in it. If education is right, then universities should not be against the universe. They should be just training places, jumping boards into the universe. If education is right, then it will not be concerned about money, and it will not be concerned about power and prestige. Then it will not be political at all.

If education is right, it will be concerned about your bliss, your happiness, music, love, poetry, dance. It will teach you how to unfold. It will not go on simply throwing information into your head. It will help you to come out of your being – to flower, to grow, to spread, to expand. It will be a totally different education.

Naturally, if education becomes involved with meditation it becomes religious. I don't call an education religious because it teaches the dogma of Christianity, or it teaches Hinduism. That is not religious. Education is religious if it makes you courageous enough to accept yourself, and live your life, and become an offering to existence in your own way, in your own unique way.

The fourth question:

Osho,
Please can you also tell us little anecdotes on sannyasin energy greed as you do on Jewish money greed?

All greed is Jewish. "Jew" is not the name of a certain race. No, anybody who is greedy is a Jew. And greed has nothing to do with money. Money is only one object of greed; anything can become the object.

Kundalini can become the object of greed; spiritual energy, psychic powers, nirvana, enlightenment, can become the object of greed – but then you are a Jew.

Remember, the word *Jew* is just symbolic: it represents greed. And there is no need to have new anecdotes. The old ones are perfectly good, and they will do.

Now that you have asked the question, you have tempted…

The new minister caught his parishioner coming out of the local tavern. "I am sorry," he said, "to see you coming out of such a place. My son, drink is of the Devil. When the Devil asks you to join him, why do you not refuse?"

"I would, Reverend," said the man. "But he might get sore and not ask me again."

You have tempted me, so I will tell you a few anecdotes. You may not ask again. And remember, these Jewish anecdotes that I am going to tell you have nothing to do with Jews, they have something to do with your inner greed. By changing the object, nothing is changed. So the question is not of changing the objects, the question is of understanding the misery that greed brings. Once you understand it, greed is dropped.

The man walking along Broadway was confronted by the business girl whispering, "Love for sale."

He said, "Sure, if you could do it the Jewish way."

She said, "If you teach me to do it the Jewish way, I will give it to you for half price."

He said, "That is the Jewish way."

Old man Feinstein's relatives gathered for the reading of his will after his death.

"Being of sound mind," read his lawyer, "I spent every last cent before I died."

"Being of sound mind I spent every last cent before I died." People really live in a very self-centered world. Naturally, if they become miserable, nobody is at fault except themselves because all great happenings in life happen when you are not a self, when you are not greedy, when you are ready to share.

Love happens when you are ready to share with another human being. Prayer happens when you are ready to share with existence. Meditation happens when you are ready to share with existence. Beauty happens when you are ready to share with a flower, or with a star, or with a bird on the wing.

Whenever you share there is beauty, there is truth, there is happiness. Whenever you hoard, whenever you live only for yourself, you don't really live. To live for oneself is to live in a grave. If you really want to live, start sharing more and more, be less greedy, and more and more life will happen to you. It is a great sharing. If you inhale and you just close your mouth and your nose, afraid that if you exhale the air will go out and will no longer be yours – if you become a hoarder of air – you will die. But you take it in, it goes out; you take it in, it goes out. The whole rhythm of life is just like in-breathing and out-breathing.

One old Jew had to have open-heart surgery. He called the medical society and asked for the best doctor in New York for this operation. They recommended the country's most famous surgeon, and old man Finkelstein went right to his office and arranged to have the operation. The operation was a complete success and the old Jew made a quick recovery.

After he was home from the hospital, he received a bill from the doctor for fifteen hundred dollars. He called the doctor and asked to see him.

Finkelstein looked at the doctor and said, "Doctor, I am an old man. For me to give you fifteen hundred dollars would mean spending almost all of my life's savings."

The doctor said, "All right. I normally get fifteen hundred dollars for this operation, but under the circumstances I will take seven hundred and fifty dollars."

Finkelstein looked very sad. He replied, "Doctor, seven hundred and fifty dollars is still a lot of money to an old man like me. After all, I don't work anymore, and it would take me a long time to save that much money again."

The doctor, completely frustrated, answered, "Okay. How about two hundred dollars?"

The old Jew said, "Two hundred dollars I know does not sound like much to you, but to me it is still a million dollars."

The doctor, completely annoyed, looked at the old man and said, "You win! I won't charge you a thing for this operation. It is on the house. There is only one thing I would like to know: before you came to me you knew I was one of the most expensive surgeons in the United States. So why did you come?"

Finkelstein replied, "When it comes to my health, money is no object."

The mind that is full of greed, the mind that is constantly obsessed with money, is already in hell. It is already out of paradise because paradise is there when you are simply not clinging to anything whatsoever. An unclinging state of mind is paradise.

Ordinarily we go on clinging. You leave the world; then you start clinging to something otherworldly. You drop out of the rat-race for money, then you start another race for spirituality, psychic powers, nirvana. But you remain the same: the same competitive mind, the same ambition to be ahead of all others.

Accept yourself wherever you are and don't think in terms of competition – you need not be anywhere else. Wherever you are, if you can be happy there, you have become religious, you have become spiritual. Spirituality knows no competition, spirituality knows no greed, spirituality knows no ambition because spirituality means desirelessness.

But people go on changing from one side to another side, from one extreme to the other. That's why Buddha insists so much on being in the middle. You can drop all your money, you can dispense with your bank balance, you can renounce the world, but then you will start hoarding some subtle money, some subtle currency of virtue, *punya*. You will start collecting: "How many fasts have I done, and how many good deeds have I done?" You will keep an account to show to God: "I have done these good things; now what is my award?"

To think in terms of award and result is to think in terms of greed. To think in terms of joy, to be joyful herenow whatsoever you are doing and never be bothered about the result of it, is to be out of greed. Then you can live in a palace and you can be surrounded with all the riches possible and still you will not be greedy. But you can renounce the world and live in a cave in the Himalayas, and if you are still ambitious, desirous, then you are greedy and you are worldly.

To be desireless is to be otherworldly.

The last anecdote:

Harry and Tilly were celebrating their fiftieth wedding anniversary and invited their three sons, their wives and grandchildren, to join them for a party.

The oldest son stood up and proposed a toast to his parents. He said, "Mom and Dad, I want you to know that no matter what I could think of to give you as a gift, I really could not think of anything good enough to give parents as wonderful as you."

The middle son stood up and said, "Mom and Dad, I hope you understand why I didn't bring you a present to celebrate this occasion. But I am sure you understand that we are in the midst of refurnishing our new summer home and we just could not find the time."

The third son, smiling, said, "Mom and Dad, I am sure you know how much I love you. Bringing you a present would not show you how sincere I am in my emotions."

The father then stood up, turned to his sons, and said, "My dear children, now that mother and I have celebrated fifty years of living together, I feel it is time to tell you something. You know, when mother and I met I was poor, she was poor, I did not have a job, we didn't even know where our next meal was coming from. Would you believe it? We didn't even have enough money to buy a marriage license."

The eldest son stood up, enraged, and asked, "Are you trying to tell us that we are bastards?"

The father smiled and answered, "Yes, and cheap ones too!"

In the ordinary world all of our relationships are money relationships. All relationships are money relationships, some power trip, some money trip, domination, ego. But if all your relationships are just money trips, trips of greed, then you don't know how to relate. And if you don't know how to relate you can never be fulfilled because it is in deep relationship that fulfillment arises.

There is a very ancient saying in Tibet: Whenever God gives you something, he never gives to you, he gives through you. I have meditated on that saying for long: it is really of tremendous significance. When God gives something to you, he never gives to you, he gives through you. He gives to you, but his way is to give through you.

So if you are not sharing, you will start missing the gifts from existence. If you are sharing, if you are non-greedy, if you simply go on sharing whatsoever you have... Like a flower shares its fragrance, go on sharing; like the cloud shares its rainwater with the earth, go on sharing; like the sun shares its rays with all the trees, and all the human beings, and all the animals – go on sharing whatsoever happens to you. Grow, and more starts coming from you.

The more you give, the more you get because existence gives through you, it never gives to you. You simply function as a passage. If you stop giving, your passage shrinks and closes. When your passage is closed nothing can enter into you.

It is almost like when you dig a well: if you go on drawing water out of it, fresh water goes on welling up in it. The well is supplied from many fountains deep in the earth; fresh water goes on coming. Then you stop drawing water, become greedy, start thinking in terms of miserliness: "If I go on taking water, one day the water may disappear and there may be no water in the well.

Then what am I going to do?" So you cover your well, you stop taking water from it. Even if you need it for yourself, you go to the river, or you go to the public place and you get your water from there, and you keep your well completely closed. What will happen to your well? Do you know? No fresh water will ever come to it now because for fresh water to come in, a space is needed. The old is filling the space, the new cannot come. And the old will become by and by stagnant, dead, and will start stinking. It will not then be possible for you to drink of it. It can become poisonous.

Stale water always becomes poisonous. It is better, if you are wise, that you not only draw water for yourself, you invite your neighbors to draw water from your well. You will feel thankful that they drew water from your well because the fresh will be coming more and more. The more you draw, the more fresh water is available.

The same is true about your innermost world: you are a well, and your fountains are connected with the divine, with the center of existence.

Share – and more will come to you. If you can share totally, not holding anything, the total will come to you. That coming from existence will be exactly in the same proportion as you have given to others.

A sannyasin is one who has dropped desiring and has started sharing. A sannyasin cannot be a Jew; and if a Jew is a sannyasin then he will have to choose either to remain a Jew or to become a sannyasin. It is not possible for you to be both. You cannot be both together: the Jew has to disappear for the sannyasin to be.

Enough for today.

7

PRANA, BREATH

THE BRIDGE FROM BODY TO SOUL

The Buddha asked a monk: "How do you measure the length of a man's life?"
The monk answered, "By days."
The Buddha said: "You do not understand the way."
The Buddha asked another monk: "How do you measure the length of a man's life?"
The monk answered, "By the time that passes during a meal."
The Buddha said: "You do not understand the way."
The Buddha asked a third monk: "How do you measure the length of a man's life?"
The monk answered, "By the breath."
The Buddha said: "Very well, you know the way."

The Buddha asked a monk: "How do you measure the length of a man's life?"
The monk answered, "By days."

A very simple question, and a very simple answer. But much is implied in the question. And the answer also shows much about the monk – his understanding, his state of mind.

When Buddha asks, *"How do you measure the length of a man's life?"* he is raising a question that can only be answered by depth. Man's life can be measured only by depth. It looks paradoxical: length can be measured only by depth.

In fact, the deeper you live, the longer you live. The length of your life depends on your depth. The quantity of your life depends on your quality. The monk could not understand it. He simply said, *"By days."* His simple answer also showed much about himself. *"By days"* means by time; "*By days*" means by the fleeting; "*By days*" means by the flux, the changing. He measures life by the momentary, not by the eternal, not by the timeless.

Life exists in time, but life does not belong to time. It penetrates time, and one day it disappears from time. It is just like when a ray of sun penetrates water, and when it penetrates the water its angle changes. That's why if you put a straight stick into water it will look curved. It will not look straight because the angle of light changes. And when the ray of light enters the medium of water, it does not belong there, it has come from beyond. It will go back, it will be reflected back because everything returns to its source, has to return to its source. Only then is the circle complete, and there is contentment.

When Buddha asked: *"How do you measure the length of a man's life?"* and the monk replied, *"By days,"* he showed his understanding. He does not know anything beyond time; he thinks life is just that which consists of time: being born, getting married, living, then old age, then death. Days go on flicking by, just like numbers on a gasoline pump.

But this is not life; this is just the very periphery. Have you observed that if you look inside, time does not exist? If you look outside there is time, but if you look inside there is no time. Have you not felt it sometimes, sitting silently with closed eyes, that inside you have not aged at all? Inside you remain the same as when you were a child, or as when you were young. Inside nothing has changed. The face is wrinkled by age, the hairs have gone gray, death is approaching – this is all from the outside. If you look in the mirror, then of course there are signs that much time has passed, that very little is left, that sooner or later you will be gone. But look within: there has never been any time there. You are exactly the same as you ever were when you were running in the garden or on the beach and collecting colored stones and seashells. Just remember.

Inside you are exactly the same this moment too. Time is a fallacy as far as the inner world is concerned because in the inner world nothing ever changes. It remains the same, its taste remains the same.

In the inner world time is simply irrelevant. And life is in the inner. It expresses itself in the outside, but it does not belong to the outside. It wells up from your within. It moves outward like ripples, it pulsates outward, but it arises from your innermost core.

When Buddha was asking, "How do you measure the life of a man?" in a very simple question he was asking a very complicated philosophical question too. And the monk was deceived. The monk said, *"By days."* But there is no day, no night. Time is a utilitarian concept, it is needed outside. When you are alone, time is not needed. It is a relationship between you and others; it is a relative concept. Try to find out, and you will be surprised that believing in time, you have been believing in an illusion – because that which does not correspond to your inner reality cannot be real.

It is just like money: if you go to the market, it has value; if you simply sit alone with your money, it has no value. The value comes only when you relate with others because the value is just an agreement between you and the others. That's why money has a beautiful name: it is called *currency*. *Currency* means when money moves it has value; when it does not move it has no value. If you go on keeping it in your pocket always and always, it is meaningless. You can keep anything else instead of it, it will be the same.

Money has value when it changes hands. From one hand to another – then there is value. Value is in its being a currency, a moving force. When it moves from you to somebody else it has value. Again, if it is stuck there it loses value. That's why miserly people are the poorest in the world: they have money, but they don't know that money has value only when it is a currency. You can hide it in your treasure chest; you will remain poor.

Time is also a currency between two people, between relationships, between societies. But in the inner world, when you are alone, it is simply meaningless.

All the concepts of time, if looked at deeply, look very stupid. But people don't look deeply into things because to look deeply creates anxiety. Then you become very anxious. Then settled things are unsettled, and whenever something is unsettled one feels anxious, one wants to be settled again.

People say time passes. But where does it pass to? From where does it come? You say it comes from the future and goes into the past? That means the future exists before it has become present? Otherwise, where is it coming from – from nowhere? From nothingness? And then you say it goes into the past? That means it goes on collecting in the past, it is still there? It still exists? Then what is the difference between present, past, and future, if they all exist? Then they are all present. Then there is no past and no future.

You say a moment that has passed is past, and a moment that has yet to come is future. You stand on a road, you have walked two miles; that has passed. But those two miles exist; you can look back, those two miles are still there. And if you want to go back you can go back. But can you go back in time?

Look back – nothing exists. Except for this present moment, on both sides there is simply smoke, and nothing. The past simply disappears, and the future appears out of nothing. And then a problem arises: if in the beginning there is nothing, and in the end again there is nothing, how can there be something between two nothings? It is impossible.

Time is not a valid concept at all. It is just utilitarian. It is accepted, it has utility. Every morning you come at eight o'clock; if there were no time it would be difficult. When would you come? How would you manage? And how would there be a possibility of me meeting you? It would become difficult. But remember it is just an agreement, it is not truth.

Truth is timeless. Time is a human invention, truth is eternal. In fact, time does not pass, we pass. We come and go; time remains. Then time is not time, then it is eternity.

Buddha was asking all these things in a simple question. The monk said, *"By days."* Buddha said:

> *"You do not understand the way."*

The man's understanding was very superficial. We can call it the understanding on the level of the body. Of course, the body has a clock in it. Now the scientists call it the biological clock. That's why if you eat every day at one o'clock, your lunchtime, then every day at one o'clock the body will say you are hungry. The body has a clock. You need not actually look at the clock. If you listen to your body, the body will tell you, "Now it is time to sleep because every day you go to sleep at this time."

And you can even put an alarm in your body-clock. When you are going to sleep you can repeat your own name loudly, three times. If your name is Rama, you can say, "Rama, listen. I have to get up at five o'clock. Help me." Talk to your body and go to sleep, and exactly at five o'clock your body will wake you. The body has a clock. That's why, every month, after exactly four weeks, twenty-eight days, the monthly period comes to a woman. The body manages very exactly unless something has gone wrong with the body – the woman may have disturbances. Otherwise, it is exactly twenty-eight days. If the clock is functioning well there will never be any problem: twenty-eight days means twenty-eight days. After nine months the body is ready to give birth to a child, exactly after nine months. If the woman is healthy and there is no complication in her body, it will happen exactly at the moment nine months are complete. The body carries a clock and functions perfectly well.

The body, of course, is measured by days. And the body shows every sign of passing time. Young, old, you can see it on the body. The body carries the whole biography.

This man's understanding was very physical, very superficial.

> *The Buddha asked another monk. "How do you measure the length of a man's life?"*
> *The monk answered, "By the time that passes during a meal."*

His understanding goes a little deeper: he is less physical and more psychological. To enjoy a meal you need a mind, to indulge you need a mind, to be sensual you need a mind. This man's understanding was a little deeper. What was he saying? He was saying that a man's life is measured by the pleasures, indulgences, sensuality, experiences that he has gathered in his life. The man is saying, "How long you live is not the point, but how much you enjoy the pleasures of life is."

There is a story about Nero, the Roman emperor. He must have been of the exact same type as this second monk. He always had two physicians with him. He would eat, and the physicians would help him to vomit. Then he would eat again. You cannot go on eating; there is a limit. So when he would feel that the stomach was full, he would order the physician to help him vomit; then he could eat again. He would eat ten, twelve times a day.

And don't think that this is very far-fetched: I have come across a few people who do it.

There was one sannyasin: after she had been here for at least two years, she told me, "I am ashamed, but I have to tell you that every day, when I eat, I vomit immediately."

I said, "Why?"

She said, "So that I can eat more. But then I vomit again."

Now vomiting has become a habit. Now she cannot resist; when she eats she has to vomit. It has become a mechanical habit. It took almost six months to break her habit.

Nero must have done it. Ordinarily, you may not be vomiting but you can go on eating too much. There are people who live to eat. It is good to eat, it is good to eat to live, but once you start living for eating then you are in a very confused state. Eating is a means, not the end.

This monk says, *"By the time that passes during a meal."* He must have been a glutton. He must have understood only one language, and that is of taste. He must have been a food addict. He says that if we count real life, then real life means those moments in which we are enjoying, indulging. It may be food, it may be sex, or other gratifications. Many people are of that type. Their philosophy seems to be: eat, drink, be merry – and there is nothing else in life.

There was a great philosopher in India, Charvak. This was his message to his disciples: "Eat, drink, and be merry. Don't bother about the other life, and the soul, and God. This is all nonsense. These are just theories invented by the priests to exploit you." He was the first Marxist; Marx came three thousand years later. He was the first Marxist, communist.

But if life is just eating, drinking, indulging, then it cannot have any meaning. That's why in the West a new problem has become very, very important, and the problem is: what is the meaning of life? All intelligent people are asking that in the West. Why? Nobody asks it in the East; but in the West the problem has become almost epidemic. It is no longer academic; everybody is asking what the meaning of life is. And they are asking at the wrong time – when they have enough to eat, enough to drink, and enough to be merry. Why are they asking this question?

In fact, when you have all that this world can give to you, then the question arises, "What is the meaning of it?" Yesterday you ate, today you are eating, tomorrow also you will eat – so what is the point? Eating and defecating – on the one hand you go on stuffing yourself, on the other hand you go on emptying yourself. Is this your whole life? And in between there is a little taste on the tongue?

It seems absurd. The effort seems to be too much, and the result seems to be nothing, almost nothing.

Man needs to have a meaning, but the meaning can come only from the higher. The meaning always comes from the beyond. Unless you feel related to something higher, you feel meaningless. Because Nietzsche said, "God is dead," he opened the door for many ugly phenomena. For example, Nazism, fascism, communism, became possible because once there is no God, that door is closed from where man has always felt meaning in his life.

Meaning arises when you feel that you are part of a divine plan and you feel that you are part of a divine flow. When you feel that you are part of a great whole, then you have meaning. A brick in itself has no meaning, but when it becomes part of a great palace, part of the Taj Mahal, it has meaning. It has contributed something to the beauty of the Taj Mahal; it is not futile, it is significant.

When God is not there, man starts finding new meaning to his life: become part of a party – the great Communist Party, or the great Fascist Party. Become part – then Stalin and Adolf Hitler become gods. Then you join hands with them so that you can feel a little meaning – that you are not alone, that you are not just accidental, that you have some mission to fulfill. Maybe you are here to bring communism to the world, a classless society to the world; or you are here to bring the kingdom of the Aryans. Then one becomes part of a Hindu religion, Christian, Mohammedan. One finds some way, somewhere, to become part of something. And people go to foolish lengths: people become Rotarians and Lions just to have a feeling that they are part of an international organization. You are somehow chosen, you are a Rotarian. Everybody cannot be a Rotarian; only very few people can be Rotarians, but you are a Rotarian. So you have a meaning, but what a foolish meaning. What does it matter whether you are a Rotarian or not? It really does not bring meaning to your life; it simply deceives you.

You can eat well, you can live well, you can have all the pleasures of life – still you will remain empty. This man, the second monk, said that life is to be measured by pleasure, by indulgence, by sensuality. But Buddha said: *"You do not understand the way."*

The way cannot be understood by the body-oriented mind, and the way cannot be understood by the mind-oriented mind. Neither can it be understood through time, nor can it be understood through experience.

The way is beyond time and beyond experience.

The Buddha asked a third monk. "How do you measure the length of a man's life?"
The monk answered, "By the breath."
The Buddha said: "Very well, you know the way."

Now in an English translation, saying "by breath" does not seem to be as significant as it appeared to Buddha when the monk said, "By *prana*." *Breath* is a translation of *prana*, but *prana* is much more meaningful than *breath*. The actual translation, closer to truth, would be *spirit*, not *breath*. And the word *spirit* exists in such words as *inspiration*, *expiration*. *Spirit* seems to be closer to home, but still not exactly true. So let me first explain to you what *prana* is; then you will be able to understand. Otherwise it looks a little absurd: the man says, "By breath," and Buddha says: *"Very well, you know the way."* The man just says, "By breath."

The first thing, if you look at yourself you will find there is the body: the first circle around you, your outermost circle. Then there is your mind: the second circle within the first circle. And then you will come to a bridge; that bridge is your breath, *prana*. By that bridge you are joined with the soul. That's why when a person stops breathing we say he is dead. The bridge is broken, now the soul is separate and the body is separate. When a child is born, the first thing he is expected to do is to breathe. Through breath the soul and body become joined together. And again, the last thing he will do when he dies will be to stop breathing. Again there will be a divorce; the body and soul will be separate.

Prana is the bridge, the glue by which you are glued together. A man can live without food for many days, you can live without water for many hours – but without breath you cannot live even for many minutes. Even seconds will seem difficult.

Breath is the bridge between matter and no-matter, between the form and the formless, between the world and the divine – or whatsoever terms you choose. Breath is the bridge, and much depends on the breath. How you breathe, what the quality of your *prana* is – much depends on it.

Watch: when you are angry you breathe in one way, when you are silent you breathe in another way. The pulse is different, the rhythm is different, the quality is different. When you are angry your breath is not rhythmic, not musical, not harmonious. It is bumpy. When you are in a passion, in sexual passion, again the breath is feverish. It is not in tune; something goes wrong with breathing. When you are sitting silently, just being peaceful, not doing anything: no desire, no passion, no anger – just full of compassion, full of love – your breathing is very soft. Your breathing has a rhythm to it, a dance to it. It has no violence, no aggression; it is very delicate.

Have you watched it? When you are in passion your breath will have a very bad odor to it; when you are peaceful your breath will have a very sweet smell to it because you are at ease, the whole being is at ease, you are at home. The breathing will carry the message that you are at home.

There are moments of deep meditation when breathing almost stops. I say almost; it does not stop really, but it becomes so silent that you cannot feel it. You can feel it only if you put a mirror close to your nose. Then on the mirror you can see it; otherwise you cannot feel it. Those are rare moments of blessing and benediction.

All the Yoga systems of the world have worked on breathing because it is through the breathing that you will pass from the body to no-body. It is through breathing that you will enter into the innermost core of your existence.

The monk is right when he says, "A man's life is to be measured by the way he breathes, by how he breathes." If you are afraid, your breathing is different; you are nervous, your breathing is different; you are sad, your breathing is different. With every mood your breathing changes. The breathing goes on showing where you are. If you can watch your breathing, you will learn the whole alphabet of your inner changing climates. You can see all the moods reflected in the breathing. Breathing is a great way to measure where you are, what you are, what you are doing. Buddha emphasized breathing very much. And his emphasis is unique: it is very different from Patanjali, it is very different from hatha yoga, it is very different from other systems, all other systems. He says: "Don't use any system for breathing because if you do something with breathing you will create something artificial. Let breathing be natural – simply watch it. Don't do anything to it. Simply be a witness, simply look at it."

Now, if you watch breathing, by and by you will see that you are different from breathing. Certainly because the watcher cannot be the watched, the subject cannot be the object, the observer cannot be the observed.

When you start watching your breathing – and Buddha says to continuously do it: walking, sitting, whenever you are not doing anything else, just watch your breathing, go on seeing it – by seeing it, a great serenity will arise in you. Because you will be standing behind breathing, and behind the breathing is your soul, you will be centered in your soul.

And if you watch breathing, you will learn: subtle changes in breathing show where you are, and breathing continuously functions as a measuring-rod. A slight change in breathing will be noted when awareness is full. And you can drop then and there, you can become more alert. If you feel your breathing is wavering a little, and you feel that this wavering is the wavering that comes when sex takes possession, then it is the moment to become more aware. And if the wavering breathing settles again, you have passed. That desire that was going to possess you will not be able to possess you. By and by, you become aware of what type of changes happen in breathing when you become angry. They are so subtle that if you can become aware when the breathing changes slightly they can be dropped from there – because they are right in the seed and the seed can be dropped easily. When they become big trees it is very difficult to drop them. You become aware of anger only when it has already possessed you. Your diagnosis is too late.

In Soviet Russia, they have developed a new type of photography: they call it Kirlian. Now Kirlian photographers say that we can catch hold of a disease six months before it really happens to the person. And if it can be done, then there will be no need for anybody to be ill. The person himself is not aware that he will be falling a victim of tuberculosis in six months. How can you be aware of that? But before it enters the body, first it enters *prana*. Before it enters the body, first it enters your energy. They call it "bioplasma" in Russia; it is exactly what we mean by *prana* – bioplasma: your vitality, your body electricity.

First it enters the body electricity, and then it takes six months to be transformed into a physical phenomenon. Then it becomes solid in the body. Then it is already too late. When you start treating it, it is already too late. If you could have caught it when it was in the bioplasma, you could have destroyed it very, very easily. There would have been no problem in it. And the body would never have suffered, the body would not even have known about it.

Buddha says that anything that enters the bioplasma first happens in your breathing. Anything that happens to your body, to your mind, first happens to your breathing. Maybe some day Kirlian photographers will be able to rediscover the fact that there is a certain association between the pulse of bioplasma and breathing. It has to be so because when you breathe deeply you have a bigger aura. That has been photographed. When you breathe deeply, you have more oxygen and more flowing energy and your body has a bigger aura, more luminosity to it. When you breathe in a dull way, the lungs are not full of oxygen and you go on carrying much stale carbon dioxide; then your aura shrinks and becomes very small.

A really alive person has a very big aura, so big that when he comes close to you his aura touches your aura. You will feel it: there are people with whom you will suddenly feel that you are attracted, pulled. They are irresistible; you would like to come close to them, closer and closer. Their aura has touched your aura.

Then there are people whose auras are almost dead, whose auras do not exist at all. They repel, they don't attract. They are like dead people; nobody feels attracted toward them.

Buddha says, "Watch, become aware of your breathing."

His yoga is called *Anapanasati yoga* – the yoga of watching the breath coming in and watching the breath going out. He says this is enough. So when the monk said, *"By the breath,"* Buddha said: *"Very well, you know the way."*

Buddha's way has ten grounds called *bhumis. Bhumi* means ground. Buddha has said that if you understand these ten grounds, and if you practice these ten grounds, you will attain to the ultimate. I would like to go into these ten *bhumis*, these ten grounds. They are very practical.

The first *bhumi* is *pamudita*; it means joyousness. Now, you will be surprised. People have a misunderstanding about Buddha and his teaching – they think that he is a very sad, pessimistic thinker. He is not. His first grounding is joyousness. He says unless you are joyous you will never reach to the truth. Joyousness, delight, celebration: that is the meaning of *pamudita*.

Be like a flower: open, dancing in the breeze, and joyous. Only joy can take you to the other shore. If you are not joyous, your very sadness will function like a rock around your neck and will drown you. People are not drowned by anything else but their own sadness and pessimistic outlook. Life has to be joyous, then life becomes spiritual.

If your church is sad, then that church exists for death, not for life. A church, a temple, has to be joyous. If you come to a saint and he has no sense of humor, escape from him, beware. He can kill you; he will prove poisonous. If he cannot laugh, then you can be certain that he does not know what truth is. Truth brings a sense of humor, truth brings laughter, truth brings a subtle happiness – for no reason at all.

Pamudita means joyous for no reason at all. You are sometimes joyous, but that is not *pamudita* because it has a reason. One day you win the race and you are very happy. What will you do? It is not going to happen every day. What are you going to do tomorrow? Or you have won a lottery and you are very happy, but this is not going to happen every day.

One day I saw Mulla Nasruddin very sad, sitting on his verandah. I asked, "What is the matter Nasruddin? Why are you so sad?"

He said, "Two weeks ago one of my uncles died and left me fifty thousand rupees."

So I said, "This is nothing to be sad about. You should be happy."

He said, "Yes, I was. And then the next week another uncle died and left me one *lakh* of rupees."

So I said, "Why are you sad? You should be dancing!"

He said, "I know. But now there are no more uncles left."

It cannot happen every day; uncles cannot always die.

Your joyousness, if it is caused, is bound to turn into unhappiness sooner or later. It is on the way already, watch out. If you have a cause to be happy, you are already getting into unhappiness because the cause will disappear. Only uncaused joyousness can be yours. Then nobody can take it away.

Only saints and madmen are joyous for no reason at all. That's why there is a similarity between mad people and saints, a little similarity, an overlapping. Their boundaries overlap. Both are very different: the saint is aware, the madman is absolutely unaware. But one thing is certain, both are happy for no reason at all.

The madman is happy because he is so unaware that he does not know how to be unhappy; he is so unconscious that he cannot create misery. To create misery you need a little consciousness. And the saint is happy because he is so fully aware, how can he create misery? When you are fully aware you create happiness for yourself, you become a source of your happiness. That's what Buddha means by *pamudita*, and he says this is the first ground.

The second ground is *vimal*. It means innocence, purity, simplicity.

Innocence – remember the word. If you become too knowledgeable, you lose innocence. If you become a pundit you lose innocence. So don't go on gathering beliefs and knowledge, otherwise your innocence will be corrupted. If you don't know, you don't know. Simply say, "I don't know." Accept your ignorance and you will be more innocent. And out of innocence much happens. Never lose your childlikeness. I don't mean that you should be childish. To be childish and to be childlike are totally different. To be childish means to be irresponsible; to be childlike means to be simple, innocent, trusting.

The third ground is *pabhakari*. It means luminousness, light.

Feel yourself as a flame, live as if you are an inner burning light, move with the inner flame. Do whatsoever you do, but always feel yourself as if you are made out of light. By and by you will see a luminousness arising around you.

It is already there. If you help, it will arise and you will have an aura. Now Kirlian photographers can even take photographs of it. It is now very tangible.

Man is made of bioelectricity; everything is made of electricity. Electricity seems to be the basic component of all. Ask the physicists: they say matter consists of nothing but electricity. So everything is nothing but different formulations and combinations of energy. Buddha says man is light. Light means electricity.

You have just to recognize the fact, you just have to cooperate with it, and you will become a great light. Not only unto yourself; you will become a light to others too: wherever you walk there will be light.

This is *pabhakari*, the third grounding.

The fourth grounding is *arsimati*: radiance, aliveness, vitality.

The religious seeker should not be dull and dead. But ordinarily you will find these people. That's why I am interested in telling you about these groundings – even Buddhists have forgotten.

If you see a Buddhist monk you will see a pale, dead, dull person – sleepy, in a stupor, somehow dragging, somehow carrying the burden of life, not interested. Buddha says, "Radiance, aliveness, vitality; this is the fourth grounding." Be alive because it is only on the wings of life that you will reach to truth. If you are dull you are lost.

Be radiant because when there is no anxiety for the future and no desire for the future, then the whole energy is available to you. Then you can burn your torch from both ends at once.

The fifth is *sudurjaya*. It means adventurousness, courageousness, challenge, welcomingness. Whenever there is a challenge, welcome it, don't avoid it. Whenever there is an adventure, don't escape. Go on the journey, go on the trip.

Nobody ever loses anything by being adventurous. I am not saying that the path of adventure is full of roses. It is not; roses are few and far between, and there are many thorns. But one grows, one becomes crystallized when one accepts a life of adventure.

Ordinarily people accept the life of security, of no adventure. A good job, a good house, a good wife, a good husband and good children – and people are satisfied. People are satisfied with living and dying comfortably, as if comfort is the goal.

Then they never grow, then they never achieve to any peaks, then they never achieve to what Maslow calls "actualization." They remain just possibilities. It is as if a seed has chosen to hide in the pod and is not ready to go into the adventure of falling into the soil. It is dangerous because the seed will have to die. It is dangerous because the seed does not know what will happen when he has disappeared. No seed has ever known what happens after the seed has died. How can the seed know? The tree may happen or may not happen.

Buddha says, "*Sudurjaya* – look at the far: *sudur*, that which is very far. Let that be your challenge." Don't be confined to the comfortable, to the familiar, to the secure; don't base your philosophy on the promises of a life insurance company. Have a little more courage, move into the unknown.

When you move into the unknown, the unknown moves to you. When you are ready to drop your securities, existence is also ready to drop its mysteries. When you are ready to be nude and available, it is also ready to be nude and available. It responds, it exactly responds to you. It never goes further than you go. If you go toward it, it comes toward you; if you escape, it also escapes. *Sudurjaya*...

Then the sixth grounding: *abhimukhi* – immediateness, face-to-faceness, encountering that which is. *Abhimukhi*, face-to-face immediateness. Don't bother about the past and don't bother about the future. Face the truth as it comes, encounter the fact as it comes – and with no preparation, with immediateness.

A man who lives by preparation is a pseudo-man. In life there are no possibilities for rehearsals. But we all live through rehearsals: before you go home you start preparing what you are going to say to your wife. Can't you be immediate? Can't you wait for the moment when the wife is there, and let what happens happen? But coming home from the office you are preparing: What is she going to ask, and what are you going to answer? Rehearsal – and then you are always clouded by your rehearsals. You cannot see that which is. You always see through your clouds. Those clouds are very distorting.

Buddha says, "*Abhimukhi*, immediateness – be alert and let there be response." Whatsoever the result, don't be afraid of it. People start rehearsing because they are afraid of the results, so they want to plan everything. There are people who plan everything. Every gesture is planned; then the life is of course that of an actor: it is not real, it is not authentic, it is not true. And if your life is not true, then it is impossible for you to come to truth.

The seventh is *durangama*: far-goingness, accepting the call of the beyond. There is a beyond everywhere. We are surrounded by the beyond. That beyond is what "God" is; that beyond has to be penetrated. It is within, it is without. It is always there, but you ordinarily forget about it because it is very uncomfortable, inconvenient, to look into the beyond. It is as if one looks into an abyss, and one starts trembling, one starts feeling sick. The very awareness of the abyss and you start trembling. Nobody looks at the abyss. We go on looking in other directions, we go on avoiding the real. The real is like an abyss because the real is a great emptiness. It is vast sky with no boundaries. Buddha says, "*Durangama* – be available to the beyond." Never remain confined to the boundaries, always trespass boundaries. Make the boundaries if you need them, but always remember you have to step out. Never make imprisonments.

We make many sorts of imprisonments: relationship, belief, religion – they are all imprisonments. One feels cozy because there are no wild winds blowing. One feels protected although the protection is false because death will come and will drag you into the beyond. Buddha says before death comes and drags you into the beyond, go on your own.

A Zen monk was going to die. He was very old, ninety years old. Suddenly he opened his eyes and he said, "Where are my shoes?"

The disciple said, "Where are you going? Have you gone crazy? You are dying, and the physician has said that there is no more possibility – a few minutes more."

He said, "That's why I'm asking for my shoes. I would like to go to the cemetery because I don't want to be dragged. I will walk on my own and I will meet death there. I don't want to be dragged. And you know me, I have never leaned on anybody else. This will be very ugly, that four persons will be carrying me. No."

He walked to the cemetery. Not only that, he dug his own grave, lay down in it, and died.

This is what Buddha means by *durangama* – such courage to accept the unknown, such courage to go on your own and welcome the beyond. Then death is transformed, then death is no longer death.

Such a courageous man never dies; death is defeated. Such a courageous man goes beyond death. For one who goes on his own to the beyond, the beyond is never like death. Then the beyond becomes a welcome. If you welcome the beyond, the beyond welcomes you; the beyond always goes on echoing you.

The eighth is *achala*: centering, grounding, immovability. Buddha says one should learn to be centered, unmoving, grounded. Whatsoever happens, one should learn how to remain unwavering. Let the whole world go into disappearance, let the whole world dissolve, but a buddha will go on sitting under his *bodhi* tree, unmoved. His center will not be wavering, he will not go off-center.

Try it. By and by, you start coming closer to your center. The closer you come, the happier you will feel and a great solidity will arise in your being. Things go on happening, but they are happening outside. Nothing penetrates to your center; if you are there, then nothing makes any difference. Life comes, death comes, success, failure, praise and insult, and pain and pleasure – they come and go. They all pass away, but the witnessing center always remains.

The ninth is *sadhumati*: intelligence, awareness, mindfulness. Buddha is very much in favor of intelligence, but remember that he does not mean intellect. Intellect is a heavy thing, intelligence is more total. Intellect is borrowed, intelligence is your own. Intellect is logical, rational; intelligence is more than logical. It is super-logical, it is intuitive. The intellectual person lives only through argument. Certainly, arguments can lead you up to a certain point, but beyond that, hunches are needed.

Even great scientists who work through reason come to a point where reason does not work, where they wait for a hunch, for some intuitive flash, for some light from the unknown. And it always happens: if you have worked hard with the intellect, and you don't think that intellect is all, and you are available to the beyond, someday a ray penetrates you. It is not yours – and yet it is yours because it is nobody else's. It comes from "God." It comes from your innermost center. It looks as if it is coming from the beyond because you don't know where your center is to be intuitive.

Buddha uses intelligence in the sense of awareness, in the sense of mindfulness. The Sanskrit word *sadhumati*, is very beautiful. *Mati* means intelligence, and *sadhu* means sage: sagely intelligence – not only intelligence, but sagely intelligence. There are people who may be rational but are not reasonable. To be reasonable is more than to be rational. Sometimes the reasonable person will be ready to accept the irrational too. Because he is reasonable, he can understand that the irrational also exists. The rational person can never understand that the irrational also exists, he can only believe in the limited logical syllogism.

But there are things which cannot be proved logically, and yet they are. Everybody knows they are, and nobody has ever been able to prove them. Love is; nobody has ever been able to prove what it is, or whether it is or not. But everybody knows love is. Even people who deny and are not ready to accept anything beyond logic – even they fall in love. When they fall in love then they are in a difficulty, they feel guilty.

But love is – and nobody is ever satisfied by intellect alone unless the heart also is fulfilled. These are the two polarities inside you: the head and the heart. *Sadhumati* means a great synthesis of both: head and heart. *Sadhu* means the heart, and *mati* means the head.

When the sagely heart is joined together with a sharp intelligence, then there is a great change, a transformation. That's what awareness is all about.

The tenth is *dharma-megha*: grace showering, becoming a cloud of truth, love and grace – *dharma-megha*.

Do you remember that just a few days ago there were so many clouds raining, showering on the thirsty earth? Buddha says unless you become a showering of grace you will not attain to the ultimate. The nine grounds are to prepare you. The tenth ground is the beginning of sharing; you start showering.

Whatsoever you get, you have to share; then you will get more. Whatsoever you have, you have to shower, you have to give it to others, you have to distribute it. All that you attain in your being has to become your compassion. Then you will get more. The more you become a spendthrift of your inner energies, the more space will be created for godliness to descend in you, for truth to penetrate you.

That's why it is very difficult to know the truth and not to share it. It is impossible. Mahavira remained silent for twelve years, then suddenly one day he burst forth. What happened? For twelve years he was silent; he must have been moving into the nine grounds. Then came the tenth; he became a *dharma-megha*, he became a cloud of truth and started showering.

You cannot do anything about it. It is just like a flower opening and releasing its fragrance to the winds. It is just like a lamp burning and showering its light all around. There is no way to prevent it; you cannot be miserly about truth.

Buddha attained to truth, then for forty-two years he continuously moved from one place to another – continuously talking, continuously saying what had happened to him. One day he was asked, "You teach us to be silent, but you go on talking."

Buddha said: I have to talk to teach you to be silent. Be silent, so that one day you can also talk. Be silent because in silence you will gather the juice. The flower remains closed until the right moment has come when the fragrance is ready. Then it opens its petals, not before it.

Be silent, be aware, be adventurous – one day all of these nine *bhumis,* these nine grounds, will prepare you to become a cloud. Then you will shower on people and you will share.

Truth has always been shared in different ways. Meera danced; she knew how to dance the truth. Buddha never danced. Chaitanya sang; he knew how to sing. Buddha never sang. It depends on the individual. Whatsoever capacities you have, whatsoever creative possibilities you have, when truth comes into you it will find your possibilities, your creativities.

Just the other night a sannyasin was saying to me, "It is very difficult; the more I become meditative, the more I like to compose music." He's a composer and he had stopped it. Now he thinks that this is like a disturbance: "What is happening? Whenever I am feeling meditative, immediately great ideas arise in me and I would like to compose. Now, what to do? Should I stop it?"

There is no need to stop. Meditation brings your creativity to an expression. Whatsoever is hidden in you will become unhidden; whatsoever you are carrying within you will be sung, will be danced – whatsoever it is. You will become a *dharma-megha.*

These three answers from the three monks show three types of understanding: the bodily, the psychological, and the spiritual. Breath means spirit – that's why I call the third understanding spiritual. If you have the first understanding then these ten *bhumis* are not for you. If you have the second type of understanding, then too these ten grounds are not for you. If you have the third understanding, then these ten grounds are for you.

And unless you can become a *dharma-megha*, remember, your life was in vain. You lived without any purpose, you lived fruitlessly, barrenly. In fact, you lived not; you only appeared to live.

So meditate on this small story of Buddha's, his asking, and the answers. Just meditate on it. I will tell you a few anecdotes to show you how we understand.

A minister asked a little girl what she thought of her first church service.

"Well," she said, after giving the matter some thought, "the music was nice, but the commercial was too long."

Now, a small girl – she knows only how to watch TV; that's her understanding. She knows music and commercials. In the church also she thought that the sermon was the commercial. She said, "The music was nice, but the commercial was too long."

The couple was married forty years. She decided to get a check-up at the hospital. When she came home, she was ecstatic.

"The doctor says I am in perfect health," she bragged to her husband. "In fact, he said I can have sex twelve times a month."

"Wonderful!" said the husband. " Put me down for two."

Now a businessman is a businessman – "Put me down for two."

Two corpses were laid out in the same room at the funeral home. One night when everybody left, one corpse sat up and asked the other, "What did you die from?"

"Cigarettes," he answered. "I just smoked too many cigarettes."

"What kind did you smoke?"

"Raleighs," he answered.

"At least, did you save the coupons?"

"Hell yes! How do you think I got this coffin?"

Even when people are dead they will continue. Naturally, it is natural that they will continue their old past, their old ways of understanding, calculation.

The girlie show was touring the army camps in Vietnam. At one outpost, arrangements were being made to feed them before leaving.

"I say," said the officer in charge. "Would you like to mess with the officers?"

"Don't mind if we do, dear," said the leading lady, "but can't we have something to eat first?"

Now a girlie show is a girlie show... Even words don't carry the meaning that they have. You put the meaning into them. Each time you utter a word, watch; each time you listen to a word, watch; each time you make a gesture, watch – and you will see that whatsoever your level of understanding, it is expressed in all the ways.

Seated in a restaurant, a priest was scrutinizing the beauty of a young lady escorted by her male companion. A layman kidded him about his female interest.

"Just because I am on a perpetual diet does not mean I can't study the menu once in a while!" said the priest.

Your inner – repressed, rejected, thrown into the basement – also goes on reflecting in your ways. Even sometimes when you avoid something, then too, your understanding is shown in your very avoidance.

The famous story of two Zen monks...

Crossing a ford they came across a woman, a very young and beautiful woman. She wanted to cross but she was afraid. So one monk took her on his shoulders and carried her to the other shore. The other monk was furious, the other monk was fiery: "It is prohibited! A Buddhist monk should not touch a woman. Now this is too much. Not only touching: he has carried the woman on his shoulder." The monk remained quiet, but he was boiling within.

Miles passed. When they reached the monastery, when they

were entering the door, the other monk turned to the first and said, "Look, I will have to talk to the master. I will have to report it. It is prohibited!"

The first monk said, "What are you talking about? What is prohibited?"

He said, "Have you forgotten? You carried that young beautiful woman on your shoulders. You should not touch!"

The first monk laughed and he said, "Yes, I carried her, but I left her on the other bank, miles back. Are you still carrying her?"

Yes, the other monk was still carrying her.

Remember that your understanding is shown in every way, and if you watch correctly, your very watchfulness will take you to a further step.

One unlucky sailor was shipwrecked on a desert island in the South Pacific. Fortunately food and water were plentiful, and the weather was perfect. So he survived in comparative comfort for six months, after which time, to his intense excitement, he spotted a small craft on the horizon. As it drifted in closer and closer, he could see that it was a ship's life raft containing one passenger. And as it got even closer he saw this passenger was a young woman. Eventually the raft splashed up on the beach and he went toward her. She was a beauty – tall and glowing and blonde, and a knockout.

"Hello, hello," said the poor lonely sailor. "Are you shipwrecked too?"

"Yes I am," she replied.

"I have been here for six months," he said.

"Six months!" she exclaimed. "Well, then I am sure I have got something you have been missing."

"Don't tell me you've got a cigarette on you!" he cried joyously.

Your own desire, your own understanding, your own greed is always there in each response, in each reaction. If you watch closely you will become aware that you go on showing your understanding or misunderstanding in each moment of your life.

Buddha's questions are very simple, and the monks who

answered may not have thought at all that they have any metaphysical significance. They may even have laughed at the ridiculous questions Buddha was asking them, but with very simple questions he had provoked their layer of understanding. The significance of the story is great. I never ask you any questions, but the questions you ask me are enough. They show everything about you. When I read your question, I am less concerned about your question than I am concerned with the questioner.

I am more concerned with the questioner, that's why I insist that you should always write your name under the question, you should always sign it – because a question in itself means nothing. It becomes meaningful only when I know who the questioner is. My answer is not for the question, but for the questioner. One may ask a question and I may answer it in one way, another asks exactly the same question, with the same words, but I will not answer in the same way because it is not the question that is important, it is the questioner.

Your question shows your understanding. Your question shows your confusion. Your question shows where you are. And I have to answer you where you are – remember it.

It happens many times in *darshan*, and it is better that you should remember it. Many people come; somebody asks a question, others listen. You are allowed to listen, but those answers that I am giving to that particular person are not given for you. Otherwise there would be great misunderstanding.

It happens sometimes that a questioner asks something. I explain it to him, I help him to understand his problem; another comes and he says, "That is exactly my question and you have already answered." I say, "No, don't be deceived so easily. You two are so different. In fact, there are no two similar persons in the world, so how can your questions be similar? You ask your question, and forget what I have said to the other." Then many times people become puzzled because they see that I can contradict myself.

Just the other night one person asked about fear: "I am afraid." I talked to him about death because I could see why he was afraid. Death was in his eyes, death was around him, he was shadowed by death. I talked much about death rather than about fear, and he understood it. I said to him, "Accept death and fear will disappear."

The next person said, "Now there is no need to ask. I have also fear in me and you have answered." I looked at the person; his fear had no relationship with death at all. His fear was fear of loneliness; it was a totally different dimension of fear. And I said, "Forget all that I have said to the other person. It was not your question and it was not answered for you. Tell me about your fear." By and by it became clear that his fear had nothing to do with death. His fear was fear of being left alone, fear that maybe his aloneness would always remain there.

The first was afraid of death, the second was afraid about whether love would happen or not. His fear was concerned with love – whether he would always remain alone, or somebody would be there who would love him. And would he be able to love? Would there be a possibility that he would be together with somebody and this constant wound of loneliness would disappear? He was not worried about death; he was worried about life. His fear was not concerned with death, his fear was concerned with life and relationship and communication and communion – love. The two persons were totally different, but they both used the word *fear*.

When I give different answers to different people, naturally you can collect all the answers and you will see: "This man is mad." The answers will be contradictory, they are bound to be contradictory. My approach is individual; my approach is person-to-person. I try to relate to you as individuals.

In the morning discourse you can meditate over whatsoever I say, but whenever you are deciding to do something, ask me in person. Don't decide it through the morning discourse because you are too many, and I am talking in a general way. The morning discourse is just to make principles clear to you. The *darshan* is to make practice clear to you, not principle. The morning discourse is just to make you aware that there are so many possibilities to grow, and how to grow. But I am not talking to you personally, I cannot. *Darshan* is so that you can ask personal questions, you can approach me and you can see your face in my mirror and I can see directly into your eyes. The morning discourse is more philosophical, the evening *darshan* is more religious.

If you can remember this difference, there will be great benefit out of it, a great understanding out of it.

Enough for today.

8

SLEEP AND AWAKE

BOTH ARE DREAMS AND MEANINGLESS

Osho,
What is more important, the practice of life or the theory? Is it possible for someone as ignorant as I am, who used to be a really devoted Roman Catholic, fifty years old, to attain to enlightenment without taking much time to study all which is between heaven and earth?

The first thing: life cannot be practiced. That which can be practiced is always the theory. Life has to be lived; there is no way to practice it, there is no way to prepare and rehearse it. Life is spontaneous. Only theories, dogmas, philosophies are to be practiced. They are unreal; the unreal has to be practiced so that you can create an illusion of its reality. The real has to be lived.

If you believe in some theory of love, then you will have to practice it. Love need not be practiced: you can simply float in it. To be in love you will have to drop all theories of love, otherwise you will never be in love. To be in the thick of life, in the intensity and passion of life, you will have to drop all philosophies of life – otherwise you will remain clouded in your words.

The problem does not arise out of life, the problem arises out of Christianity, Hinduism, Jainism, Buddhism. The problem arises out of the "ism." Life is very simple. Even animals can live it; it must be simple. Even trees are living it; it must be simple, it cannot be very complicated. Even birds, even rocks and rivers are living it. Why has it become so complicated for man? – because man can theorize about it, man can weave and spin doctrines around it. Those doctrines are poisonous.

If you are a Christian, you cannot live life. If you are a Hindu, no, life is not for you. To be alive one need not be a Hindu or a Christian, one simply needs to *be*, one needs just to be.

The two explorers were going through the jungle when a ferocious-looking lion appeared on the track in front of them.

"Keep calm," said the first explorer. "Remember what we read in that book on wild animals: if you stand absolutely still and look a lion straight in the eyes, he will turn tail and run away."

"Fine," said the second explorer. "You have read the book, I have read the book, but has he read the book?"

Books create problems, books puzzle you. The thing is very absurd: they puzzle you in the name of trying to clarify things, they puzzle you through their explanations. You are caught in those explanations because you think that unless you have the explanations, how are you going to live?

Have you heard the famous anecdote about a centipede who

was walking? It was a sunny morning and it was beautiful, and the centipede was happy and must have been singing in his heart. He was going along, almost drunk with the morning air.

A frog sitting by the side was very puzzled – he must have been a philosopher. He asked, "Uncle, wait! You are doing a miracle. A hundred legs! How do you manage? Which leg comes first, which comes second, third – and so on and so forth, up to a hundred. You don't get puzzled? How do you manage? It looks impossible to me."

The centipede said, "I have never thought about it. Let me brood." And standing there, he started trembling and he fell down on the ground. He himself became so puzzled – a hundred legs! How is one going to manage?

Philosophy paralyzes people. You are paralyzed by your philosophies. Life needs no philosophy, life is enough unto itself. It needs no crutches, it needs no support, no props. It is enough unto itself.

This is the first thing I would like to convey to you. This is my understanding, not my theory; this is how I feel life to be. It is not a mind thing, it is my existential experience. Trust life, and if you trust in life, I call you religious. Trust in life is trust in existence. God is a theory; when you dissolve that theory only life is left in its tremendous mystery, shimmering – just surrounding you within and without.

And you are part of it, part of its ecstasy.

"What is more important," the questioner has asked, "the practice of life or the theory?" Practice is needed only for a theory. Life needs no practice. You have simply to live it without brooding, without bringing the mind in. Once you bring the mind in you have started distorting life.

"Is it possible for someone as ignorant as I am to attain to enlightenment?" It is possible only for those who recognize their ignorance because those who recognize their ignorance are the innocent people. The recognition of ignorance is the very door to enlightenment. If you think you know, then you will be debarred.

Pundits have never become enlightened. They cannot; they have too much knowledge, they are too burdened with knowledge. They are like donkeys carrying scriptures – that's what Jalaluddin

Rumi has said. A donkey remains a donkey, whether he carries a Koran on his back or not does not matter. You can carry scriptures in your memory, but memory is not knowledge. To memorize a thing is not to know it. To memorize a thing is a way to avoid knowing it. It is very cheap, a computer can do it; there is nothing human about it, nothing special. A computer can do it better. All that your mind can do, a computer can do better, so there is nothing special about it, nothing human, nothing divine. It is a mechanical thing.

You can remember, you can memorize as much information as is available, but that is not going to help you. You can become a walking *Encyclopaedia Britannica*, but the donkey will be carrying the Koran unless you become aware that life is a mystery to be lived, not a problem to be solved. Then you approach in a totally different way. The approach becomes qualitatively different, then you approach through awareness, not through knowledge. Then you approach immediately, directly. You look into life without any clouds hindering your eyes – Christian, Mohammedan, Hindu. No clouds, just pure eyes, just looking like an innocent child.

To become that innocent child the first requirement is to understand that you are ignorant. It is one of the most difficult things. It is simple to renounce riches, but very difficult to renounce knowledge.

Many people renounce riches: they renounce their families, their homes, the world; but they don't, they never, renounce their knowledge.

I used to know a man who renounced the world. We were together in the university. After a few years I came across him in a city; I went to see him. He had renounced everything, he had become a Jaina monk. I asked him, "Are you still a Jaina?"

He said, "Why not? I am a Jaina, I was born a Jaina."

I said, "I was thinking you had renounced everything, but you have saved knowledge? You have renounced your parents, but you have not renounced that which your parents have taught you. This is something – you have renounced your home, but you are still carrying subtle impressions of the home. That's what being a Jaina is. If you had been brought up in a Mohammedan family, you would have been a Mohammedan. If you were never told by anybody that you were a Jaina, you could not have become a Jaina.

You have renounced the family, you say. You say, 'I have renounced my mother, father, my wife, my children.' Then why are you carrying knowledge that was given by them? Renounce that too."

He looked puzzled. He said, "That is difficult."

It is easy to renounce riches because they are outside; knowledge is an inner richness. It is easy to renounce the worldly things because they are like clothes – you can undress. But to renounce knowledge is like renouncing your skin; it is not so easy. It is painful, very painful.

From where does the pain come? The pain comes from the ego because knowledge is the food for the ego. It is the subtlest food for the ego. The more you know, the more you feel powerful.

Lord Bacon said, "Knowledge is power." It is very difficult to renounce power. Money too is power, but nothing compared to knowledge because money can be stolen: the government can change, communists can come, money can be distributed. You cannot rely on the money; the bank can go broke.

But knowledge is more secure: no government can take it away, no change of politics can take it away, nobody can rob you of it, and you cannot go so easily bankrupt. Knowledge seems to be more secure. You can produce money any day if you have knowledge – not otherwise. Knowledge can bring money, not otherwise. Money may not be able to bring knowledge, so knowledge is more of a richness, a greater wealth, more powerful – and the subtlest possession inside. The ego feels very good: "I know." That's why it is one of the most difficult things to recognize: "I don't know." The moment you recognize that you don't know, you become innocent, you become available. The ego disappears.

The question is from Deva Geeta. She is an old sannyasin, and she asks, "Is it possible for someone as ignorant as I am to attain to enlightenment?" It is only possible for those who know that they are ignorant – this is the beginning of real knowledge, the first sunray of wisdom penetrating into the darkness of your soul. The ego is the darkness, and this recognition that "I don't know" is the first ray of wisdom.

Socrates is reported to have said, "When I was young, I thought I knew everything. When I became a little more mature I started to feel that I knew only a few things. When I became old, one day I recognized that I didn't know anything at all." That day he declared, "My ignorance is utterly ultimate and profound, and I don't see any way that I can get out of my ignorance." Truth is mysterious and unknowable, and cannot be analyzed and dissected. There is no way to know it. You can be the truth but you cannot know it because for knowing, distance is needed. For knowledge, truth has to be there as an object, you have to be there inside as a subject, and knowledge happens between the two. Knowledge divides the world into three parts, a trinity: the knower, the known, and knowledge.

Truth is one. Neither is there anything to know, nor is there anybody to know it, so how is knowledge possible? Truth is, existence is, life is, and we are part of it.

Socrates says, "Now I can say I don't know anything." The day he declared this, the oracle in Delphi said to some people, "Socrates is the greatest man of wisdom alive on the earth." Those people came back and said to Socrates, "You are blessed! The oracle of the temple of Delphi has declared you the greatest wise man of the world."

Socrates laughed and said, "It is too late now. I know that I know nothing. There must be some mistake – at least this time the oracle has missed. Go back and tell the oracle that Socrates himself refuses it."

Those people were very puzzled because they were thinking they were bringing good news. What more could there be? When the gods declare Socrates to be the wisest man of the world, what more can you want? And here is this fool – he says, "I don't know anything. And it is too late. Go and say that something has gone wrong. The oracle is not right."

Those people, puzzled, confused, went back. They said to the oracle of the temple, "Socrates denies. He says, 'I am absolutely ignorant.'" There was laughter in the temple, and the oracle said, "That's why we declared him the greatest and the wisest man in the world. That's why. There has been no mistake."

If you can understand this, then ignorance becomes innocence. Don't call it ignorance; ignorance has a wrong association. Ignorance means that you are still thinking in terms of knowledge, you are still thinking that something is missing, something is lacking. Drop that word. That word is not right.

Innocence, childlike innocence – and I know Deva Geeta is a childlike old woman.

"Is it possible for someone as ignorant as I am to attain to enlightenment without taking much time to study all which is between heaven and earth?" There is no need to study anything. Everything is revealed. You just need clear eyes; study is not needed. You are not to go into the books, you just have to see the greenery of the trees, smell the fragrance of the flowers, listen to the birds, and the sound of running water, and the beautiful clouds floating in the sky.

Everything is so perfect and everything is so tremendously beautiful. Just approach this great shrine of God. God is enshrined here in every stone, and every stone is a sermon, and he is flowering in every flower, and he is breathing in every heart. Just approach with innocence, and everywhere you will find it is holy ground.

Every bush is afire with God because life itself is what God is all about; the totality, the wholeness of life is what God is all about. You just approach with clear, childlike, innocent eyes. That will do. The universe is your university. The Koran and the Vedas and the Bible and the Gita are irrelevant – God's greatest book is just in front of you. Turn its pages.

When you move from the trees and you look up to the sky you have turned a page. When you look at the sun, you have turned another page. When you look at your child, into his eyes, you have turned another page.

This is what the real Veda, the real Koran, the real Bible is. This is *the* book, and all other books are man-made. Only this universe is the book that God has written himself.

Have you observed that all religions claim that their books are not man-made? Hindus claim that the Vedas are *apourusheya*: not made by man but made by God himself, and Sanskrit is the divine language, not human. You will find the same type and the same foolish claim everywhere. Mohammedans say the Koran descended from God, and so with Jews and Christians. Everybody is trying to claim that his book is the divine book and nobody bothers to look at the real divine book.

You are also a page in that divine book, and everything is part of it. These books are beautiful; I am not saying that anything is wrong with them. The Koran is beautiful – recite it, sing it. The Vedas are beautiful, but remember, don't be lost in them. Let them be stepping-stones toward the real book of life.

The second question:

> *Osho,*
> *In answer to a dream I sent you, you said dreams are dreams, without any meanings. Why say such a thing? I don't understand.*

I am not only saying that dreams are dreams, I say that whatsoever you see when you think you are awake is also a dream. The dreams that you see with closed eyes in your sleep and the dreams that you see with your open eyes in your so-called awake state – both are dreams and both are meaningless.

The questioner must have felt hurt because you would like even your dreams to have meaning. That's how psychoanalysis has become so important. People are foolish: they want their dreams to have great meaning. Even their lives are meaningless, and they think their dreams are meaningful.

You don't have any meaning right now – you cannot have. Meaning arises only when you are in flow, flowing with existence. Meaning is a happening between you and existence, when you are in tune; there is no other meaning. All other meaning is just illusion.

Try to understand what I mean by "meaning." Meaning is when there is a harmony between you and the whole. When there is a subtle dance and you are in step with the whole, there is meaning. Life is an orchestra, and if you start playing your flute solo and you forget the orchestra then there is no meaning. Then you are a nuisance, and whatsoever you are doing is not only meaningless, it is against meaning. It is better that you stop; for god's sake, stop! When you are flowing with the total and there is no individual left, no ego left, there is meaning. With the ego there is no meaning – because ego is a jarring note, ego is a noise, ego is a resistance against the whole.

The ego says, "I am separate and I have my own private destiny." Hence, egoistic people always feel deep down that their lives are meaningless. In the West now, meaninglessness has become almost a common thing, a cliché. Everybody is talking about meaninglessness.

People are rich, people are well fed, they have good shelters. In fact, for the first time in history a few countries have come to a point where they are free of poverty, of all the ugliness that comes through poverty and all the limitation that poverty brings. They are free. But the moment they become free, they start feeling meaningless.

Poor persons are not so aware of meaninglessness because they have to earn money – there is meaning. They have to send their children to the university, there is meaning. They are going to make a good house somewhere in the future; they are accumulating, by and by, a little money for it. They will have Cadillac car someday, there is meaning.

One day suddenly you have all: a good life, good clothes, good food. Then meaning disappears. A poor man always seems hopeful, you can always see a glimpse of hope in the eyes of a beggar. But rich men's eyes become dim, dull; the hope disappears.

The rich man's eyes become like a desert with no oasis, with no hopes. What happens? – all that he had been thinking up to now as meaningful has become meaningless because he has achieved it. And suddenly he becomes aware of the total emptiness within.

Meaning happens, real meaning happens only when you start falling in tune with God, or the whole, or call it cosmos, existence, or whatever. When you are in tune with the whole there arises great benediction. Great grace surrounds you. Your heart is full, fulfilled; a deep contentment and peace and serenity. There is meaning.

That's why I said that dreams are dreams; don't be too bothered by them. If you want to have some meaning, you can have it. You can go to the Freudian psychoanalyst – he will find meaning in it. He has some meaning already prepared for you. Whatsoever dream you bring, he will enforce his meaning on it.

Did you see the Taj Mahal in your dream? He will say these are phallic pillars, so the dream is sexual. Go to a follower of Adler: he says that all problems arise out of an inferiority complex. You have seen the Taj Mahal so you want to be like the Taj Mahal – superior, great, unique. Go to the Jungian and he will find some other meaning. You can go to many psychotherapists and they will all find different meanings, and this is something that nobody looks at. The whole thing is that the meaning is not coming from your dream, the meaning is coming from the analyst.

I have heard about President Sukarno of Indonesia. He was strictly a sex man, strictly a libido man, strictly Freudian. He could never pass a statue without patting it on the derriere. All his conversation away from the affairs of state – and he had some of the greatest affairs in his state – was always about the ladies. Here is his description of women:

A woman of twenty is like the continent of Africa – wild and untamed.

A woman of thirty is like Asia – hot-blooded and passionate.

A woman of forty is like the USA – overly-trained and too well-techniqued.

A woman of fifty is like Europe – decaying and falling apart.

A woman of sixty is like Australia – everybody knows where it is, but who wants to go there?

So you can go and take your dreams to some Sukarno – he will find nothing but sex. Even geography becomes symbolic only of sexuality. Even Europe, Asia, Africa, Australia – suddenly they have a totally different meaning you have never heard before. You project.

I am not a psychoanalyst. But people feel very good when they go to a psychoanalyst and the psychoanalyst listens very attentively to their nonsense. Nobody listens to your nonsense so attentively. Why should anybody listen? But the psychoanalyst has to listen; you pay for it, so he listens very attentively, it is your time. Otherwise, who bothers? Even the psychoanalyst just pretends that he is listening.

I have heard an anecdote about Freud.

A young apprentice was working with him. He was young and

full of energy, however to listen to people's nonsense dreams the whole day is tiring business, uninteresting, boring. But he was always surprised to see Freud: he was always full of energy, never bored. One day, in the evening when he was leaving his master, he asked Freud, "You are old, aged, but you are never tired. And from the morning to the night you are continuously listening to neurotic things, meaningless. But I get tired – after two, three patients, I'm completely exhausted."

Freud laughed. He said, "Who listens?"

You just have to pretend that you are listening, you just have to learn the trick of pretending that you are listening, that you are tremendously interested. You are interested only in the money that he is going to pay.

But the patient feels very good: "Here is somebody who listens so attentively." There is a great desire in human beings that somebody should listen to their miseries. It unburdens them, and it gives them a feeling that somebody loves, cares. That's why you go on talking about miseries. Everybody goes on talking about his miseries, illnesses, this and that, and wants the other to sympathize. You feel you are not alone. And when you are telling nonsense dreams and the psychoanalyst brings beautiful explanations, great theories, suddenly you feel you are very meaningful, you are no ordinary person. Just see what beautiful dreams you have. Maybe you have not created a great painting like Picasso and you have not written a great book like Shakespeare, but so what? You have dreamed such beautiful dreams that even a Freud, a Jung, an Adler is interpreting them – and they really interpret very beautifully.

But this whole business is nonsense; a dream is a dream. The whole effort in the East has been totally different: we have never bothered about the meaning of dreams. Our whole effort is to make you aware so that dreams disappear.

I have been telling you again and again a famous Zen anecdote...

A Zen master woke up in the morning and he saw a disciple passing by. He called him, "Come here! I had a very beautiful dream. Would you like to interpret it?"

The disciple said, "Wait. Let me bring a bucket of water. Please wash your face."

The master waited. The disciple brought a bucket of water and the master washed his face. By that time another disciple was passing, and he called. He said, "Listen, come here! I had a beautiful dream. Would you like to interpret it?"

He said, "Wait. Have you washed your face? I will bring a cup of tea for you." And he brought a cup of tea.

The master was very happy and he said, "If you had tried to interpret, I would have thrown you out of the monastery!"

This is the right interpretation: you had a dream? Wash your face, be finished. Still lingering a little? Have a cup of tea, but get out of it. It is a dream. What is there to interpret?

Only one thing has to be remembered: that you dreamed because you were unconscious and now you are trying to interpret it, still you are clinging to it.

It happened because you were fast asleep. For a buddha, dreams disappear; they don't happen, they cannot happen because he becomes so alert that even in sleep a subtle layer of awareness remains. He never loses his awareness. That's what Krishna means when he says in the Gita, "When everybody is fast asleep, the yogi is awake."

It does not mean that the yogi just stands in the room and remains awake. He would go mad. He also sleeps, but somewhere deep down a substratum remains alert, a small lamp continues burning inside – and in that light, no dreams can penetrate.

Buddha is reported to have said that dreams are like thieves: if the house is dark and there is no lamp inside, the thieves become interested in the house. They come closer, they look in the windows, and if the master is fast asleep, then even better. And if the guard is no longer on duty today, then perfect – they enter.

Dreams are like thieves. When there is a guard sitting at the door, thieves stay away. When the light is on inside the house and the windows are full of light, they don't dare to come close. When they see that the master is fully awake and moving and there is talk and singing and people moving around and shadows, they don't come at all.

Dreams happen because you are not aware in your sleep. And dreams continue to happen in your waking state also because then too your awareness is just so-so, very lukewarm, nothing much. So think of dreams only as symbolic in this sense. They prove that you have not yet become alert enough – that's all. That's the meaning when I said to you that dreams are dreams, without any meaning.

The questioner had written a long letter relating a dream. This was my message: that dreams are dreams, without any meaning. Don't be too bothered by them. Only one thing is important: when dreams are happening in your sleep, you lose all your consciousness. In the daytime also you are not very conscious. So become more conscious. Don't pay much attention to dreams, otherwise it can become a very dangerous game. You start playing with dreams – their meaning, their symbols, their myth – and you go in and in, one layer upon another layer, and you will be lost.

Mulla Nasruddin was walking into town one evening when he suddenly came across a pile of cowshit on the path. He bent over slightly and looked at it carefully.

"Looks like it," he said to himself.

He leaned closer and sniffed, "Smells like it."

He cautiously put his finger in it, then tasted it, "Tastes like it. I'm sure glad I didn't step in it!"

Beware of analysis!

The third question:

> *Osho,*
> *The observer is not the observed – then where does the observed spring from? And what about our continual projections? Is it all illusion? And yet, can't the nature of the illusion throw light on its creator-observer?*

The word *maya* has to be understood. In English there is no equivalent word; *illusion* is not right.

In the East, we call real that which is eternal, timelessly there – has always been, will always be, there was never a time when it was not. This eternal we call the real, the true. Exactly opposite to it is the unreal, the untrue – which has never been, will never be. Between the two is maya. Maya means that which appears to be and yet is not. It is just in the middle of the real and the unreal. It is a lie, but it appears like truth. It is a decorated lie, and very convincing. When it is there it appears absolutely true; you know it.

In the night when you dream you never suspect. Even very skeptical people, atheists, don't suspect. In a dream there is nobody who suspects. Even great doubters who suspect everything don't suspect the dream. When the dream is there it appears absolutely true.

Absurd things also look true. When the dream is there it is real. It is so real that even absurdity does not make you doubt. In the morning, when you open your eyes, suddenly it is unreal. Now from where had it come? – it had come from your own unawareness. It was your projection. It was not there outside you, it was inside you. It was your game, and when you were so lost in it, it became real. In the morning you are awake, the projection is withdrawn; you can see now that it was unreal.

Now what to call a dream? Call it real? It is not real because there was a time when it was not, and now again there is a time when it is not. Should we call it unreal? But then it was there in the middle. In the evening it was not, in the morning it is not again, but in the night it is there. So how can you call it unreal? So in the East we invented a new term. We call it maya: what is unreal but appears as real because of our unconsciousness.

Maya is almost like magic – something which is not, but can be made to appear as if it is. It shows something about you. A dream shows something about the dreamer. For example, if you dream about women, sex, and things like that, that simply shows that in your waking life you must be trying to be celibate, or you must be trying to go beyond sex. You must be repressing sexuality. The repressed bubbles up in your dream, becomes a projection. If in the night you dream always about fasting and dinners and things like that, that simply means you must be trying to starve yourself in some way or other. You must be fasting, or you may be a food maniac. You must be doing something wrong; your body is not satisfied. That dissatisfaction arises in your dream. Or you are repressing something that arises in your dream. It simply shows that your life is not going rhythmically. There is something disturbing its rhythm. That disturbance arises in the dream, becomes a projection. It shows something about the person who is dreaming.

"The observer is not the observed – then where does the observed spring from?" It springs from the observer – but the observer is fast asleep, has not yet become really an observer, is only potentially an observer, not actually. Out of that sleepiness, slumber, stupor, arise all sorts of illusions: you create them.

"And yet can the nature of the illusion throw light on its creator-observer?" Yes, it throws some light.

Let me read you a very famous story of Idries Shah. Listen to it very attentively.

A certain quiet dervish often used to attend the weekly meals given by a cultivated and generous man. This circle was known as the "assembly of the cultured." The dervish never took part in the conversation but simply arrived, simply shook hands with all present, seated himself in a corner, and ate the food provided.

When the meeting was over he would stand up, say a word of farewell and thanks, and go his way. Nobody knew anything about him, though when he first appeared there were rumors that he was great saint. For a long time the other guests thought that he must indeed be a man of sanctity and knowledge and they looked forward to the time when he might impart some of his wisdom to them. Some of them even boasted of his attendance at their meetings to their friends, hinting at the special distinction which they felt in his presence.

Gradually, however because they could feel no relationship with this man developing, the guests came to suspect that he was an imitator, perhaps a fraud. Several of them felt uncomfortable in his presence. He seemed to do nothing to harmonize himself with the atmosphere, and didn't even contribute a proverb to the enlightened conversation which they had come to prize as a necessary part of their very lives. A few, on the other hand, became unaware that he was there at all, since he drew no attention to himself.

One day the dervish spoke. He said, "I invite all of you to visit my monastery. Tomorrow night you shall eat with me."

This unexpected invitation caused a change in the opinions of the whole assembly. Some thought that the dervish, who was very poorly dressed, must be mad, and surely could provide them with nothing. Others considered his past behavior to have been a test. At last, they said to themselves, he would reward them for their patience in bearing with such dreary company. Still others said to one another. "Beware, for he may well be trying to lure us into his power."

Curiosity led them all, including their host, to accept the hospitality. The following evening the dervish led them from the house to a hidden monastery of such size and magnificence that they were dazed. The building was full of disciples carrying out every kind of exercise and task. The guests passed through contemplation halls filled with distinguished-looking sages who rose in respect and bowed at the dervish's approach. The feast which they were given surpassed all powers of description. The visitors were overwhelmed. All begged him to enroll them as disciples forthwith. But the dervish would only say to all their entreaties, "Wait until the morning."

Morning came and the guests, instead of waking in the luxurious silken beds to which, clad in gorgeous robes, they had been conducted the night before, found themselves lying stiff and stark, dispersed on the ground within the stony confines of a huge and ugly ruin on a barren mountainside. There was no sign of the dervish, of the beautiful arabesques, the libraries, the fountains, the carpets.

"The infamous wretch has tricked us with the deceits of sorcery!" shouted the guests. They alternately condoled with and congratulated one another for their sufferings and for having at least seen through the villain, whose enchantments obviously wore off before he could achieve his evil purpose, whatever that might be.

Many of them attributed their escape to their own purity of mind. But what they did not know was that by the same means which he had used to conjure up the experience of the monastery, the dervish had made them believe that they were abandoned in a ruin. They were in fact in neither place.

He now approached the company as if from nowhere and said, "We shall return to the monastery." He waved his hands and all found themselves back in the palatial halls. Now they repented, for they immediately convinced themselves that the ruins had been the test and that this monastery was the true reality. Some muttered, "It is as well that he did not hear our criticisms. Even if he only teaches us this strange art it will have been worthwhile."

But the dervish waved his hands again and they found themselves at the table of the communal meal, which they had in fact never left.

The dervish was sitting in his customary corner eating his spiced rice as usual, saying nothing at all. And then watching him uneasily, all heard his voice speak as if within their own breasts, though his lips didn't move.

He said, "While your greed makes it impossible for you to tell self-deceit from reality, there is nothing real which a dervish can show you – only deceit. Those whose food is self-deceit and imagination can be fed only with deception and imagination."

Now, all that you come to experience in life is nothing but your own desire. Because you want to experience it, your mind conjures. Mind is a great magician. It is very tricky, it is the greatest magic show: your own mind. If you want to conjure something you will convince yourself. Even an ugly woman can become beautiful if you are full of desire.

Mulla Nasruddin always goes to a hill-station. Sometimes he goes for three weeks but comes back in ten days; sometimes he goes for four weeks and he's back within two weeks.

I inquired of him, "What is the matter? You had gone for six weeks and you are back within ten days."

He said, "There is a way to decide how long I should stay there."

I said, "Tell me what is your way? How do you decide?"

He said, "I have kept a very ugly woman to take care of my house there on the hill-station. She is so ugly and nauseating, repulsive. When I go to the hill-station, this is my way to judge how long I should stay: when by and by I start seeing beauty in that woman, I escape."

Sexuality goes on accumulating, your desire to have a woman goes on accumulating. Then there comes a point when you don't see what is. You see what you want to see; then even an ugly woman, nauseating, repulsive, can become the most beautiful woman, can become a Cleopatra.

It is your desire that creates the trick. You can force yourself to believe anything whatsoever.

This mind is the origin of maya, of all the illusions that you live through. Once you start becoming aware of the mind, awareness is totally different from the mind. Then the observer arises, then you become an awareness.

When you become an awareness and you can see the games of the mind that have been playing with you for so many lives, suddenly you start laughing at the whole ridiculousness of it.

It depends on you. You kiss a woman's lips, you think it is very beautiful – it depends on you. There are tribes in the world, primitive tribes, that never kiss. When they came to know that people kiss each other, they laughed. They could not believe it.

In Thailand there is a primitive tribe which has, down through the centuries, never kissed because they say it is so ugly to put lips on anybody else's lips and to exchange saliva. It is so ugly; if they ever came to know about the French kiss they would die laughing. Tongues moving into each other's tongues!

But ask a Frenchman. In fact, the French people think only they know how to kiss; nobody else knows. It is just a conditioning. These same people, this primitive tribe which has never kissed, rub noses with each other – and they like it very much. It is their kiss. Now, you will feel a little awkward if somebody comes and starts rubbing his nose with your nose. You will say, "What are you doing? Have you gone crazy or something? Lips can be rubbed, but not noses. What are you doing?"

In love, you can kiss each other. There are tribes who salute each other by touching each other's tongues; that is their salute. Westerners have been laughing about it. Just see: each tribe has managed to believe its own way. Many African tribes don't like women with hair. The women are shaved, then they become beautiful. Now, you cannot think women beautiful when they are shaved. They look like Buddhist nuns, and one feels an urgent desire to escape from them. Skulls without hair look ugly – but that too is an idea. Thin lips are thought to be beautiful, but in Africa they like thick lips. They hang weights on their lips to make them thicker. Girls hang stones on their lips so their lips become very, very thick. You will think this is ugly, but this is beauty to them.

What is beauty and what is ugliness? – just a mind concept. Nobody has yet been able up to now to define what beauty is, and nobody is ever going to be able to define what beauty is because beauty is nothing but your idea of it. You create beauty and you can believe in it; then it is beautiful. You can believe in ugliness, and it is ugly.

Just watch, and you will see that your mind conditions you toward certain things. Then you start looking for those things. Then you will project in your dreams – and by and by while you are awake, you will project.

This is now a scientific finding: if you are left alone, in isolation for three weeks, you start conjuring up all sorts of dreams. If you are just left in a cave, everything supplied to you, but you are not allowed to talk to anybody – food comes from a hole, water comes from a hole, and you are comfortable in the cave, you see no human being for three weeks – just after the fourth day you start talking a little loudly. Ordinarily you talk inside, you go on chattering. But after four days of isolation your lips start moving. After the first week you start talking very loudly. What is happening?

And by the second week you are not only talking, you start answering too. You also talk for the other person who is not present. By the third week you are almost insane. What is happening? What happens in just three weeks' time? Left alone, the mind is starved of all outside things. It cannot remain without occupation, it creates its own occupation. It finds an image; it starts thinking a woman is sitting by your side. First you will laugh, "This is just a play." First you will say, "I know that it is just to find occupation." But by and by you will forget completely, and the woman will become real. You may start making love to the woman; you may start fighting, talking, quarreling. Now you are fully awake, with your eyes open, and the dream has become real. Modern research about isolation and what happens in isolation is tremendously revealing.

Bring more awareness to your mind, otherwise you are always on the verge of going mad, of becoming mad. There is not much difference between mad people and sane people. Sanity and insanity are only different by degrees. If you are sane you can become insane any moment. The bank goes bankrupt, or your wife dies, or your daughter elopes with somebody – just a little push and you go mad.

Madness is boiling within you. You are just close to it; become aware. Mind is what maya is – and all that is created by the mind is illusory, *mayic*, magical. Mind is a magician, and if you watch this magician you will be surprised. It is beautiful to watch what beautiful games and dramas it creates. Watching it, by and by, it subsides. One day, mind disappears; there is body and there is soul, but mind disappears.

When there is only body and soul and the mind has disappeared, you are enlightened. Enlightenment means the disappearance of the magician.

The fourth question:

> *Osho,*
> *I am always looking for signs of movement, different energy states, telepathic happenings, even new gray hairs will do. Spiritual materialism? – Yes. But what to do?*

The mind is always hankering. The mind is nothing but hankering, desiring something to happen. Sometimes it is thinking about money, to have more money, to have bigger houses, to have more respectability, to have more political power. Then you turn toward spirituality; the mind remains the same. Now you want to have more psychic powers – telepathy, clairvoyance, and all sorts of nonsense. But the mind remains the same – you want more. And if you want more you will remain ill.

Health is in being contented with this moment. Health is when you are totally in this moment and happy and blessed. Illness is if you are asking for more.

You can change the objects; that's very simple. That's what we go on doing. Small children play with toys and we tell them that these are toys. They have small cars, toy cars and toy trains and toy airplanes, of course. But watch: when your boy has a toy airplane he goes out to show everybody in the neighborhood. To the other boys he says, "Look what I have got. I have an airplane." He feels tremendously great.

What are you doing later on? – those toys disappear; bigger toys appear. Now if you have a big car, you would like everybody to become aware of it – otherwise what is the point? Now if you have an airplane, you would like to advertise it so that everybody knows that you have such a big airplane. The same game continues.

Now it is telepathy, or clairvoyance, or psychic powers: "If you can do this, I can do more than this. I can read people's thoughts thousands of miles away."

There is a Zen story. It will be good for you to meditate over it...

A man came to Master Lin Chi. The man said, "My master is a great psychic man. What do you say about your master? What can your master do, what miracles?"

Lin Chi asked, "What miracles has your master been doing?"

The disciple said, "One day he told me to go to the other bank of the river, and I stood there with a piece of paper in my hand. The river was very wide, almost one mile. He was standing on the other bank and from there he started writing with a fountain pen, and the writing came on my paper. This I have seen myself, I am a witness! What can your master do?"

Lin Chi said, "My master does greater miracles than this; this is nothing. When he is hungry he eats, and when he is sleepy he goes to sleep."

The man said, "What are you talking about? You call these miracles? Everybody is doing that!"

Lin Chi said, "Nobody is doing that. When you sleep you do a thousand and one things. When you eat you think a thousand and one things. When my master sleeps he simply sleeps: no tossing, no turning, not even a dream. He simply sleeps, he is totally in sleep. Only sleep exists in that moment, nothing else. And when he feels hungry he eats. He is always wherever he is."

The man was puzzled. He said, "I cannot see yet what there is in this."

Lin Chi said, "But this is the miracle, the greatest miracle!"

What is the point of writing from one bank to another bank? It is just foolish. Only foolish people would be interested in it. What is the point?

Somebody went to Ramakrishna and said, "My master is a great man. He can walk on the water."

Ramakrishna said, "Foolish! I can simply go to the ferryman, and with just two paisa he takes me to the other side. How many years did your master have to practice to do this miracle?"

He said, "Eighteen years."

He said, "This is too much; just two paisa is the value of it. Your master is a fool. Go and make him aware that he should not waste his life. It can be done so easily."

Yes, this is what Ramakrishna is saying: all miracles are ego trips. A real man of religion is a miracle, but his miracle is very subtle.

Mulla Nasruddin came to me the other day and he said, "Osho, I ran a hundred yards in six seconds!"

I told him, "Nasruddin, but that is not possible; the world's record is more than nine seconds."

He said, "That's right, but I know a shortcut!"

First you become interested in miracles, and when you don't know how to do them you find a shortcut, you start deceiving. Then you start playing tricks with people. That's what your Satya Sai Babas and others are doing. They have found shortcuts – just deceiving, cheating.

But there are foolish people who will be impressed by these things. In fact only a fool can be interested and can be impressed by these things. Otherwise what is the point? There is no point in it. Life in itself is a miracle, but the ego is not ready to accept that. It wants to do something special, something that nobody is doing, something extraordinary.

The husband was primping before the mirror before leaving for his big speech. He was a political leader.

"I wonder how many great men there are in the world?" he mused.

"One less than you think," said his wife.

Always remember that whenever the idea arises of how many great men there are in the world, always remember there is one less. At least you should not get into that nonsensical trip.

"I am always looking for signs of movement, different energy states, telepathic happenings, even new gray hairs will do. Spiritual materialism? – Yes. But what to do?" It is neither spiritualism nor materialism; it is simply stupidity. Drop it because to live with stupidity any longer is dangerous. One tends to become accustomed to it, one tends to make a habit of it.

Whenever you feel that something stupid is there, immediately drop it, drop it like poison. Don't go on playing with it, not even for a single moment because even that single moment can prove fatal. In that single moment the stupidity can enter your bloodstream, can become part of you, can start hiding somewhere.

One thing has to be remembered as a criterion: this moment is all. If you can live in this moment you will have an allness, and if you ask for the next rnoment you will have an illness. Just this moment is enough.

This continuous hankering for the next moment is a subtle discontent. "This moment is not fulfilling, so maybe the next moment…" Hope for the next. My suggestion is live this moment, whatsoever it is. Even if it is painful, live it because that is the only moment there is. The next moment never comes. Don't wait for it. Ambition always waits, ego always waits.

Mulla Nasruddin was sitting in the audience once, listening to some poor soul drone on until there was nobody left but him.

"This is terrible," the speaker said, looking out at the empty seats. "I really don't know what to say."

"You could say goodbye," the Mulla shouted up.

"Anyway," the speaker continued, "it is nice of you to stay."

"What's nice?" the Mulla growled. "I'm the next speaker!"

Waiting for the next moment – waiting, bored – but waiting for the next moment: waiting, exhausted, tired, but waiting for the next moment. Only death will come. The next moment is death. Life is this moment.

So don't try to hide your old desires in new names; don't call it telepathy, don't call it clairvoyance, don't call it spiritual power. It is the same – it is the ego. Spirituality knows nothing of power. Spirituality is a tremendous peace. I am not saying it is powerless, but it knows nothing of power. It is tremendously powerful, but there is nobody to feel powerful in it. The ego has disappeared; you are gone, gone forever. Only godliness is.

Of course, God is powerful. The Jews call God, Elohim, it comes from a root *el*. The root is the same as from where the Mohammedan word *Allah* comes. It means the source of power, the powerful. *Allah* means the powerful; *Elohim* means the powerful.

God, is powerful – when you are not, he is there. But there is nobody to claim power. A spiritual man is powerful, but there is nobody to claim it. When the claimer goes, only then does the power come. They never meet together.

So forget about all your spiritual desires. Simply be in the moment. That's what I call being spiritual.

The last question:

Osho,
While you are sitting in Chuang Tzu auditorium telling stories about me, I am sitting in the Turkish bath telling my disciples stories about you. All I have to do is mention the name Osho, and everyone bursts into uproarious laughter.
Mulla Nasruddin.

That's true: I am nothing compared to Mulla Nasruddin, he is a great storyteller. He can manage to tell stories in such a way that even the mention of a name is enough.

Let me tell you one anecdote...

The large and friendly prison was getting a new warden. On the last day of office the old warden was introducing the new warden to the inmates, and made his farewell speech. In closing he said, "A little anecdote: number twenty-eight." The crowd of prisoners burst into wild laughter and applause, and the old warden stepped down.

Afterward, the new warden who had listened to the proceedings, asked the old warden about his final remarks, especially why the mention of number twenty-eight seemed to be so hilarious.

"Well, you see," the old warden said, "these men have been here so long and have heard my jokes so many times that instead of telling them the whole story, I just tell the number. The men remember the story and laugh accordingly."

"Amazing," the new man said. "You must write them all down for me and I will use one tomorrow in my opening talk."

The next day the new man made his first speech to the inmates. He was a little nervous and decided a joke would be good.

"In conclusion," he said, "a little anecdote – number fifteen."

A hush fell over the crowd. The warden became more nervous, smiled, and stepped down from the rostrum. Afterward he asked the old warden, who had stayed to see if all went well, "What happened? Yesterday they seemed to love your story. Today I fell flat on my face."

"I guess," said the old warden, "some people can tell a story, some people can't."

Mulla Nasruddin is superb. There is no comparison to him. He can tell a story just by mentioning the name. The way, the gesture, his whole presence may create a great hilarious situation.

It is said about Mulla Nasruddin that when he was a small student in school, the headmaster cursed him because whenever he went to school he would start telling stories, little stories. Children would giggle and laugh, and it was a great disturbance. All the teachers were very annoyed.

One day the headmaster went to see what was going on. Mulla Nasruddin was telling the class something – he was sitting in the last bench – and the whole class was laughing uproariously.

The headmaster cursed Mulla Nasruddin: "Let this be my curse. Wherever your name is ever mentioned, people will start laughing just hearing your name. And if somebody tells one story about you, at least seven stories will be told immediately – somebody will tell another, and somebody else will tell another."

And this has continued; the curse has been working.

Once Mulla Nasruddin went to a meeting. Of course he was hoping that they would receive him, but the meeting had already started. The great Tamerlane was sitting in a chair, he was the chairman. Nobody paid any attention to Mulla Nasruddin. He sat where people had put their shoes, but he started telling jokes. By and by, people turned. All the people turned toward Nasruddin, and they had their backs to Tamerlane.

Tamerlane became very angry and he said, "Nasruddin, stop all this!"

He said, "I cannot because wherever I am, I am the chairman. It makes no difference where I am sitting."

He may be telling stories about me in his Turkish bath. Naturally, it has to be so: I pay him so much respect; he has to pay respect to me.

Enough for today.

9

PROVISIONS FOR THE JOURNEY

The Buddha said:
Those who study the doctrine of the buddhas will do well to believe and observe all that is taught by them. It is like unto honey; it is sweet within, it is sweet without, it is sweet throughout; so is the Buddha's teaching.
The Buddha said:
O monks, you must not walk on the way as the ox that is attached to a wheel. His body moves, but his heart is not willing. But when your hearts are in accord with the way, there is no need of troubling yourselves about your outward demeanor.
The Buddha said:
Those who practice the way might well follow the example of an ox that marches through the deep mire carrying a heavy load. He is tired, but his steady gaze, looking forward, will never relax until he comes out of the mire, and it is only then that he takes a respite. O monks, remember that passions and sins are more than the filthy mire, and that you can escape misery only by earnestly and steadily thinking of the way.

The seeker has to go alone on his pilgrimage. Otherwise is not possible; it is not in the nature of things. Truth is not something outside you; otherwise you could go in company. It is within you. Truth is not objective, so it cannot be collective. It is subjective. Truth is subjectivity; it is your innermost core. Only you – and only you – can penetrate it. Nobody else can go with you. The path has to be traveled in tremendous aloneness. A master knows that he is pushing you in a journey where you will be left alone. Buddha particularly is very much aware of it; he has not uttered a single word against it. He has never said, "I can lead you to the ultimate." You will have to go alone. The tour is going to be absolutely unguided, with no maps, with no guide to show you the path.

Then of course you have to be prepared for it. You have to provide for all emergencies, all accidents on the way, all possibilities of your going astray. You have to carry provisions for the journey. Buddha has called these provisions *parmitas*; the word is beautiful. *Parmita* means: that which can lead you beyond, the provisions for the other shore. The journey is going to be alone. The moment you leave this shore you will be left alone in a great and wild ocean, and you will have to fight the ocean, and you will have to find the way absolutely on your own. No knowledge that you have gathered before is going to be of any help because each person comes to truth in his own way. The perception of truth is absolutely unique and individual. No two persons have known truth in the same way because no two persons are ever the same. They are different: their vision is different, their perception is different, their interpretation is different, their expression is different. So all that you have gathered about truth is not going to help you much. In fact it may hinder you, but it cannot help you. It can become an obstacle.

So Buddha says, "Don't carry knowledge." Then what does one have to carry? If the journey is going to be alone, then you have to create some qualities, *parmitas*, which can follow you like a shadow. These ten *parmitas* have to be understood very deeply.

The first *parmita* is *dana*: generosity, sharing. Ordinarily mind is a miser. It tries to hold, to possess. Mind is not generous, and if you go with this mind you will be lost because a miser's mind is a very closed mind. Miserliness is a sort of closing in; you are not open to the world, you don't allow your windows and doors to bring more light from the outside, you don't allow your windows to bring new breezes from the outside – because you are constantly afraid that something you are holding inside may escape.

Mulla Nasruddin was standing in the court of the City Magistrate. He was saying, "Now it is too much, and I cannot tolerate it anymore. We have a small room to live in, only one room. I live there, my wife lives there, my twelve children live there, and my wife is obsessive. She has a few goats in the room and a dog also sleeps there. It is becoming so ugly and so dirty. It stinks! And I cannot live anymore. So I have come to ask for a separation."

The magistrate said, "But don't you have any windows? Can't you open your windows?"

He said, "What! And let my pigeons out?"

When you are holding something you cannot open the windows, you cannot open the door. You are afraid, but if you don't open the windows of the mind you will be in trouble because when you are alone in the ocean, fighting with the waves, a closed mind will be a blind mind. You will need all openness there because only out of openness can the response be right.

So Buddha says *dana*, generosity, sharing, has to be learned. While you are on this shore, learn as much sharing as possible. Share whatsoever you have to share because nothing really belongs to you. Your possession is a crime. Whatsoever you possess, or claim that you possess, is a crime against the whole. You can at the most use, but you cannot claim possession. Things have existed when you were not here, things will be here when you are gone and completely forgotten. Who is the possessor? We come empty-handed and we go empty-handed. So while you are in the world don't become like a fist; remain open-handed. An open-handed person is an open-minded person too. In fact, the hand is nothing but an extension of the mind.

The right side of your mind is joined with your left hand, the left side of your mind is joined with your right hand. When you move your right hand your mind moves, when you move your left hand the other side of your mind moves. When your hand is like a closed fist, then your mind is also closed like a fist. Yes, this expression "open-handed" is beautiful: an open-handed man is also open-minded.

So Buddha says the first *parmita*, the quality that can take you beyond, is sharing. He does not mention what to share because it is not important what you share. Whether you share a song, or a dance, or you share your love, or you share your experience, your meditation, your money, your house, your clothes, your body, is not the point. But sharing should become essential.

Ordinarily hoarding is essential. A hoarder will remain clinging to this shore. He cannot go to the other shore because a hoarder, in the first place, cannot leave this shore. All his hoarding belongs to this shore. See the point of it. Somebody says, "Come, there is a bigger house," but you will say, "First I will have to carry the treasures which I have hidden in this house. I cannot go right now. I have much involvement with this house. My whole life's savings are here. I will have to take it with me, only then can I come." But the other shore is such that you cannot take anything from this shore.

This is a beautiful paradox: you cannot take anything from this shore, but if you are sharing enough, and if you share all that you have on this shore, you can carry a sharing mind. You cannot carry your house, you cannot carry your money, but you can carry your love, your compassion. That compassion will be helpful.

Buddha says if you have love and compassion in your heart, existence also behaves in the same way. Existence always reflects you. If you share, existence shares with you. If you are hoarding, that means you are against existence. A hoarder is against: he's afraid, he does not trust. "Who knows what is going to happen tomorrow?" He does not trust existence. He trusts his own bank balance, his trust is in things that he has created or that he has accumulated. He does not trust the vast, the infinite.

Buddha says if you trust, then existence also responds in the same way. Existence is a mirror: it echoes you. If you go as a hoarder then you will be in trouble because then everywhere you will see the enemy – in the waves of the ocean, in the infinite journey. A thousand and one problems will arise and you will be at a loss. There will be no guide, there will be no guidebook, and you will be alone, absolutely nude and alone, with no hoardings of your own, no securities, no insurance. It will be difficult for you to go.

Buddha says you can go only when you have already dispossessed all that you have. Now, you can dispossess in two ways. You can dispossess only as a means, so that you can possess on the other shore; but that is not true dispossession, that is again just a trick of the mind. That's what many Buddhist monks, Jaina monks, Catholics and others are doing. They are ready to renounce, but their renunciation is out of calculation. It is not out of love, it is out of calculation. They calculate that nothing can be saved on this shore, so why not renounce it and save something on the other shore, in the other world? Money cannot be saved, it is going to go; so why not have virtue in your possession? But the possessiveness remains the same.

Buddha says, "Be nonpossessive; possess neither on this shore nor the other. Be always sharing." So there is a very specific teaching. Buddha has said to his disciples that when you meditate and you come to beautiful spaces in your being, immediately share them. If there is nobody, then just close your eyes and shower that blessing on the whole existence. But don't become a possessor of it – even of meditation, even of wisdom. Don't become a possessor.

There is a beautiful anecdote.

A young man came to Buddha. He was attracted by Buddha's presence. By and by, he started meditating, but there was one problem. One day he came and he said, "There's only one problem; the problem is, you say that when meditation flowers then you have to release all the fragrance to the whole world. I can do this with just one exception: I cannot shower it on my neighbor. I can do it on the whole of the world, but just give me permission not to shower it on my neighbor."

Buddha laughed and he said, "You fool, that is the whole point. You can shower it on the whole universe because you are indifferent to the whole universe. You cannot shower it on your neighbor because you have an enmity. Love knows no enmity. First shower on your neighbor; only then will the universe receive it. There is no other way. First shower on your enemy, first befriend your enemy, then the whole universe will befriend you."

That's the meaning when Jesus says: love your enemy, love thy enemy as thyself. Jesus also says: love thy neighbor as thyself. Maybe, in almost all cases, the enemy and the neighbor are the same person; they are not different people. The neighbor and the enemy are almost always the same person because he who is very far away from you cannot be your enemy. To be your enemy somebody has to be very close to you. To be an enemy somebody has to be just on the boundary of your being, has to be your neighbor. Then he pinches you, then his very existence becomes an anxiety, then he interferes, then his very existence is nonacceptable.

Buddha says, "Shower your meditation, otherwise you have missed." Now, this is a very new teaching – Patanjali has not said so. This is a very new insight. Buddha says if you attain to meditative states, shower it immediately. If you don't shower it, then you have not attained to the space that you think you have attained. Then you are in a deception, you are in an illusion because a meditative state is, by its very nature, sharing. If you cannot share, then you must be in a deception somewhere. Then the state is pseudo, then the space is not real. A real meditative space, by its very nature, wants to be shared. If your meditation does not become compassion, then somewhere something has gone wrong.

This is his first *parmita*, a quality on which you can ride and go to the other shore. But ordinarily we live very clinging, afraid. Our attachments are more to things than to persons, and our attachments to persons are also very self-motivated. There is no compassion in them.

So many people come to me and they say, "I am in love with this woman or with this man," and I look into them, and I see that they are in love only with themselves. Nobody seems to be in love with anybody else – hence so many problems. If you really love a woman or a man, love will be enough. There will be no problem in it. Love knows no problems. If problems arise, that simply shows that somewhere love is not true, or it is something else just pretending to be love. Everybody is trying to exploit the other. It is not a sharing thing; you are using the other as a means. Sooner or later the other starts feeling it too, that he or she is being used as a commodity. Then there is rebellion, reaction, revenge, conflict.

People you call "lovers" are continuously trying to dominate each other. We possess things, we possess people, and in this race – this mad race for possessions – we lose our own selves. One is lost in his possessions. If you really want to know who you are, you will have to become a little loose from your possessions.

A rabbi and a Catholic priest were fishing in separate boats some distance apart. The priest got a bite and was so nervous that he fell out of the boat. He sank twice, and as he was coming up the second time the rabbi rowed over and called out, "Father, can I have your boat if you don't come up again?"

We may not be so direct, but this is how we are: just waiting. How can we possess more? – just waiting. How can our territory become a little bigger? Even if others suffer for it, even if they have to die for it, we are ready to sacrifice the whole world. For what? – for things which you will not be able to carry to the other shore. Death will come and shatter all your arrangements.

Buddha said: before death takes things away from you, share them. At least there will remain some gratitude in people's hearts for you, at least they will remember you; death will not be able to efface your memory completely. By sharing you will become open. And by sharing you will become more trusting – and trust becomes the boat to the other shore. Trust people because people are nothing but a manifestation of the universe, a manifestation of the universal soul. When you share with somebody, in fact you are sharing with existence because *everybody* is a manifestation of existence. When you water a tree and the tree feels happy, and the leaves seem to be delighted, and the tree starts swaying and dancing in the breeze, it is existence you have watered. Existence was thirsty in the tree; you have watered, and existence is happy.

Whatsoever you do to people, to trees, to animals, you are doing to existence. And of course existence repays a thousandfold. When you are totally alone and there is nobody with you, only existence all around, it will repay you. Buddha says this is the first *parmita*.

Oscar Muscovitz and Sidney Margolis had a profitable little business going, importing artificial flowers for the ladies' dress trade. Mainly, it was profitable due to their seldom, if ever, paying Uncle Sam taxes. But to their loft came, as it must to all men, the agents of the Internal Revenue Service. Finding Oscar in charge, as Sidney was on a buying trip, the first agent tried to explain the nature of the visit.

"Mr. Muscovitz, you people are doing business and failing to report to the government."

Oscar turned purple: "Report? What report? What is to report?" he demanded.

"Well," the agent replied, "first of all, we would like to know about your dependents, that is, your family exemptions."

Oscar proceeded to tell them all about Harriet, his wife, dependent number one, and all the trouble and aggravations she had been giving him lately; then he got to his son and described in great detail how Freddie had gotten this girl in trouble, and the ensuing problems from that scene; dependent number three, his daughter Marjorie, a good girl, but no beauty, and how much she was costing.

Finally, after absorbing as much of the detail of Oscar's private life as he could stand, the agent said, "Mr. Muscovitz, let us forget all that for a moment and concentrate on the business itself."

Replied Oscar, "Like what, exactly?"

"Like how much business you are doing, what the assets are worth, how much profit you made…"

"What!" screamed Oscar, hysterically. "Are you crazy? I don't even tell my partner that!"

You don't give, even to those who are very intimate with you. You don't give, even to those who love you. You don't give to your father, your mother, your wife, your children. You simply don't give; you don't know the language of giving. You know only one language: how to get more. How to get more, how to get from everybody else. You know only one way of thinking, and that is "get-think."

Buddha says to learn "give-think." Learn the ways of giving and you will flower. That flowering, that fragrance, will follow you. That will be one companion on the infinite pilgrimage.

The second is *shila*.

Shila means discipline, *shila* means grace in living. Buddhists have misinterpreted *shila* in many ways; they think *shila* means a rigid character. It does not mean that. The very word means a graceful life, a life that has grace in it, elegance. What life can have grace in it? – only a life of compassion, love, gratitude; only a life that is responsible, a life that cares for others. Now, you can be nonviolent, but it is not necessary that your nonviolence will be a grace. I have seen so many Jaina monks. They are nonviolent, but very ungraceful. The beauty is missing, and the fruit is the proof of the tree – there is no other proof. If they were nonviolent there would arise a tremendous beauty: their eyes would show it, their very vibe would show it; there would be a constant soundless music around them. But it is not there, everything seems to be dull and dead. They are nonviolent, but their nonviolence is not graceful: it has not happened spontaneously, it has been forced. Their nonviolence has a violent element in it, it has been violently forced. They have tried hard to become nonviolent, they have managed somehow to become nonviolent, but the nonviolence is not like a natural flowering; it is cultivated.

The Buddhist word *shila* is very beautiful; it means graceful.

There can be two types of stillness. You can force yourself according to Yoga methods, you can learn a certain posture. By and by, you can manage to force your body into that posture. First it will be uncomfortable, but by and by the body adjusts. The body has tremendous capacity to adjust to any situation. Then you can force your body to sit unmoving –and if you go on doing it, by and by after a few months you will become like a buddha statue. But that will be violence, and there will be no grace in it. Deep down you will be boiling; deep down there will be hellfire; deep down you have not changed. How can you change just by changing the body? The real phenomenon has to be just otherwise: the within has to change, then the outward thing follows. And then it has grace.

It is not a question of forcing the periphery because the center will not be affected at all by forcing the periphery. You can keep quiet; that does not mean you are quiet. But if you are quiet that certainly means you can keep quiet. This difference has to be understood. This is one of the most vital distinctions in a person's religious life: the way is not from out to in, the way is from in to out. Don't force things from the outside, and don't think that by changing your body and your outward demeanor you can change your inner qualities. No, it doesn't happen that way. Change the inner, and the outward follows. Then there is grace.

Buddha says the second *parmita* is grace in living, a discipline that has arisen out of understanding.

The word *discipline* is meaningful. It comes from the same root as *disciple*. It means readiness to learn. *Disciple* means one who is very ready to learn, very open to learn. When one is open to learn, that means one is very aware because learning is possible only when you are aware. When you are not aware you cannot learn anything. People who are aware can learn everywhere, anywhere.

Just the other day I was reading about a Sufi mystic, Sibli. Sibli was asked, "Who guided you on the path? Who was your first master?" The questioner was surprised because Sibli said, "A dog. One day I saw him almost dead with thirst, standing by the water's edge. Every time he looked at his reflection in the water he was frightened and withdrew because he thought it was another dog. Finally, such was his necessity that he cast away fear and leapt into the water, at which point the other dog vanished. The dog found that the obstacle, which was himself – the barrier between himself and that which he was seeking – melted away. In this same way my own obstacle vanished when I knew what I took to be my own self was just a reflection, not the reality. And my way was first shown to me by the behavior of a dog. He was my first master."

A man of understanding learns from everywhere. A man of understanding learns and becomes a disciple. A discipline arises, and Buddha says unless you have discipline, the capacity to learn, to receive – the awareness – you will not be able to go to the other shore. Knowledge will not help, but the capacity to learn will help. And the difference is clear. Knowledge is borrowed; the capacity to learn has to arise in you; it is your capacity. You cannot borrow the capacity to learn. You can borrow knowledge; knowledge is cheap. The capacity to learn means a great transformation in your being: you will have to drop the ego and you will have to drop accumulating. You can accumulate knowledge, you can accumulate information; learning is not accumulation. You never accumulate learning. You simply remain learning; no treasure arises out of it. It is just like a mirror: something comes before it, it reflects it; when the thing has moved it remains quiet – again a mirror, again simple, innocent. It does not collect. You cannot ask a mirror, "How many people have looked into you?" He does not collect, he is simply a mirror – he mirrors. Learning is like a mirror, and knowledge is like a photoplate. It also mirrors, but only once; it is caught in the reflection, then it is destroyed.

Buddha says *shila* is the second *parmita*.

The third is *shanti*. *Shanti* means patience. Of course, the journey is vast, and you cannot be in a hurry. If you are in a hurry, you will never be able to move to the other shore. The journey is timeless; great patience is needed, infinite patience is needed. Nirvana cannot be something instant.

Sometimes people come – very foolish people – and they say, "I have come only for three days. Is meditation possible?" They don't know what they are asking; even three lives are not enough. When you are in such a hurry, even three hundred lives will not be enough because in such hurry your mind is very tense. Slow down, relax a little bit, don't be impatient – and then it is possible.

Maybe it can happen in three days. You see the point? Try to see the point: it can happen in three days, it can happen in three seconds, it may happen in a split-second – but then you will need oceanic patience. How much time it takes will depend on how much patience you have. The more patience you have, the less time will be needed; the less patience you have, the more time will be needed. If you really want to have it, drop all impatience. Forget all about when it is going to happen. Simply enjoy the moment. Enjoying the moment, being totally in it, one day suddenly it is there. In fact, it has never left you. It was always there but you were so much in a rush that you could not see it. The day you relax and sit silently in your room, suddenly you become aware of the presence. It is there, the whole room is full of it. The whole world is full of godliness. Yes – every bush is afire.

The Jews have a beautiful story about Moses going to Mount Sinai, and there Moses saw a green bush afire. He was puzzled, he could not believe it because the fire was there and the bush was not burning. Then God spoke to him: "Don't be afraid, Moses. I am your God, your Lord. This fire is my fire." And, of course, how can God's fire burn a bush? The bush is also God's fire. Moses saw one bush afire on the mountain, and I would like to tell you: every bush is afire. There is no need to go to Sinai. Just look in this garden; every bush is afire with God because all greenery is his fire, all life is his fire, each breath is his fire.

Patience – then suddenly you start feeling godliness is present. Impatient, and you are rushing madly, and in your mad rush you cannot see. It is almost as if you are carrying a beautiful camera, and running around you are trying to take some pictures, and you go on rushing and running. What is going to happen? – you won't have any pictures; you may have only a few destroyed plates, the whole film will be just a chaos. When you are taking a picture you have to hold the camera absolutely still, it should not be shaky. Then a clear-cut picture comes out of it.

When you are not rushing anywhere and your inner being is just still, herenow, the divine reflects. Then all chaos disappears, all questions disappear. Buddha says *shanti*, patience, is the third *parmita*.

The fourth is *vidya*. *Vidya* has many meanings: it means energy, it means courage. Certainly courage is needed, and certainly energy is needed.

One has to be continuously aware that one's life energy should not be wasted unnecessarily. One should not have leakages. We are leaking, we are never a reservoir of energy. Infinite energy is given to you, but you are a leaking vessel. In every way you dissipate energy; you never sit silently.

Buddha used to call his meditation *jhan*. *Jhan* is a Pali term for the Sanskrit *dhyan*. From *jhan* came the Chinese *ch'an* and the Japanese *Zen*. In Japan, Zen became the crescendo. What

Buddha had planted as a seed flowered in Japan, came to its climax. What Buddha had started came to a conclusion. Zen people say meditation is nothing but sitting silently doing nothing. That's what Buddha was doing – doing nothing – when he attained. That's what he was doing, sitting under the *bodhi* tree. What was he doing? – he was not doing anything. He was simply sitting so silently that there was no leakage of energy. That energy started rising higher and higher and higher, that energy was reaching peaks. And then the energy rushed and touched the *sahasrar*, the seventh chakra; it came to the ultimate. Suddenly there was a flowering; Buddha became a lotus flower.

You have the same energy but you go on throwing it away. Whenever you have energy, a great desire to throw it away arises in you. You may call it "sexual urge" or you may call it something else, it makes no difference. But whenever you have energy a great desire arises to relieve oneself.

In the West, sex is thought of as a release. In the East, we have taken the sexual energy in a totally different perspective. There is no need to release it; it is your energy. Because you go on releasing it, you remain empty. If you allow it sometimes to gather, if you simply let it gather inside you, the sheer quantity comes to a point when there is a qualitative change. The gathered energy rises higher and higher, the level goes on becoming higher and higher, and you touch higher altitudes of your being. A point comes when the energy has touched the climax of your being. That's what *samadhi* is.

Buddha says *vidya* is the fourth *parmita*. One should learn how not to dissipate energy. Remember, he is not telling you to become a miser because he has given you the first *parmita*: never be a miser. When he says, "Gather energy," he is not teaching you any miserliness; he is simply teaching you wisdom. He knows how it happened to him.

Share whatsoever you have, but don't leak. Leaking is not sharing. That's why I see that two persons can make love to each other and still there may be no sharing. Both leaked. They use the other just as a help to leak, that's all. Sharing is totally different; it is not a leaking. This has to be remembered: when you leak you simply lose, nothing is gained out of it. When you share you give something very ordinary, and you gain something very extraordinary. In sharing you never lose.

The fifth, Buddha calls *dhyan*: meditation, silence, sitting, doing nothing.

Let that penetrate your life more and more. Whenever you have time, whenever you have nothing to do – don't create unnecessary, unneeded occupations – just sit silently, watch life flow by. Look at the trees or at the stars, or just look at your nose, or at your navel; or close your eyes and just look at the inner silence, or inner thoughts. Just be, and let things pass; sit silently. Buddha says if you can sit silently for even a few moments without doing anything, glimpses will start coming to you.

Now, modern psychologists also agree that if a person can be allowed just to sit silently, that's enough. Nothing else is needed. All else is just a help to sit. Somebody gives you a mantra and says, "Sit silently and do the mantra." Now there is much research work going on about Transcendental Meditation, and Mahesh Yogi thinks it is because of the mantra that things happen. That is not true. It is just because you sit silently for twenty minutes that things happen.

The mantra is not relevant: you can sit without the mantra and the same thing will happen. Maybe the mantra gives you an excuse to sit – because you are so foolish that you cannot sit, you have to have something to do. So if somebody says, "Say, Rama, Rama, Rama," you have some excuse to sit silently for twenty minutes because you are doing "Rama, Rama, Rama." Whatsoever results come – your blood pressure goes low, your breathing becomes more silent, there are changes in the oxygen content of your body, even your heart beats with a different rhythm; you feel very relaxed, the alpha waves are created, and out of those alpha waves you feel very quiet and refreshed – they have nothing to do with the mantra, or with any mantra in particular. You can do "Rama, Rama," you can do "Om, om," you can do "Allah, Allah," or "Ave Maria," or anything. Or you can create your own mantra, you can repeat your own name – even that will do. In fact, it has nothing to do with any mantra; it has nothing to do with a mantra as such. If you can simply sit for twenty minutes without doing anything, the result will be the same. So whatsoever psychological investigations have revealed about TM, it is nothing about TM. It is simply about sitting silently.

Just sit silently and you will see: you are growing a new quality to your being; you are becoming more collected, more centered, more fulfilled. Your face will change, your eyes will change, you will have a serenity around you. Even others will start feeling your serenity. Even they will start feeling that something has happened to you because wherever you move you will bring a certain cool breeze with you. And the situations will remain the same.

Somebody will insult you, but now you will be able to laugh. No anger will arise, not that you are controlling it. In fact it is not arising: you can see the whole absurdity of it; you can see the point that that man, that poor man who is angry and insulting you, is in bad shape. It has nothing to do with you. You have to be more compassionate to him. You will feel compassion rather than being angry. Rather than being destructive to him, you will feel much pity for him – a totally different quality.

Worries may be the same, they continue; through your meditation the world is not going to change. The world will be the same but by your meditation you will be different, and when you are different the world is different because it is your world, it depends on your vision, on your interpretation. Everything will be the same, but nothing will be the same anymore because you have changed.

Buddha says, on this lonely journey to the other shore you will very much need to learn how to sit silently.

Ordinarily we are almost obsessively occupied: you cannot sit silently, you have to do something. Doing is a madness. If you have nothing to do you feel at a loss, you start boiling within: you start reading the same newspaper again, or you go and start gossiping to the neighbor, and you have talked about these things a thousand and one times, and again you are there. You have to do something. You cannot remain quiet, you cannot remain unoccupied.

In the West you have a very absurd proverb: the empty mind is the Devil's workshop. This must have been invented by the Devil himself because the empty mind is God's workshop. This must have been invented by the Devil so that nobody remains empty and the Devil can continue his work well. If you are really empty the Devil cannot enter you because thoughts function as horses for the Devil. He cannot come – without thought, evil cannot enter you. Without thought, there is no possibility of anything entering you. All that enters you from the outside enters through thought. When there is no thought, the outside disappears. You are just an inside. That's what I said in the beginning: truth is subjectivity.

The sixth *parmita* Buddha calls *pragya*. *Pragya* means wisdom. It is different from knowledge. Knowledge is that which is not based on your own experience; wisdom is that which is based on your own experience. Rely only on that which you have experienced. Don't rely on anything else, otherwise when you are left alone all your knowledge will disappear and nothing will be left. That which has come from others is not going to be with you when others have left you. Only that which is yours will be yours.

A disciple was leaving his master. It was a dark night and it had become late; the disciple was a little apprehensive because he had to pass five miles of dense forest to reach to his village. The master saw that fear. He said, "Are you afraid of the darkness?"

The disciple said, "Yes, I am afraid, but I couldn't gather courage to say so."

The master said, "Don't be afraid." And the master lit a candle, gave the candle to the disciple, and said, "This will do. Go."

When the disciple was going out of the door, the master suddenly blew the candle out. The disciple said, "I don't understand what you have done. Just a moment before you lit the candle for me with such compassion. Now why are you so cruel? Why have you blown it out?"

The master laughed. He said, "My candle will not be of much use to you."

Buddha has said: "*Appo deepo bhava* – be a light unto yourself."

"The night is dark, I know, and I would like to help you in every way; but I cannot do anything that is impossible. Only your light will help you in the dark night, so rely on yourself. Go with my blessings. Go into the dark night with my blessings. Rely on your own consciousness. Remain alert, let that be your light because nobody else's light can help you."

This is a beautiful parable, of infinite significance.

Wisdom is that which is your own experience – remember it. Throw away, burn all that you have gathered from others. That which is yours is true; that which is not yours is untrue. A truth is truth only if you have experienced it. Even a truth becomes a lie when you have not experienced it. When I say a truth to you, it is truth when *I* say it. When you hear it, it becomes a lie because for you it will not be based on your experience. So drop all that luggage that you have been carrying; it is useless, it is not going to help.

Buddha says in this journey to the other shore, drop all the weight that you have gathered from others. Just take that which is yours. Of course you cannot drop it, you will have to take it; there is no way to drop it. Can you drop anything that you have known? Can you drop it? How can you unknow what you have known? – there is no way. If you have experienced something in meditation, how can you drop it? You cannot drop it because by experiencing it, it has become part of your being. That's what *pragya* is. *Pragya* is some experience that has become part of your being, is no longer a possession; it is just your very being. How can you carry that which you have not experienced? You cannot carry it. Only that is yours which has been experienced by you.

Beliefs have to be dropped. Only wisdom can be of help.

There is a Hasidic story...

Without telling his teacher anything of what he was doing, a disciple of Rabbi Barukh's had inquired into the nature of God, and in his thinking had penetrated further and further until he was tangled in doubts and what had been certain up to that point became uncertain.

When Rabbi Barukh noticed that the young man no longer came to him as usual, he went to the city where he lived, entered his room unexpectedly and said to him, "I know what is hidden in your heart. You have passed through the fifty gates of reason. You begin with a question and think and think up an answer – the first gate opens, and to a new question. And again you plumb it, find the solution, fling open the second gate – and look into a new question. On and on like this, deeper and deeper, until you have forced open the fiftieth gate. There you stare at a question whose answer no man has ever found, for if there were one who knew it, there would no longer be any freedom of choice. But if you dare to probe still further, you plunge into the abyss."

"So I should go back all the way to the very beginning?" cried the disciple.

"If you turn, you will not be going back," said Rabbi Barukh. "You will be standing beyond the last gate. You will stand in faith."

That's what Buddha calls wisdom.

Belief is from others, faith is your own. Don't be deceived by dictionaries; dictionaries say *faith* means *belief*, *belief* means *faith*. They don't mean that; they are not synonymous. They are really opposite to each other, antagonistic. Belief is just faith in appearance; deep down there is doubt because you have not experienced. How can the doubt disappear? You are simply pretending that you know. Without knowing, the doubt will remain there deep inside your heart. One day or other you will have to face it. And the time that you wasted in repressing it is a sheer wastage. You should have encountered it in the first place.

Doubt encountered, not repressed, disappears. Then faith arises. Faith is the Jewish term for the same thing that Buddha calls *pragya*, wisdom. By belief you trust others, but others cannot go with you. Don't lean on others: that is Buddha's fundamental message. Lean on your own self because you will be left alone in the final stage and only your own eyes, your own wisdom, will be of help.

Another Hasidic story I would like to share with you…

A woman came to Rabbi Israel, the maggid of Kosnitz, and told him with many tears that she had been married a dozen years and still had not borne a son.

"What are you willing to do about it?" he asked her.

She did not know what to say.

"My mother," so the maggid told her, "was aging and still had no child. Then she heard that the holy Baal Shem was stopping over in Apt in the course of a journey. She hurried to his inn and bade him pray that she might bear a son.

"'What are you willing to do about it?' Baal Shem asked her.

"'My husband is a poor bookbinder,' she replied, 'but I have one fine thing that I shall give to the Rabbi.'

"She went home as fast as she could and fetched her good cape, her *katinka*, which was carefully stored away in a chest. But when she returned to the inn with it, she heard that Baal Shem had already left for Mezbizh.

"She immediately set out after him, and since she had no money to travel, she walked from town to town with her *katinka* until she came to Mezbizh. Baal Shem took the cape and hung it on the wall. 'It is well,' he said.

"My mother walked all the way back from town to town until she reached Apt. A year later, I was born."

"I too," cried the woman, "will bring you a good cape of mine so that I may get a son."

"That won't work," said the maggid. "You heard the story. My mother had no story to go by."

Old answers won't help, others' answers won't help. You cannot repeat in life; life is unrepeatable. You can read the Vedas and the Koran and the Bible, it won't help. It may help the *rishi* who wrote the Veda, but it won't help you because it is a borrowed thing to you. The *rishi* had never read any Veda, Mohammed had never read any Koran. You cannot have that which Mohammed gained because he had never read any Koran. And you are trying to gain it by reading the Koran? No, it is not possible.

Buddha says, "Remember, life is unrepeatable, truth is unrepeatable." Nobody else's answer is going to help. You have to find your answer, depend on only your experience. Sort it out in your mind: all that is not yours, throw it out, go and throw it in the river. Keep only that which you know, which you know on your own, and that will become a provision, a *parmita*.

The seventh is *upai*. *Upai* means: skillful means. Buddha emphasizes very much that not all means are good; only very skillful means have to be used. What does he mean by "skillful"? – he means an *upai*, a method which can be dropped when its use is finished. Otherwise, one can become too burdened by the method itself. He used to say: "You use a boat to go to the other shore, but then you leave it. You don't carry it on your head. You don't say, 'This boat has brought me to this shore, so now how can I be so ungrateful and leave it here? I will carry it on my head for my whole life.'"

Buddha says, "Use things, and drop them when their work is finished." When you have utilized them, go ahead. Leave things behind.

All methods have to be dropped by and by. Ultimately, finally, before you reach to the other shore, you have to drop all. Meditations, disciplines – everything has to be dropped. So be very skillful, otherwise there is a tendency to be caught by the method.

I know people – even a person like Ramakrishna was in a difficulty...

He used Mother Kali for his meditation and he became obsessed with her. Then whenever he would close his eyes, Kali would be standing there. Her image would come – beautiful – but this was trouble. Now he could not be alone, now there was no way to be totally silent. The Mother was always standing there, so there was always company. And when the Mother was standing there, of course Ramakrishna had to say something: praise her, sing a song, pray, do something. He became very disturbed: "What to do about it?" He himself had cultivated it. For years he had cultivated it, for years he had prayed before her image, saying, "Come into my dreams." For years he had been asking, crying and weeping, "Mother, when I close my eyes, why don't you come to me?" Then it started – not that the Mother heard; there is nobody to hear. Not that the Mother took compassion; there is nobody. But constantly asking, constantly remembering, he became hypnotized. It was an auto-hypnosis, but tremendously powerful – he was a powerful man. Now Kali was always standing there, in the night, in the day. It was difficult to have any privacy. Even if he went in, Kali was there; his inner space also became occupied. He became burdened.

But how to drop Kali? Even the idea of dropping her was difficult. Then he asked a very great saint who was passing by. He told him, "Something has to be done now."

The saint could see the point. Ramakrishna had used a method but had used it unskillfully, so he had become too obsessed with the method. It was good it had been used, but one should always remember that every method has to be dropped one day, so don't become too attached. Now he had become too attached.

The saint told him, "Close your eyes and when Kali appears, take a sword from inside and cut her in two."

Ramakrishna said, "What are you saying? Have you gone mad? How can I cut Mother Kali? No, that is not possible. I cannot do it, I cannot even think about it!"

Then the saint said, "Then you will be always obsessed with this idea. You will never attain to real *samadhi* because real *samadhi* is when consciousness is absolutely pure and there is no content in it. The mirror is absolutely pure, nothing reflects." He said, "Then it is for you to decide."

Now Ramakrishna was in much doubt about what to do. He wanted to attain to *samadhi*, but this attachment was coming in the way. Finally he decided: "Okay," he said, "I will do it. But from where to get the sword?"

The saint laughed and said, "From where you have got your Mother Kali, from the same place! It is imagination, so imagine a sword – and imagination can cut imagination. This Mother Kali is your imagination, your sword is your imagination. Cutting Mother Kali and her falling apart is also imagination. To destroy imagination, a real sword is not needed. For only an unreal thing, an unreal thing will do."

Ramakrishna tried many times, but would not succeed. The saint got fed up. He said, "Now tomorrow I am leaving. This is the last time. I will do one thing to help you: I'm going to bring a piece of glass, and when Mother Kali arises…" – because whenever the Mother Kali would be there, immediately you could see it from outside also: Ramakrishna would start swaying and tears of happiness would start rolling down his face. The saint said, "When I see that now you are in your hypnosis and Mother Kali is there, I will cut you on your third-eye center with my piece of glass. Blood will flow. At that moment – this is to remind you not to forget the sword – as I am cutting you, cut your Mother Kali. Try it, otherwise tomorrow I will go." He was threatening to go, and it was difficult to find a man like him. His name was Totapuri, a very rare *paramahansa*.

Ramakrishna tried, crying and weeping, and when Totapuri cut his third-eye center, he also took courage and cut the Mother inside. Suddenly, all disappeared, Mother and sword and all. He was in absolute silence.

Buddha says, "Use all means and methods in a very unattached way so when the time is right to drop them, you can drop them. Everything has to be dropped."

The eighth is *pranihan*, surrender. Buddha says, "Remember, you have to do much, but the ultimate always happens when you are not doing anything." It happens in a let-go. *Pranihan* is the state of let-go. Do all that you can do. It will help, it will prepare the ground, but it cannot cause the truth to happen. When you have done everything that you can do, then relax; then nothing more is left to be done. In that relaxing, in that let-go, the truth happens. Truth is not something that we can bring. It comes, it descends, it happens; it is nothing of your doing.

The ninth, *bala*, is power. After surrender is power. Now, see the difference.

At the fourth Buddha said *vidya*, energy. It was not power, it was simply energy, human energy. Now after surrender there is *bala*: power, divine power. When you have surrendered and your ego is dropped, suddenly you are full of unknown power. You have become a receptacle.

The tenth, *ghyana*, is seeing into the nature of things, or awareness. Buddha uses the word *ghyana* in a very specific way: seeing into the nature of things. When you have surrendered and the power of the divine or the power of the whole has descended on you, then there is that encounter, that vision, that realization – nirvana.

These ten are the *parmitas*. They have to be practiced.

Now, the sutra. The sutra is to remind you of how you have to work for these ten *parmitas*.

> *The Buddha said.*
> *Those who study the doctrine of the buddhas will do well to believe and observe all that is taught by them. It is like unto honey; it is sweet within, it is sweet without, it is sweet throughout; so is the Buddha's teaching.*

This is one of the things to be understood. This is very significant, and Buddha has repeated so many times, "My teaching is like honey; sweet within, sweet without, sweet throughout; sweet in the beginning, sweet in the middle, sweet in the end. My teaching is like honey." He has repeated that a thousand and one times. Why? There is a very significant message in it.

Ordinarily, whenever you feel happy, unhappiness comes afterward. When you indulge, you have a glimpse of happiness. Then there is pain and frustration. So it is sweet in the beginning but bitter in the end. Seeing this, many people have tried the reverse, the extreme opposite. That's what ascetics do. They say, "Fasting, austerities, discipline is painful in the beginning, but very sweet in the end." These are the two ways in the world: the way of the worldly man who hankers for pleasure even if in the end it brings pain: "It's okay, we will see. Right now, why miss?" Even if a drop of honey is there, he's ready to suffer for years for it. The worldly man thinks of the momentary and suffers for it.

And then the so-called religious man, seeing this absurdity, stands on his head. He turns the whole thing upside down. He says, "If in the world this is experienced, if you enter a blissful, peaceful, happy state and in the end you become frustrated, then the happiness is for a moment, and for years afterward you remain frustrated." He tries the other: he says, "First I will move into pain – I will fast, I will move away from all pleasure, I will go to the Himalayas, I will stand in the cold, or in the hot sun. I will move into pain myself – and then comes pleasure." And yes, that's true. It happens because pain and pleasure are two aspects of the same coin. If first you look at one side, you will have to look at the other side later on.

Buddha says, "My teaching is totally different – it is neither of the worldly nor of the other-worldly; it is neither of one extreme or of another extreme. It is sweet in the beginning, it is sweet in the middle, it is sweet in the end." He says it is not a question of choosing between pain and pleasure. If you choose pleasure, pain will come; if you choose pain, pleasure will come. But on the whole, both are there.

"My teaching," Buddha says, "is of choiceless awareness." Don't choose, you should not choose – neither pain nor pleasure. Then the whole coin drops out of your hand. Then pleasure and pain both disappear, and that which is left behind is what bliss is, or peace, or serenity. But it is sweet: *It is like unto honey; sweet within, sweet without, sweet throughout; so is the Buddha's teaching.*

> *Buddha said:*
> *O monks, you must not walk on the way as the ox that is attached to a wheel. His body moves, but his heart is not willing.*

If your heart is not willing then there is no need. Then the time has not come for you to move on the way or to go in search for the truth. Then you still need to live in the world and get a little more mature. But don't go against the heart because that going is useless. If your heart goes with you into the search for truth, only then go.

> *His body moves, but his heart is not willing. But when your hearts are in accord with the way, there is no need of troubling yourselves about your outward demeanor.*

Buddha says if your heart is ready, if you have experienced life and the pain of it, if you have suffered life and understood the frustration of it and your heart is ready to move to the other shore – you have experienced this shore and have found that it is just empty, just illusory – if you are ready to move to the other shore without looking backward, not even a slight desire for this shore has remained in your being, then you are ready.

"Then," Buddha says, "you are free of all discipline. Then there is no need; then this much is enough: your heart is in accord with the way." Discipline will come. This is enough; discipline is needed because your heart is not in accord with the way. "But then," Buddha says, "that discipline is not of much use."

Remember, Buddha is not ready to take you on the way if you are immature. Maturity is a must. What do I mean by "maturity"? By "maturity" I mean a man who has looked into life and found that it is just a dream. When the reality that you think is real starts looking like a dream, you are mature. Then it is very simple to move to the other shore alone. There will be no difficulty; your heart will be in accord with the way, you can go dancing, you can go singing, you can go laughing – you can go joyous, cheerful. You will not go reluctantly, you will not go resistantly, you will not go against yourself. In fact, you will not be going; you will simply be moving with the stream, like timber.

> *Buddha said:*
> *Those who practice the way might well follow the example of an ox that marches through the deep mire carrying a heavy load. He's tired, but his steady gaze, looking forward, will never relax until he comes out of the mire, and it is only then that he takes a respite. O monks, remember that passions and sins are more than the filthy mire, and that you can escape misery only by earnestly and steadily thinking of the way.*

Buddha says that first great effort is needed, and then great surrender too. That is the meaning of the Zen people saying that "effortless effort" is needed. A great harmony is needed of effort and no-effort. If you rely on your effort you will never reach; if you rely only on God's grace you will never reach. The possibility to reach arises only when you have done all that you can do. Only at that moment does the universe shower on you, not before. Then you can relax.

So Buddha says to first do everything that you can do. Never ask for help before that. Don't be lazy, don't be lethargic; bring all your energy into action. Become totally involved in the spiritual work. Of course, remember also that this is not going to give you the ultimate. A moment will come when you will have to surrender. But you can surrender only when you have done all that you can do. God helps those who help themselves.

There are two types of people. The first type says, "If it is going to happen by his grace, it will happen. When he needs, or when he wants, it will happen. I will have to wait." Their waiting is impotent, their waiting is of no worth. They have not earned it, they have not taken even a step toward God. It is not going to happen.

Then there are egoistic people. They say, "It is going to happen by our effort. There is no God, there is no grace, there is no possibility of the universe helping us; the universe is absolutely indifferent to human beings. We have to do all that we can do, and it is going to happen only by our effort."

Buddha says these people will also never reach. They are too egoistic. The first type is too lethargic, the second type is too active, and the reality is just in the middle: be active and yet ready to surrender.

These are the differences among the three religions in India. Hinduism is of the first type, Jainism is of the second type, Buddhism is of the third type.

Hinduism believes it will happen by God's grace, that whenever he wills, it will happen – nothing can happen without his will. Not that what they say is wrong, but they don't earn it.

Jainism says it will happen by our will, our power. There is no grace, no help coming from the universe, so we have to fight and struggle. So Jainism becomes a very egoistic trip.

Buddha says you have to do all that you can do. Be a Jaina first, and then be a Hindu. That is the greatest synthesis ever brought to the world: be a Jaina first, and then be a Hindu.

In Buddha, the whole East came to a synthesis. Buddha's contribution to the world is unique. And that's my teaching too – be a Jaina first, and then be a Hindu. First make all the effort that you can, go to the very end that you can, and then relax. Then you have earned; now the grace will be coming.

Effort plus surrender, struggle plus surrender, brings one home.

Enough for today.

10

AWARENESS

ALWAYS BEGIN WITH SIMPLE THINGS

The first question:

Osho,
You are my favorite meditation. Do buddhas mind being gazed on for more than three seconds at a time?

The question is from Maneesha. It is tremendously important to understand.

Jesus was taking his leave from his disciples. The last night, when he was going to be arrested, breaking the bread he said, "This is my flesh, this is my meat; eat it." Pouring the wine he said to his disciples, "This is my blood; drink it."

What he is saying looks very crude, but the meaning is very significant: a disciple has to become a cannibal. He has to eat his master, his master's vibes. The very presence of the master has to be swallowed, chewed, digested. A buddha exists only for that, so that you can eat him. Of course, it depends on you what will happen after you have eaten a certain vibe. The transformation will happen within you; you will have to be very careful.

There are people who eat food – you can give to them the best of foods – and they will only produce manure and nothing else. There are people who will produce something more: thinking, philosophy, mind. There are a few more, very rare, who will produce something still higher: poetry, music, love. And there are very rare souls who will produce something even higher: prayer, meditation. And there are only a few, few and far between in the history of humanity, who will eat the same food you eat and will produce godliness, or nirvana. It is the same food that we eat. The poet eats the same food that you eat, but something becomes poetry out of that food. An essential part of the food becomes poetry, it bursts out in song. A dancer eats the same thing as a soldier, but the soldier only produces violence and the dancer produces grace. It depends on you how you will use my presence.

Meditate as much as you can: that is the most basic thing; everything else is secondary. There is no limit to it; as much as you can digest, digest. There is no excess in it, there cannot be. The more you do, the more you will feel you can do still more. Until your whole being is transformed into the same kind of presence as your master, go on meditating.

Another scene…

Bodhidharma lived in China for many years, and then one day he decided that now the time had come for him to go back to his home. He wanted to return to the Himalayas, he wanted to die in the Himalayas. He gathered his disciples, the four foremost disciples, and he asked them, "What is truth?"

The first said something which was philosophical, logical, very systematic, but Bodhidharma was not happy. He looked very sad. He said, "You have only my skin."

He asked the other; the disciple said something. His answer was a little better than the first one: more intuitive, less intellectual, more poetic, more musical. Bodhidharma said, "You have my flesh," but still he was not very happy.

He asked the third the same question: What is truth? The third was still better; he said something which was more existential, had a glimpse of realization in it, just a ray of light. Bodhidharma was not unhappy, but not yet happy. He said, "You have my bones."

Then he asked the fourth, and the fourth said nothing. The fourth answered with silence. Bodhidharma looked into his eyes: they were like an infinite abyss, a bottomless abyss. The disciple fell unto his feet without uttering a word. Bodhidharma must have danced in his innermost being. He was tremendously happy; at least one had understood him totally. He said, "You have my marrow, my very soul."

Those four were all cannibals; they were eating the master. But one produced only the skin, the other produced flesh, the third produced bones, the fourth exactly reflected the master – gave birth to the master again in his being.

So while you are here with me, let it be your deepest meditation. I speak to you – not that there is something to be told to you. It is just a device. It is just a device so you can be close to me; it is just a device so you can be engaged in listening and your being can be in deeper contact with me. You have learned the ways of language. It is very difficult for you to sit silently with me: if you sit silently you will be faraway, you will be lost in your thoughts. There will be a great distance between me and you. I have tried that.

I used to sit silently with people, but I found they were faraway, thousands of miles away in their thoughts. They just look physically close; spiritually they are not there at all. Somebody is moving into his past, somebody has already moved into some imagination in the future. I used to look into them and I found they were not there, they were somewhere else. Only their bodies were there – empty shells, hollow. Their minds were not there, and if your mind is not there it is very difficult for your soul to be there.

I talk to you so your mind becomes engaged in my thoughts. While you are engaged in my thoughts, at least you will be able to avoid your thoughts. You will be closer to me – closer than you can be while you are thinking your thoughts. At least my thoughts are mine: they come from a deep emptiness, they carry the flavor, they have a subtle vibe in them. While engaged with me in a verbal communication, listening to me attentively, your mind becomes engaged and cannot go to the past and cannot go to the future. It has to be here, it has to be attentive, it has something to do here. While the mind is engaged in my words, I can communicate on a different level too; your being is close to me and just being close is enough.

That's the meaning of *satsang*: just to be close to someone who has disappeared, just to be close to someone who is no more, just to be close to someone who is just a tremendous nothingness.

Coming closer to this nothingness, you will also start disappearing and melting. It is natural. There will be a few moments when you will suddenly disappear. Those are the moments when you have tasted something of me. When you disappear, when you are completely lost, when the mind has simply stopped functioning, you are just pure attention – then you and I are not two. Then there is no I-thou relationship. Then only one exists in which the I and the thou have both dissolved. Then we overlap each other: then your center is my center and my center is your center.

The more these moments come to you, the more you will produce the highest possibility: your destiny. So Maneesha, go on meditating on me as much as you can.

And I know her – she has been doing it; she has been very attentive, very aware. With great care and love, she has been absorbing me.

You ask, "Do Buddhas mind being gazed on for more than three seconds at a time?" They cannot mind because they don't have any mind. In fact, if you don't gaze at them, they feel sorry for you. If you look here and there and don't look directly to them, they feel sorry for you. You are thirsty and pure water is available, but you go on looking sideways. You don't look straight, you don't look directly, you don't look immediately. You will miss.

Look at me not only looking – because eyes can absorb the

subtlest vibe. It is a way of eating. Eat me, be cannibals. Remember, what I am saying is not important at all. What I am being here is important. So don't be lost in my words; they are just toys to play with. Listen to my being, to my presence.

The second question:

Osho,
Why must everybody who wants to do meditation or hear the lecture pay for this?

Why not?

The rabbi climaxed his sermon with, "Life is like a glass of tea."
Later, one of the congregation asked, "Rabbi, why is life like a glass of tea?"
"Why not?" answered the rabbi.

I also say to you: Why not? You pay for everything in life, why not for your meditation? You pay for everything in your life, why not for God? Why do you want God for free?

In fact, you don't want God. You are ready to pay for whatsoever you want. You know that you have to pay. You don't want meditation. If it is given free, and even with *prasad*, then you will think about it. You are ready to go to the movie and pay for it; why should you not pay for your meditation and the lecture if you want to hear it?

The question comes, naturally, from an Indian – and a non-sannyasin – who does not understand me at all, who must be a newcomer. The Indians think they are the most religious people in the world. All bullshit: they are the most irreligious people in the world; they just have an egoistic idea that they are very religious. If you are really religious, you will be ready to pay for your meditation with everything, even with your life.

What is money? If you pay five rupees for something, and if you earn ten rupees a day, then you have paid with half the day. Money is just a symbol that you have devoted half your day's labor for it. You go to the movie and you pay ten rupees for a ticket; you earn ten rupees per day. You are saying that this movie is worth it – "I can stake one day's labor for it." But you are not ready to stake anything for your meditation, prayer, for religion. In fact, religion is the last thing on your list. You want it for free. Basically you don't want it; if there is a price to it you start feeling uneasy.

You ask why you have to pay here. The price that is asked is nothing; it is just the beginning of learning a certain lesson: that one has to pay for everything, and certainly for prayer, certainly for meditation because it is the highest thing in life. Those few rupees that you have to pay are very symbolic, just symbolic, just token – they indicate something. If you are ready to pay something, then I know you will be persuaded to pay more. By and by, one day you will be able to stake your whole life for it. If you are not ready to even pay five rupees, it is impossible for you to stake your whole life.

Gurdjieff used to ask a lot of money for his lectures – and not only money, he would create all sorts of obstacles. For example: no lecture would be declared beforehand. If the lecture was going to be this morning at eight o'clock, you would receive a phone call early in the wee hours, at five o'clock, "At eight o'clock reach a certain place" – and the place would be twenty miles or thirty miles or fifty miles away – "and Gurdjieff is going to talk, and we have to pay for it."

People used to ask, "Why do you create trouble? Why can't you say beforehand so we can manage?" And Gurdjieff would say, "If you can manage, then it is not of worth." If you can come suddenly, dropping all that you were going to do… Maybe you were going to see the Prime Minister at eight o'clock, and suddenly now there is an alternative. Either you go to Gurdjieff or to the Prime Minister – and you go to Gurdjieff – then something is going to happen. You have staked for it, you have taken trouble. Then too it was not certain that Gurdjieff would speak. He might come and he would look around, and he would say, "Not now. No, not today. I will inform you later on."

Once it happened in Paris that for eight days he called people, and for eight days he canceled. The first day there were near about four hundred people; the last day near about five or six people. When he looked at them he said, "Now only the right ones are left.

The crowd is gone, now I can say whatsoever I want to say to you."

I am also not interested in the mob, in the crowd. I am not interested in casual visitors. I am interested only in the few sincere seekers. They have to show their mettle.

And the money that you have to pay is just the beginning. It is just the alpha; by and by I will persuade you to pay with your life. Unless you have that much courage, nothing is going to happen. Religion is not cheap, certainly not free.

But the Indian mind is very money-minded. They talk about being religious, but they are very money-minded people. Their whole outlook about things is money. No Westerner has ever asked this; they understand: the ashram has to be maintained, the place has to be ready for you – some musician has to prepare for the music, somebody has to conduct the meditation, the gardens have to be looked after, the buildings have to be built. All needs money – where is it going to come from? And you know well that I don't do any miracles.

There are only two ways. One is somebody else should donate for you. But why should somebody else donate for you? You will meditate and somebody else will donate for you? Why? If you want to meditate, you pay for it. And if you really want to meditate you will be ready to pay for it; there should be no hitch about it. If you don't have money, go and earn it. If it is absolutely impossible, then come and work in the ashram and pay that way, work-wise. But don't ask to come for free.

This idea of getting religion for free has entered so deep in the mind that people think they have a claim. People come to the office and they say, "Why are we not allowed?" But why should you be allowed? You have to earn it to be allowed. Just because you want to come in does not mean much.

You have to show that you are sincere, you have to show that you are not just here out of curiosity. What is the way to check someone? The easiest way is money because the greatest greed is for money.

The greatest greed is for money, so whenever you have to lose your money you have to lose a little part of your greed. When you pay five rupees for entry, you are paying by dropping a little greed. The money is not the problem, the problem is greed; you are dropping a little greed. And this is just a beginning – because meditation can happen only when all greed disappears. A slight greed inside you and meditation is not possible. For a greedy mind there is no meditation; meditation happens only in a non-greedy mind. If you don't have money, then work. Pay by your work and show your sincerity.

But the person who has asked must have money; otherwise he would not have been allowed to enter here.

He must have paid – must be greedy, must want to have everything free, at least about God. Nobody bothers about God.

I have moved in the masses for years. I did not decide in a hurried way to drop out of the mob. I saw that it was absolutely absurd: you go on talking to people who are not ready to listen; you go on talking to people who are not seekers, who are not in any search. You go on talking to people who have come just for entertainment. Why should I waste my energy and time? I tried in every way to be available to bigger crowds, but then I found it was impossible. They come as entertainment, and they hear through one ear and it is lost from the other.

There is a story about Bayazid, a Sufi mystic...

He was passing through a cemetery and he came upon a heap of skulls. Out of curiosity he took one skull. He had always been of the thought that all skulls are almost the same, but they were not the same. There were a few skulls whose ears were joined together; there was a passage. There were a few skulls whose ears were not joined together; there was a barrier between the two. There were a few skulls where both of the ears were joined to the heart but not joined together – there was a passage running to the heart.

He was very surprised. He prayed and asked God, "What is the matter? What are you trying to reveal to me?" And it is said that he heard a voice. God said, "There are three types of people: one, who hear through one ear; it never reaches anywhere. In fact they don't hear, just the sound vibrates and disappears. There is another type who hear, but only momentarily; they hear through one ear, and it is lost into the world again through the other ear. There are a few souls, of course, who hear through the ears and it reaches to the heart."

God said, "Bayazid, I have brought you to this heap of skulls just to help you remember it when you are talking to people. Talk only to those who take whatsoever you say to their hearts. Otherwise don't waste your energy, and don't waste your time. Your life is precious: you have a message to deliver."

One day I also understood – not by going to a cemetery and coming across a heap, but by looking into alive people. There are three types; Bayazid is right. The story may be true or not, that is irrelevant. I looked into thousands of people and I found that there are only a very few who will take the seed to the heart, who will become soil to it, who will absorb it. Others are just curiosity-mongers, just entertaining themselves. Maybe the entertainment is religious, but it is meaningless.

So here I don't exist for the masses. Let it be known once and forever: I am not interested in the crowd, I am interested only in individuals. You have to show your mettle.

And this is just the beginning of the ashram. Once the ashram is established rightly, there will be more and more difficulties for new people to enter.

The third question:

Osho,
What is the test or confirmation that a man has followed the path of awareness? In my life, although I am not very certain to say that I was in the practice of awareness, at times I have felt, "Why am I eating? Why am I doing this and that?" Please comment.

"Why" has nothing to do with awareness. The "why" leads into a totally different dimension: the dimension of analysis – and analysis is not awareness. Once you ask the question "why," you have moved from the fact already.

You are confronting something – for example, anger has arisen in the sky of your mind. There is a cloud hovering around, it wants to settle on you, wants to get roots in you, and you feel disturbed; the anger is coming. Now, to be aware means just to see it; not to do anything. Just to see it without any condemnation and without any evaluation. Just to see it. Not to ask for a cause or from where it is coming: "Why, why should it be?" And don't ask how it should be avoided because the moment you ask how it should be avoided, why it has come, you have moved away from the fact. The fact was that just a cloud of anger was surrounding you. Remain with the fact without any questioning, without even any tacit judgment. Don't say it is bad because the moment you say "bad" you have started going away, you don't want to see it. Don't say that you are against it, that it should not be because if you are against something you cannot face it. Just remain aloof, neutral, indifferent.

The questioner says that he thinks this is some sort of awareness. It is not; it is analysis. Analysis is not awareness; analysis is of the mind. Awareness is not of the mind, awareness is something beyond the mind. When you ask "why," you have allowed the mind to interfere.

You see a roseflower – you don't ask "why," you don't ask, "Who has planted this bush, who is the gardener?" If you ask these things then the rose is no longer there, you are clouded by other thoughts. A real understanding of the rose is possible only when you don't even say, "It is beautiful," because these words will become a barrier. You don't even say, "This is a roseflower," because this labeling is dangerous. The moment you say, "This is a rose," all the roses that you have seen before have come in. They will be standing there in a queue, the very word *rose* will revive all the memories connected with the rose. Not even a single word needs to be there. One has to be just an openness to see whatsoever is there.

Watch the roseflower without any language, without any appreciation, judgment, without saying anything, without asking any questions and without trying to find any answers. Otherwise, you have moved into the mind.

What is mind? The thinking process is mind. "Why" creates the thinking process. Awareness means just be a witness.

There is a beautiful story about the Sufi mystic, Master Jalaluddin Rumi…

He was standing on the bank of a river one day. Suddenly he spotted a fur coat floating downstream in the middle of the current. He hollered over to a scholar who was standing there on the bank too.

"Hey man, there is a fur coat in the middle of the river. See it? Grab it man!"

The scholar jumped in the river out of his greed, and swam out. Rumi was a little nearsighted; all he could see was a lot of commotion and flubbing around out there.

"For Christ's sake, what are you doing out there. Bring it on in."

Finally the scholar heard his hullabaloo, and shouted back between gasps: "You cockeyed fool! This ain't a fur coat out here, it's a bear. And the more I struggle with him, the deeper his claws go. And he won't let go!"

"Friend," said Jalaluddin Rumi, "that bear is reason."

If you ask the question "why," you are caught, you are caught by the bear of reason. And the more you ask questions, the more you will get entangled – and the claws will go deeper into your body, into your being. Don't ask any question. If you want to be aware, just be aware.

Awareness is a simple process with no questions, no answers. One simply watches. And rather than starting with complex things, start with very simple things – because there are people who start immediately with complex things. They never go to the primary school, they never go to the secondary school, they never go to the college; they simply go to the university, to the post-graduate school. Of course they fail because to enter a post-graduate class you have to prepare.

Listening to people like Krishnamurti, or Ramana Maharshi, listening to them speak about awareness… And awareness is all – it is the very essential religion, the central core of all religion – so when you listen to them speak about awareness, and you listen to Ramana Maharshi, Krishnamurti, Buddha, Gurdjieff, and everybody is praising it, you become greedy. You say, "So I must have this awareness too. I cannot allow it to go, I must have it. These people are enjoying so much awareness and they are feeling so blissful, in such great benediction, I must have this commodity too." So you start grabbing. But you start wrongly, you start with complex things.

Somebody is suffering from sexuality; he starts trying to become aware of sex. This will not be possible. You have taken a very complex thing. Or somebody is suffering from anger, and has suffered his whole life, and his whole life is destroyed by anger and the poison that is created by anger. Now listening about awareness, suddenly he will try it on anger. This won't do – and if you fail, you lose self-confidence; that is very dangerous. Start with very simple things.

Buddha used to say, "Start with breathing because that is the simplest thing in the world, so simple that you don't do it at all. It happens on its own." You don't breathe. In fact you are never aware of breathing unless something goes wrong. You have some breathing trouble? Then you become aware. Otherwise breathing goes on its own: you can go on sleeping and the breathing continues. It is good; otherwise if you had to take care about it, life would be impossible. Someday you would sleep and you would forget to breathe, and – gone. And there is no way to undo it; once gone, you are gone forever. Breathing is spontaneous, it is a very simple process: the breath just goes in, goes out – nothing much in it. Buddha says, "Watch it, become aware of it. Sitting silently, simply see the breath going in, the breath going out." You will feel very bored because it is very monotonous: the same breath coming in, the same breath going out.

So the first problem has to be very simple, like breathing. And the second problem will be that you will have to face boredom. If you can face boredom, boredom disappears and there is tremendous calm behind it. So start awareness with the breathing process.

At least for one hour every day, sit silently just watching your breathing, doing nothing – not even chanting a mantra because then you are making it complex. Simply see the breathing; it is a natural mantra: it goes in, goes out, goes in, goes out. You are not to say that the breathing is going out. You have to simply go with the breathing. It is going out, the consciousness goes with it; it comes in, the consciousness comes in. You simply sense its going in and coming out. You try to remember it.

You will find difficulties even in this simple process. For a few seconds you will be aware, then you will forget. Then your mind has taken you away – to your business, to your woman, to your children, or a thousand and one problems are there. Again after a few minutes you will remember: "I have forgotten; I am not watching my breath" – then again come back. There is no need to repent, there is no need to fuss about having forgotten because now if you fuss about it, again this time is being lost. Whenever you recognize that you have lost track of breathing, come back; again start watching it. Doing it slowly, slowly, one day you will be able to watch your breath. If a person can watch his breath for forty minutes continuously, then there is no problem in life. He can watch any problem. And by watching, any problem can be dissolved.

But first you have to learn how to watch. So don't start with complex things, but with very simple things. Buddha says two things: watch either breathing or walking. Buddha himself did both: for one hour he would sit under the *bodhi* tree and watch his breathing, and when his limbs would feel tired, cramped, then he would walk for one hour and watch his walking – one foot goes, another foot, another; then he would turn. If you go to Bodhgaya, where Buddha became enlightened, just near the *bodhi* tree there is a small path on which he used to walk.

The breathing awareness in Buddhist terminology is called *anapanasati yoga*, and the walking meditation is called *chankamana*. These are two simple processes – and both are tremendously beautiful. Breathing can be watched sitting silently, and walking can be watched being active. But the walking process is very simple: you need not worry about it, you need not plan about it. Everybody is capable of walking; you need not even learn about it. Small, simple, spontaneous processes have to be made aware first. And then, when you have attained a certain capacity, you can try it on other things: anger, greed, sex, possessiveness, jealousy – there are millions of problems. Then you can try on other problems, and you will be surprised by the miracle of it. It is a very magical process: if you watch something silently, it disappears.

A great sexual desire arises in you; simply watch it arising. It is throbbing in your body, it is moving in your mind, it is stirring fantasies in you – just watch, with neither condemnation nor indulgence. Just watch, and you will be surprised: the more watchful you become, the less power there is in the sexual urge. There comes a moment when you are fully aware; you have become a light unto yourself. In that moment the urge has completely disappeared. This is not repression because you have not repressed the sexual urge. If you repress you will be getting into trouble. All repressed people sooner or later are bound to become insane. So this is not repression. You are not against the sexual urge, you don't have any attitude about it. Simply watch it, and by just watching, the energy changes its quality; the sexual urge becomes a fuel for awareness, and awareness burns bright. And there is no residue, there is no wound, no repression.

This is how *shila* arises, the graceful discipline Buddha talks about: one is no longer indulgent and one is no longer repressive.

The world has known only two things up to now: either you indulge or you repress. Buddha has shown a totally different path. Neither do you indulge nor do you repress; you simply watch.

But always start from the very small things. Never try the first time on some big enemy, otherwise you will be defeated and once you are defeated you will lose confidence, and you will lose trust in the miracle of awareness too.

The idiot of the village was employed by the priest as a church cleaner. One day, while he was cleaning the altar, a big crucifix fell on his head. Luckily he was not hurt very badly. The day after, the priest found him in a corner of the church with a heap of small, smashed crucifixes.

"What on earth are you doing?" he asked furiously.

Said the idiot, "Much better to kill them when they are still small!"

Remember it; it is much better.

Just first try with very small things which you can easily destroy through your awareness. Then great confidence arises, great certainty that "Yes, it works." Trust overwhelms you; now you have a secret key in your hands. But don't be in a hurry – go on trying with small things, small problems, simple problems and then go on, by and by...

The tendency of the mind is just to try the most important problem. Once you have the key, you want to open the ultimate door immediately, you want to unlock the mystery. Just having the key does not mean anything: you have to learn how to use it. And the ultimate lock is very complex. You may destroy your key. It may not work.

Start with small things, and never ask "why" because we are not interested in analysis. That is the difference between the Eastern psychology which I call the psychology of the buddhas, and the Western psychology, the analytical process. This is the difference: if you go to a Freudian, or a Jungian, or an Adlerian, or other types of therapists, they will immediately start analyzing. They will say, "Tell us, what is your problem? Tell us in detail." In Freudian psychoanalysis, the patient talks and talks and talks, and the analyst simply sits by the side listening to his talk, and analyzing in his mind what is what. Then finally he gives the solution: "This is the problem." But this is an interpretation. It may show more about the psychoanalyst than about the patient. It is his analysis.

You can try it; go to different therapists and they will always interpret your problem differently. If you go to Adler, he will interpret everything as an inferiority complex; that is his base. If you are in politics, he will say that you are inferior, that's why the power urge. If you go to Freud – you are the same person – and you say, "I am very ambitious, and I want to become a great politician, a great political leader," he will analyze it through your sex. He will say that maybe you are becoming a little impotent or something – because whenever a person starts becoming a little impotent, he wants some power to substitute for it.

So political leaders are very dangerous nearabout the age of forty-five, fifty. Beware because when they start losing their sex power, then they have to prove themselves somewhere else.

There is every possibility that Adolf Hitler was impotent, and to prove that he was potent he became destructive. If you go to the Freudian he will analyze it in that way. If you go to the Jungian he will find very occult meanings, mythological meanings. He will go into the mythologies of the world and find the meanings.

The Eastern approach is totally different. It says "why" is not the question; the fact is there, the fact is enough. We don't go into the history of it, it is not going to help, it will make it more complicated. Why go into the past, or why go into the future? The fact is here. It is present in front of you. Face it, be beware of it.

"Beware" means: be aware of it. Just look at it.

This is a totally different approach. The buddhas have said – and it is now one of the most existential and experiential foundations of Eastern psychology – if you watch a fact rightly, penetratingly, it disappears just by observation. Exactly as you bring light to your dark room, darkness disappears. And with darkness, all those problems disappear that existed with darkness.

For example, if you enter a dark house sometimes you stumble upon the furniture and you become angry, and you beat the furniture and you say, "Some enemy exists here." Then you grope in the dark; a painting falls on you and then you are furious and you want to smash everything. But all these problems are created by darkness.

Bring light, bring awareness, and then suddenly darkness disappears – with darkness disappearing, you no longer stumble upon the furniture, and the painting does not fall on you. There is no anger and no rage, and you are not furious, and you don't go insane. Those problems were concerned with darkness; they disappear with darkness.

In the West, they start trying to analyze: "Why did this painting fall?" Now, it is a very costly affair to go to a psychoanalyst and get analysis. "Why did this painting fall in the first place? There must have been something wrong in your childhood between you and your mother, otherwise why did the painting fall? Why did you stumble on the furniture? You must be accident-prone because other people have passed through the same room and they have not stumbled on the furniture. So it shows something about your childhood trauma: maybe when you were being born you were stuck, and the doctor had to pull you out. So since then you have been stumbling, and you go on stumbling. Now the trauma has to be dissolved." These things – you laugh, but they have become very serious philosophies in the West. There are great propounders of them, and everybody claims that he has found the final solution.

In the East we have not worked that way. We don't ask "why." We say, "The painting has fallen, so the painting has fallen. Now I am struck by it, so I am struck. The problem is not with the painting, the problem is not with the furniture, the problem is that the room is dark." Of course, you never stumble upon darkness – see the point – you stumble upon the furniture. You never stumble upon darkness. A painting falls on your head and hurts you – darkness never falls on your head and hurts you. But darkness is the real problem. If you pay too much attention to the problems that are happening, you will go in a wrong direction because they are not real problems. The real problem is that the room is lacking light. Bring light in.

Awareness is not a question; it is just trying to become more alert, more mindful.

I have heard...

A woman came before the local judge complaining that her husband had made a murderous attack on her with a large pair of scissors. "Judge!" she cried. "He rushed at me and slashed my face to pieces!"

The judge looked at her face, on which not the slightest mark of conflict appeared.

"When did you say this happened?"

"Only last night, Judge."

"But I don't see any marks on your face," said the puzzled judge.

"Marks?" roared the woman. "What do I care about marks! I have got witnesses!"

Now, as if witnesses can prove it, as if just having witnesses is enough.

You can find out why you stumbled on the chair, why the painting fell upon you, but nothing will be solved by it. The darkness remains untouched. You can go on finding one explanation, another explanation – not that in the East a few people have not tried it. A few people have tried it. It has never been a main current of the Eastern approach, but a few people have tried it. That's what the theory of karma is: it is an effort to find an explanation.

You are in business, you go bankrupt; now you ask why: "Why are others succeeding and I have gone broke? Why?" Now there is a constant question inside you – "Why?" Then you go to a religious man, to the priest, to the astrologer. He looks at your hand and he says, "In your past life you have done something, that's why you have failed." Now you feel very relieved. You remain broke, it doesn't change anything. Your bankruptcy will remain there, but you feel satisfied just by the explanation that in your past life you have done something wrong and that's why you are suffering. Now there is an answer and the answer satisfies your question, but the problem remains untouched. The problem is that you are bankrupt. It does not make any difference what explanation you get.

Somebody is poor and he always feels, "I am good, honest, sincere, and I am poor." Then somebody explains, "This life you are good, honest; of course in the next life you will be paid enough for it, there is no injustice." "There may be a little delay," they say in India, "but there is never any injustice. God will pay you. Wait, trust." But the man says, "But I am poor, and I am hungry." And then they will say that in the past life you have done something wrong, bad karma, so you are suffering. That makes things clear.

That's why in India there has not been a single revolution in five thousand years' history – revolution has been killed by the explanation of karma. There cannot be any revolution here. There is no need for revolution. Explanations are enough: the poor man is poor, the rich man is rich; the rich is rich because he has done good karma, and the poor is poor because he has done bad karma. Now, if the poor man tries to start some revolution he will suffer even in future – again bad karma, violence, this and that. "So at least now, don't do anything bad. Suffer, and in the next life..." And nobody knows what happens in the next life, so it is a very beautiful explanation.

Yes, Marx is not wrong when he says that religion is the opium of the people; it has been used that way. Not that religion as such is really so, but religion has been used as an opium. Then people can be drugged.

I would like to say this to you: never bother about explanations; see the fact, and be aware of the fact, and don't be too concerned about explanations. Otherwise you will go on and on – you did something wrong in your past life, that's why you are so violent, aggressive, full of anger.

But have you never asked the other question? – "Why did I do something wrong in the past life?" Then they will say, "Even further back you did some wrong"; but that goes on and on. The question is: why, in the first place, did you do wrong in your first life? There is no explanation unless God himself made you in such a way that you had to do something wrong. But then God is the culprit; you are not. Why should you suffer? Let God suffer if he has committed a mistake.

These explanations are poor efforts to console oneself. Somebody dies and you are hurt, and you are in much pain, and you want somebody to console you, and somebody comes to console you – because wherever there is demand there is supply. That is an economic law, it applies everywhere. If you are crying and weeping, some foolish, stupid person is bound to come, and he will say, "Don't cry. The soul is immortal." Now, that doesn't change anything. Your wife has died, and you cannot make love to your dead wife. The problem is there, you will miss her. The immortal soul cannot cook food for you tomorrow and you have to look after your children. The immortal soul is not going to come, but somebody says, "The soul is immortal." It gives a sort of consolation: "So she has not died really. So she must be somewhere and there is a possibility to meet someday, somewhere, and it will be good." You start dreaming, and it consoles. But this explanation is like a tranquilizer, a sedative, like alcohol. It intoxicates you.

If somebody has died and you are in pain, what do I say to you? I say, don't ask for explanations. Look at this pain. Death has happened; watch it. It has hurt you deeply; watch it. Beware, be aware, be mindful of how fragile life is, how everything ends. Just see the flux-like phenomenon of life, the momentary dreamlike existence. Just see, and don't try to explain, and don't try to escape, and don't try to avoid – and don't try to get occupied somewhere else. Just look: death has happened, you are sad, great sorrow has happened to you. Look into it, and by watching and becoming aware of it, much will be revealed to you. The sorrow, the sadness will disappear – and with it will disappear all attachments because you will be able to see that all attachment brings sorrow.

It is not the death of your wife that you are sorry for. It is not because of death; if she had been somebody else's wife there would have been no problem. She was your wife – it is not the question of death that you are troubled with. Some part of your being is snatched away: you had become too attached, you feel uprooted. You will feel a gap in your heart, an empty space.

Watching the sorrow that death brings, you will become aware that behind the sorrow is not death but attachment. And seeing the facticity of attachment you will relax, you will become a little loose in your attachments. Next time death happens there will not be so much sorrow. A day comes when death happens and there is no sorrow. You know this is how things are; you have accepted it. You have known the reality of life, that it ends in death. And there is nothing else to do. You have become aware.

The fourth question:

> *Osho,*
> *What does my greed for money, to have money and to see that I am able to make money, mean?*

It simply means that you are greedy.

There is no need to go into great philosophy about it. It does not mean anything else than what it means: you are greedy. And greed says that you must be empty, so you want to stuff yourself with something or other.

Money is a way to stuff oneself with things. Money can purchase everything, so money becomes very important. Then you can stuff your emptiness with everything. You can have as many women as you want, you can have as many palaces as you want, as many cars, airplanes – whatsoever you want. You can go on stuffing yourself with things.

You are empty. An empty person is a greedy person, and nobody is ever fulfilled by greed. Nobody is ever fulfilled by anything because things are outside and the emptiness is inside, and you cannot take outside things into the inside. So you can become rich, but you will remain empty. Your treasure chest may become full, but your heart will remain empty. Your bank balance will go on increasing, but your soul will not increase. In fact it may start decreasing because each time you run after money you lose some soul; it is a great risk. By losing your soul you earn money. By destroying your inner purity, your inner virginity, you go on selling your inner for the outer, you go on exchanging. In the end you have piled up a lot of money and many things, but suddenly you realize that inside you are a beggar.

The inner can be fulfilled only by the inner. I am not saying to renounce your money; that too is foolish. To continuously run after money is foolish, to renounce money is also foolish. Nobody can fulfill his inner emptiness with money, and nobody can fulfill it by renouncing money because both are outside. Whether you accumulate money or renounce, both are outside. That is not looking into the problem directly.

You are empty inside; something has to be done there. A prayer has to fill it, a meditation has to flower there; only the fragrance of existence will be able to give you fulfillment. So I am neither for money nor against money. Money can purchase many things. All that is outside can be purchased with money, there is no problem in it. But money cannot lead you to the inner contentment, and that is the problem. You have to work for that.

My own observation is this: the more money you have, the more is the possibility of becoming aware of the inner emptiness because the contrast makes things very clear. A person who is poor inside and poor outside does not know his inner poverty. That's why poor people look happier, beggars look happier than rich people, than millionaires. Why? – because the beggar is poor in both ways: poor inside and poor outside. There is no contrast. It is as if you have written on a white wall with white chalk; you cannot read it. A rich man has much richness around him, and just in the middle of it all is emptiness, poverty. Because of the contrast, it hurts. It is as if you are writing with white chalk on a blackboard; it comes clear and loud.

So I am not against money. In fact, my whole approach is that only rich people can be religious. A poor person cannot be. It is very difficult for a poor person to be religious. To be poor and to be religious needs great intelligence, very great intelligence, unique intelligence. Only then can you be religious. To read something written with white chalk on a white wall you need very penetrating eyes, but to read on a blackboard is very simple.

My analysis of the whole of human history is that a country

becomes rich whenever it is irreligious. A country becomes rich whenever it is irreligious, and a country becomes religious whenever it is rich: this is how the wheel moves.

India was religious one day, when it was a golden bird – very rich. In the days of Buddha, it was the richest country of the world: the whole world was jealous. Then it was rich and religious. But whenever a country becomes religious it starts becoming poor because a religious person does not care about outward things. When you don't care, the outward disappears; then the country becomes poor. Now India is poor, and religious only for the name's sake.

The sun will rise in America; the future of religion is in America, not in India. India is bound to move on the path of communism. It cannot avoid it, it is already on it. It is moving slowly. It is a very old country so it moves very slowly, at an old man's pace. But it is moving; slowly, slowly it is moving. It is dropping democracy, it is dropping freedom, and it is becoming more and more materialist, socialistic. That is the first step; then by and by it will be a communist country. By becoming communist it will become rich again; by becoming rich it will become religious again.

America has become rich and will become poor, sooner or later. You can see the hippies: they have already moved. They have dropped out of the rich society because they have seen the futility of it. It is meaningless. They talk about love, not about war. The moment you start talking about love and not about war, your country is going to become poor because to remain rich one has to remain continuously violent and aggressive. They are talking of the simple life, but a simple life cannot be a rich life. Technology will disappear. If technology disappears, richness will disappear. America is rich, will become religious, and by becoming religious, by and by, it will lose its richness.

There is a possibility of Russia, somewhere in the next century, becoming very rich and suddenly becoming religious. The wheel of history is very dialectical – thesis, antithesis: this is how it moves.

I am not against richness; I am in favor of religion. If you are very intelligent, then even in your poverty you can see the futility of riches. But then you have to be very perceptive: you have to think about something that you don't have and you have to recognize that it is meaningless. Without having it, to recognize it as meaningless is very difficult. Having it and recognizing that it is meaningless is simple. So I would like to repeat it again: if a poor man becomes religious, he shows intelligence and if a rich man remains irreligious, he shows stupidity. A rich man who is not religious is simply a fool. A poor man who is not religious simply needs sympathy. He is not a fool, you can forgive him. No rich person can be forgiven if he is not religious; that shows he is stupid. He has riches, and yet he has not been able to see that they are futile.

Your greed simply shows that you are feeling empty. Now, you can fill it with things but it will never be filled, or you can start growing into your inward consciousness and it will be filled.

People can continue for their whole lives wasting all their energies in greed. This ambition is not going to help you.

Mulla Nasruddin and his neighbor were talking about the problems of raising their boys.

"Is your son very ambitious, Mulla?" asked the neighbor.

"Yes," said Nasruddin. "He has such big ideas about being rich and successful that already he has begun to look on me as a sort of poor relation."

Just the idea that he is going to be very successful and rich, and already he has started looking at his father as some sort of poor relation!

You can go on an ego trip if you start on the path of greed – and that can take your whole life. People remain greedy to the very end; they are dying and they remain greedy; even death does not make them aware.

Solomon and Irving were partners in the dress business. They had the worst season of their careers, and were at a complete loss as to what to make that would sell. There was not a dress to be cut in their cutting-room. They both decided the only way out to leave their families any money was to agree to a suicide pact. They drew straws and Solomon was to jump first. Solomon jumped out of the thirtieth-floor window, and as he was falling he noticed that every cutting-room on every floor he passed was busy.

He yelled back to Irving, "Don't jump! Cut velvet!"

Even to the very end – you can be dying, but the business, the business of greed continues. Once you are on the trip it is very difficult to get out of it. One gets more and more involved, and on the path of greed you are insulted many times, humiliated, but still you get up again. And again you rush.

There was a long line waiting in the early morning in front of a clothing store that advertised a special sale. A man walked to the front of the line. The people grabbed him and pushed him back to the end of the line. Once more he headed for the front of the line, and they kicked him and pushed him into the gutter. Finally he got up, brushed himself off, and said to a man at the end of the line, "If they do that once more, I am not going to open the store."

Still he is ready to open the store. They have thrown him in the gutter, but people go on rushing, almost insane. Greed is a sort of insanity.

Use money, but never be greedy. As a means, money is perfectly good; it is a great means of exchange, very utilitarian. Use it, but don't be used by it: possess it, but don't be possessed by it. Remain the master.

The last question:

> *Osho,*
> *After your touching discourse today, I went up rather solemnly to where you had been sitting, to prostrate and say thank you. But when I prostrated, I found myself laughing instead.*

That's how it should be. That's the way to thank me, that's the way to be grateful to me. I am against seriousness. If you come closer to me, come laughing. Even sometimes when you come solemn and serious, I will make you laugh. Laughter to me is prayer. Serious faces are ill faces. Never go toward the divine seriously; go laughing and dancing, and your prayer will be heard and your thank-you will reach to the address.

It was good that you came to thank me and you started laughing. That is the right way, the perfect way. Like a flower, it opens.

Have you ever seen a solemn, serious flower? They are always laughing; through their laughter, they are offered to existence. Except for man nobody seems to be serious on this earth, and except for man nobody seems to be in misery. Except for man nobody seems to be puzzled. Animals, birds, trees, rocks, rivers, mountains – nobody seems to be serious, they are all laughing. In their laughter they are praying. Join hands with them.

Remember it always: the deeper your laughter, the deeper will become your prayer. If you can dance, you have entered the shrine, you have come close to the ultimate.

Yes, dancing is the only way to reach the divine.

Enough for today.

11

BUDDHA

THE GREATEST ANARCHIST IN HUMAN HISTORY

The Buddha said:
I consider the dignities of kings and lords as a particle of dust that floats in the sunbeam. I consider the treasure of precious metals and stones as bricks and pebbles. I consider the gaudy dress of silks and brocades as a worn-out rag. I consider this universe as small as the holila fruit. I consider the lake of Anavatapta as a drop of oil with which one smears the feet. I consider the various methods of salvation taught by the buddhas as a treasure created by the imagination. I consider the transcendental doctrine of Buddhism as a precious metal or priceless fabric seen in a dream. I consider the teaching of buddhas as a sky flower before my eyes. I consider nirvana as awakening from a daydream or nightmare. I consider the struggle between heterodox and orthodox as the antics of the six [mythical] dragons. I consider the doctrine of sameness as the absolute ground of reality.

Buddha is the greatest anarchist in human history. He does not believe in any rule from the outside. To help you become free of the outside, he teaches you an inner rule, an inner discipline. Once you have learned the ways of the inner discipline, he's there, ready to destroy that too because you are ruled. Either from the outside or from the inside, you are a slave. There is freedom only when there is no rule.

So the inner discipline is just a step to get out from the outer domination of the society, of the state – of the masses, civilization, culture, etcetera. Once you are free of the outer domination, then Buddha starts destroying your inner discipline too. That's why I call him the greatest anarchist ever. There have been people who have taught that no outside rule should exist, but Buddha is alone in teaching that even the inside rule is a form of slavery, a subtle slavery. No-discipline is his discipline. When a person is absolutely without any discipline, then there is beauty because then there is freedom. Then one acts spontaneously, not according to any rule imposed by others or imposed by oneself. Then one simply acts out of nothingness. Then the response is total: nothing is being held back and there is no enforcement of any sort, there is no violence. There is tremendous grace, there is benediction because now the actor has completely disappeared, the doer is no longer there. If you are trying to discipline yourself, the doer remains in a subtle way. If you are trying to discipline yourself, you remain schizophrenic, you remain divided. A part of you disciplines you, another part is being disciplined by you. So one part becomes the master and another part becomes the slave. Again there is division, again there is duality, again you are not one.

There is bound to be conflict in this duality because in reality you are one, and this is a fiction. Who is trying to rule whom? Who is there to be dominated by whom? There is only one existence inside, one being. To bring any sort of discipline means to divide that unity, and that division is misery, that division is hell.

So, first Buddha says there is no God – because if there is a God and any belief in God, then man can never be free because then there is a dominator, a dictator. With a God in the world, there can be no democracy. Impossible. If God has created man, then of course he is the ultimate power. If he's omnipotent, omnipresent, omniscient, then how can freedom exist? You are never left alone; he's everywhere. That's what the so-called religious people teach; they say, "He's looking at you wherever you are. In the most private situation also, he's there watching you constantly. His eyes follow you."

This seems to be a very dangerous teaching: it means you don't have any freedom, it means you don't have any privacy. God is like a universal Peeping Tom: he's always there at the keyhole, you cannot escape from him, his very presence is destructive. His presence means that man has no freedom.

Nietzsche's declaration that "God is dead and now man is free," has a Buddhist tone to it. That's what Buddha said, "God is not, and there is freedom." Freedom means you are not created by anybody and you are not dominated by anybody and you are not manipulated by anybody. To Buddha, freedom is God. Try to understand it. It is difficult because Buddha uses such terminology that it becomes very difficult for childish minds to understand. The childish mind can always understand that there is a God dominating you, looking after you: compassionate, kind, great – the Father, the Mother. These are childish ways to understand the truth.

Buddha says there is no God, and freedom is absolute. That absolute freedom is Buddha's God. Freedom is God, freedom is divine. So first he takes away all outer beliefs. There is no need to believe in a God; the belief itself will become the barrier.

Just the other night a sannyasin came from England, and she was very nervous, trembling, shaking. And she said, "I am very much afraid because I cannot yet believe in you." I said, "Who expects you to believe in me?" She was afraid because she thought that she doubted. The ordinary religions have taught people that you become religious only when you believe; if you don't believe you are irreligious. The West is completely unaware of a great religion that has existed in the East which does not require any belief. In fact, this religion says belief is a barrier. A religion without belief is very difficult for a Christian or a Mohammedan or a Jew to conceive. It was even difficult for Hindus and Jainas to conceive.

Buddha is a great revolution, a very radical outlook. He says all beliefs are dangerous. You should not believe; you should see.

I told the sannyasin, "Don't be worried, doubt is perfectly okay. Doubt is better than belief. Doubt can never hinder you; doubt remains open. Belief is a closing of the mind; then the aperture is closed, then you don't look." In fact, a man who believes becomes afraid to look. Maybe the truth is against his belief – then what to do? He closes his eyes; it is easier to protect one's belief with closed eyes than with open eyes. Who knows? The truth may not coincide with your belief, the truth may shatter your belief, the truth may be against your belief. It may not be Christian, it may not be Hindu, it may not be Mohammedan. Then what will you do? So it is better to remain with closed eyes.

A man with belief becomes afraid: he does not seek and he does not inquire and he does not search. He never explores. He remains stuck with his belief. He holds his belief to his heart. This is out of fear.

Religion is not out of fear – at least real religion is not out of fear. At least, it *should* not be out of fear. Real religion is fearlessness. Buddha says with a God, how can you be fearless?

The Jewish God says, "I'm very jealous. Don't worship any God other than me; I'm very jealous. If you worship any other God, I will destroy you."

Now, these words look very political, and very stupid. And to put these words into the mouth of God himself is sheer nonsense. God saying "I am very jealous"? Then God seems very human, even below human because human beings have existed who are not jealous. A Buddha has existed who is not jealous. Buddha seems to be in a better state of consciousness than the Jewish God. Jealous? Prohibiting his followers not to worship anybody else? "Because I am jealous, and I will destroy you"? What the Jewish God says is simply unbelievable. He says. "If you commit something against me, for ten generations I will torture you. Not only you: ten generations of your children will be tortured. But if you worship me, for a hundred generations the rewards will be coming to you."

Now, what type of God is this? Your child has not done anything – you commit some crime, you disobey God, and for generations your children will suffer, and for a hundred generations your children will get the reward if you have done something good. And "something good" means, in Jewish terms, if you have obeyed the omnipotent God. If you disobey it is sin; if you obey it is virtue.

There seems to be no real value. God may be saying something absurd, but if you obey it is virtue, if you disobey it is sin. And this threat, that "For ten generations I will take revenge," and this bribery, that "For one hundred generations I will reward" – look at what type of mind has worked out this concept of God. It cannot be very divine. It is not divine at all; it is in fact sub-human.

Buddha says there is no God – don't be afraid. To make man fearless, Buddha says there is no God. And to make man an explorer of truth, he says there is no need for any belief. Belief is not a requirement; it is an obstacle. Be open. Explore. Doubt, think, meditate, experiment; and when a mind comes to experience truth without any belief, the mind itself becomes true because then there is a communion between truth and the mind.

Be fearless. There is no need for anybody to dominate you. Freedom is the very substratum.

First he drops outer beliefs: in God, in hell, in heaven – because your hell and heaven are just your projections. If you knew about different hells and heavens you would understand. The Tibetan's hell does not have fire in it because the Tibetan's hell has to have more cold, more ice. They know; they suffer from cold, so hell has no fire at all. Of course the Hindu's hell has fire; Hindus suffer from heat. The Hindu's concept of heaven is almost of an air-conditioned heaven. The sun is never hot, and cool breezes are always blowing, and shady trees, and the flowers are like diamonds – and everything is cool. Of course, a hot country, suffering for centuries from heat, dreams.

But things continue... They are your projections. There are as many hells in the world – and as many heavens – as there are climates because it will depend on the experience of your own climate. For a Tibetan, fire in hell will look almost like a heavenly gift. No, fire has no existence in hell; it is absolutely cold, you will be frozen to death by coldness. Fire exists in heaven. There everything is warm.

Now, what do these concepts show? They show your mind. They don't show anything about heaven or hell. Man continues in his dreams, in his projections.

If you die, you may be dying as far as your body is concerned, but your mind continues. In fact, the Buddhist approach is that the idea of heaven and hell has arisen because during his whole life a man projects, thinks, about the afterlife. If he has been committing many crimes and sins, he becomes guilty; he feels that he is going to hell. He becomes very afraid. By the time he's dying the fear arises: "Now there is no time left to put things right." Now he is going to hell, and he has an idea of hell, of what hell is. So when a person dies, when he is free of the body, the projections become very real. He starts dreaming. So when a Hindu dies, certainly he dreams after death. Immediately he dreams either of heaven or hell. It depends: if he was a good man, virtuous, a worshipper, then of course he is very self-confident. When he dies, he knows that he is going to heaven. Immediately after death, the mind starts dreaming. The time between one death and another birth is used in dreaming.

You live in a dreamworld – exactly as you live in the night. What happens when your body relaxes and you go to sleep? – you start dreaming. You forget your body in your sleep. Sleep is a tiny death, a very mini-death. You forget your body, you don't remember your body at all. You become just your mind, as if the mind is no longer burdened by the body and the reality of the body. The mind is freed: there is no pressure on the mind of bodily reality, of objective reality. Mind is freed. Suddenly, you start dreaming. Of course, your dream is your dream – it has nothing to do with any reality whatsoever.

When you die this is exactly what happens, and it happens in a bigger proportion. Once you die all the pressure of bodily reality and objective reality disappears. The mind is free to dream. Even in sleep there is a burden, even in sleep you are connected with the body, but in death you are disconnected completely. Now the mind is completely free. Like a balloon, it starts rising into its projections. So if you have lived a bad life…

When I say "if you have lived a bad life," I mean if you think your life has been bad, if you have been taught that this life is bad. For example, if a Jaina has been eating meat, he will suffer hell after his death – but not a Mohammedan, not a Christian, not a nonvegetarian who has never thought about it. He will not suffer hell. But a Jaina is bound to suffer hell. If he has eaten meat, his idea will make him guilty; the guilt will be there, the guilt will project, and he knows what hell is; hell will be projected.

Between death and birth there is a great dreaming time, and you can live long in that dream time because dream time is absolutely different from your waking time. Have you sometimes observed that you are just sitting in your chair and for a minute you fall asleep and you dream? And the dream is so long that it takes years – in dream time. Then suddenly you are awake and you look at the clock and only one minute has passed. Now you are puzzled. How, in one minute's dream, could you see a projection of many years? You were a child, then you become young, and then you went to the college and the university, and you fell in love and were married, and you were just coming out of the church – and the dream is broken. There is such an expanse of many years. How has it happened in a single minute?

Dream time is different from actual time: it can happen in a single minute. So maybe between death and birth there are only a few minutes, or a few days at the most, or a few hours. But they will look very long; you can dream infinite dreams: you can dream of hell, you can dream of heaven – but you continue.

I have come across a beautiful anecdote sent to me by a few of my sannyasins…

Once upon a time, there was a playboy named Shiva. One day, he suddenly died. His friends thought of inquiring if he had reached hell. Of course, naturally, they thought he must have reached hell. So they rang up hell.

The phone was picked up and a voice boomed, "Hello, the Devil speaking."

"Hello, Mr. Devil, has Shiva come to hell?"

"No, try the other place. We have enough playboys here, and we don't need any more trouble," said the Devil.

So they rang up heaven and a very, very holy voice said, "Hello, Virgin Mary speaking."

"Has Shiva come to heaven?"

"No, not yet," said Virgin Mary. "Try tomorrow."

So they rang up again the next day, and the same pure and holy and saintly voice said, "Hello, Virgin Mary speaking." They again asked about Shiva and she said, "No, not yet. Try tomorrow." And her voice was as sweet as honey; sweet in the beginning, sweet in the end, sweet throughout!

So next day, they tried again and a wonderful and sexy voice came, "Hello, Mary speaking."

The friends looked at each other and said, "So, he has reached."

Your hell is your hell; your heaven is your heaven. It is your projection, it is your personality projected in dreams. These are not realities.

Buddha is tremendously existential. He's the first religious man who has said that there is no heaven and no hell; it is just in the dreams of humanity that heaven and hell exist. If you have stopped dreaming while alive, then there is no heaven and no hell. In fact, there is no sin and no virtue. He's the greatest iconoclast, the idol-breaker. He takes everything away from you because he knows that unless everything is taken away, the mind continues. Mind needs props. If all the props are taken away, the mind collapses. And in that collapse, reality arises in its true color, in its true tone.

Reality is only when the mind is not. Mind is a distorting faculty.

Now these are the last sutras. Of tremendous import, each sentence is like a sword, and it cuts the roots of the mind. And when it comes to cutting the roots of the mind, Buddha excludes nobody, not even himself. That's his authenticity. It is not that he is against other philosophies, he's against philosophy as such – against his own philosophy too. That's the authenticity of the master. It is very easy to be against others' philosophies, but to be against one's own philosophy means the man has no philosophy of his own.

He's simply asserting a truth: that philosophy is not the door to reality. He's against all methods, including his own.

You will be surprised: "Then why does he use methods?" The methods are to be used only because of you, because you are not ready to take the jump. The jump is too big, and you take it in small doses. Hence, he has to invent methods. The same is true about me. I would like you to take the quantum jump without any methods, but you cannot take it. Now the abyss is too big and fear possesses you. So I have to make small steps for you. Slowly, slowly, I persuade you. The more you become ready, the more I push you into no-method, into no-mind, into no-religion.

The essential religion is no-religion, and the greatest method is no-method. And to come to a state of no-mind is to come to awareness. Buddha has to talk to many categories of people, but these sutras are for those disciples who have come of age, who have become mature.

It happened once…

I was chatting with Mulla Nasruddin, who was a rabid fisherman. I told him, "I notice, Nasruddin, that when you tell about the fish you caught, you vary the size of it for different listeners."

"Yes," he said, "I never tell a man more than I think he will believe."

That's what Buddha is doing too. If you have come to him with a childish mind, he will give you some toys to play with. If you have come with a little better, a little more grown-up mind, a little more mature, he will not give you those toys. And if you are really mature enough to listen to truth, unafraid, then… Then these sutras.

Today's sutras are the last. They are meant only for very grown-up people, so listen to them very attentively.

It is said that once Jesus' disciples asked him, "Have you brought a message of peace to the world?" He said, "No. I don't bring peace, I bring a sword." A sword? Christians have puzzled over it down through the centuries because it doesn't look right. Jesus is the messenger of peace and he says, "No, I have not brought peace to you, but a sword." He says, "I will teach you how to hate your mother and how to hate your father and how to hate your wife and how to hate your husband and how to hate your children. And unless you are ready to hate your father and your mother, you cannot follow me."

Now these words, coming from Jesus who says, "God is love," look very contradictory, very inconsistent. It is difficult to sort out what he means. It has been difficult for Christians; they avoid these sentences. But if you understand this sutra of Buddha, you will be able to understand Jesus too. By "sword" he means: each master brings a sword into the world to cut the roots of the mind. And when he says, "Unless you hate your father and your mother and your family, you cannot follow me," what is he saying? He's saying that unless you drop that mind that has been given to you by your mother, by your father, by your family; unless you drop your past; unless you forget completely what the society has given to you – the idea of good and the idea of evil; unless you drop the whole conditioning that society has given to you, you cannot follow him.

These sutras are like swords: they cut, and they cut totally. Buddha is very hard because he has great compassion. He will not allow any loophole from where you can find your slavery again. So first drop all outer discipline, and then drop the inner discipline too. In that undisciplined state is freedom, is nirvana, is *moksha*. And out of that freedom, whatsoever happens is virtue. Out of slavery, whatsoever happens is sin.

> *The Buddha said:*
> *I consider the dignities of kings and lords as a particle of dust that floats in the sunbeam.*

He says all political power, all power as such, is stupid. Don't rush after it, don't be ambitious because all ambition collects dust and only dust. If you are not disillusioned by dust, you will not be able to know what truth is. A man obsessed with ambition is not capable of knowing truth at all. Eyes full of ambition never see what is; they only see what they want to see. The ambitious mind is the wrong mind; the nonambitious mind is the right mind.

What does it mean to be nonambitious? It means that you are not hankering for the future, that you are not hankering for the next moment; that you are not hoping for the next moment, that you have abandoned hope; that you live in this moment, that you don't have any future, that the present is all that is. A nonambitious mind becomes still, and that stillness comes of its own accord – not that you still yourself. A nonambitious mind is still; there is nowhere to go, nothing to hanker after. Then reality is available.

For an ambitious mind reality is not available because reality is available only in the present and the ambitious mind is always somewhere else. Always somewhere else, the ambitious mind is never content. Discontentedness is its very base. Buddha asks, "For what are you desiring? Desiring for kingdoms? You want to become great kings and dignitaries?"

I consider the dignities of kings and lords as a particle of dust that floats in the sunbeam. Why does he say: ...*that floats in the sunbeam*? Have you seen sometimes, a sunbeam enters through the roof, the whole room is dim and dark and just one beam of sun enters the room; then you can see dust floating, dust particles floating in it. They shine, they look like diamonds. They are ordinary dust. If the sunbeam were not there you would not even see them, but in a sunbeam they look like diamonds. They shine, they become radiant.

Buddha is saying when you project an ambition, when the sunbeam of ambition is there, dust particles look very precious. They are not precious in themselves. And he should know: he was born a king. Then he left those palaces. The day his ambition dropped, suddenly the sunbeam disappeared and he saw only dust and dust.

The night he left his palace and his kingdom and his newly born child, the charioteer took him out of the kingdom not knowing where he was going. And he was not supposed to ask. But when Buddha stepped down from the chariot and he told the charioteer, "Now take my clothes back, and please give your dirty clothes to me," the charioteer could not understand what he meant.

He said, "What are you doing? Have you gone crazy?" He was an old man, the age of Buddha's father, and he said, "I have looked at you and I have loved you from your very childhood. What are you doing? I am just like your father; tell me, what is your agony? Why are you leaving these beautiful palaces, this kingdom? You are the happiest man in the kingdom. Where are you going?"

Buddha said, "I look at those palaces; they are on fire.

Everything is burning, the whole world is burning and I want to walk in the cool shade." The charioteer, of course, was not able to understand what he was saying.

He said, "What are you talking about? I don't see any fire anywhere. What are you talking about?"

Buddha said, "You may not understand, but I have seen the fire. Everything is on fire, everything is burning because everything is moving toward death."

Just the day before, he had gone to the town, his capital town, to inaugurate a youth festival. And on the road he had come across a dead body. He had not seen a dead body up to that moment. He asked, "What has happened to this man?"

The story is beautiful. The story is told in an Eastern way, in a mythological way. The story says that the charioteer was prohibited by Buddha's father ever to talk about death, and ever to answer such questions – because the father had been forewarned when the Buddha was born that if ever he came to know about death, he would renounce the world. So the charioteer was not going to say anything. But the story says that one god, seeing this, entered the charioteer's body. Seeing that the moment had come when Buddha was ready to renounce, and only through that renunciation was he going to realize – that rare moment of existence had arrived – the gods helped. They forced the charioteer to say the truth.

The charioteer said, "The man is dead, sir."

Buddha asked, "Is this going to happen to me too?"

The charioteer had to speak because the gods were forcing him – so he said, "Yes, this is going to happen to you too, sir.

Buddha said, "Then return home. There is no point in going to inaugurate the youth festival. I am no longer young. Seeing death, I have become old. Seeing death, I have died." A great glimpse, a great insight happened. And Buddha said the next day, "The whole world is on fire. I have seen death and when death is coming, then what is the point? I would like to find something which is beyond death."

I consider the dignities of kings and lords as a particle of dust that floats in the sunbeam.

But we don't see death; our ambition prevents us from seeing it. Even if death came right in front of you, you would not be able to see it because your ambition would function as a barrier. It won't allow you to see, it is like a blindfold.

I have heard...

A rich manufacturer from New York suffered a nervous breakdown.

"You must rest," advised his doctor. "Go to Florida, lie around under the sun, go swimming. You will be better in a month."

The businessman followed the doctor's advice and went to Miami, got into his swimming shorts, and strolled the warm sandy beach. Then the water was too much to resist and he went for a dip. But he had overestimated all the years he had gone without exercise and before he realized it he was over his depth, and could not swim back.

"Help! Help!" yelled the businessman. "Save me! I'm drowning!" An alert lifeguard heard the cry, dived into the water, and towed him to safety.

The manufacturer's wife came running to the scene on the beach. "Irving, baby, are you alright? Speak to me."

"I'm alright," wheezed Irving, dripping water, "but I've got to ask you something in private, please. Bend down."

The worried wife stooped over. "Yes, Irving, what is it that you want to ask me?"

"Tell me, how much do I tip for a thing like this?"

He had faced death, but he asks his wife, "Tell me, how much do I tip for a thing like this?" Life is not the problem; money is the problem: "How much do I have to tip?" Even facing death a man never realizes that the very existence of death makes his whole life meaningless. Money has no meaning when death is there.

But the ambitious mind lives in a very different world. The sunbeam of his ambition makes dust particles shine like diamonds. Once the sunbeam disappears, once the ambition is not there, everything falls flat and you can see where you were going, what you were hankering for. If life is going to disappear – and it is going to disappear, it is going to move into the desert of death sooner or later; it is only a question of time – then whatsoever you are hankering for is meaningless. Death will take everything away from you.

Buddha says, "Seek something which death cannot destroy."

> *I consider the treasure of precious metals and stones as bricks and pebbles.*

All your money, all your precious stones, all your bank balances, Buddha says, "I consider as pebbles." You are children playing on the seashore of life, collecting pebbles – colored of course, they look beautiful of course, but they are pebbles on the seashore, of no significance. And while you are collecting them life is rushing out of your hands, slipping by. You are taking a great risk. This opportunity is not to be destroyed in only collecting pebbles.

A man who took his two little girls to the amusement park noticed that Mulla Nasruddin kept riding the merry-go-round all afternoon. Once, when the merry-go-round stopped, the Mulla rushed off, took a drink of water, and headed back again. As he passed near the girls, their father said to him, "Mulla, you certainly do like to ride on the merry-go-round, don't you?"

"No, I don't. Rather, I hate it absolutely and am feeling very sick because of it," said Nasruddin. "But the fellow who owns this thing owes me a hundred rupees, and taking it out in trade is the only way I will ever collect from him."

Money seems to be the greatest obsession in the world. Money seems to be the greatest madness in the world. We go on selling our lives and collecting pebbles. We call it money. One day we simply disappear and the money is left here, and the life that you wasted in collecting that money could have been used in a more creative way. It could have become a song, a dance; it could have become a prayer, a meditation; it could have become a realization of truth, freedom... But you missed.

Buddha says:

> *I consider the gaudy dress of silks and brocades as a worn-out rag.*

All that you go on desiring seems foolish. There are people who live only to eat; there are people who live only to dress; there are people who go on playing with things – good when you are a child, but it seems that very few people ever become grown-ups. They certainly grow old, but very few people become grown-ups. To grow old is one thing, to become grown-up is quite another. A grown-up person is one who can see through things: what a toy is and what is not a toy. Small children playing, you laugh at them, but have you looked into your own life? Have you grown up at all? Maybe you have changed your toys – children are playing with toy cars and you are playing with real cars – but the play remains the same.

There are people...

Once I was a professor in a university, and a professor used to live just across from me. He had a car but it was always sitting there, and he would clean it and wash it every day, religiously. I became puzzled by and by because it never came out of the porch.

I inquired. He said, "You see, the traffic is such, and the car is so beautiful, and it is risky to take it to the university – you know the students: somebody may scratch it."

"Then why did you purchase the car?"

He said, "I love it."

Now, think of loving a car... But there are people who love cars, who love houses. It is not very difficult to see what has happened to them. These are the people who cannot love a person. They can only love a thing because you can manipulate a thing, control a thing better than a person. A person is always dangerous. If you love a woman it is always dangerous, if you love a man it is always dangerous – because a man or a woman is a freedom, intrinsic freedom. You cannot totally control. Man has tried in every way by creating marriage, and laws, and this and that, and creating respectability around them, and punishment and awards, and everything just to make one thing certain: that the woman is no longer a freedom, that the man is no longer a freedom. When a man is a husband he is no longer a person, and when a woman is a wife she is no longer a person. The freedom has been killed. Now, a husband is a thing, and a wife is a thing – they can be controlled more easily. If the wife does something, you can go to the court. The magistrate will help you, the police will help you to force the wife back into her "thinghood."

People love things, and people are afraid of people. Then they can go to absurd limits. Now, a car has a utility; certainly it has a utility – but to be in romantic love with a car is absurd. And this was romance: I would see him washing it every day for half an hour, completely absorbed, and the car was never used. He went to the university on a bike, and the car went on sitting there. But he felt very happy that the car was there. He looked at the car as if he were looking at his woman, he touched the car as if he were touching a human body. I watched him: his eyes would suddenly become aglow when he looked at his car; something great happened around the car. It is absurd; not only absurd, it is insane.

> *I consider this universe as small as the holila fruit. I consider the lake of Anavatapta as a drop of oil with which one smears the feet.*

Buddha says if you become aware, the whole universe looks very tiny because awareness is bigger than the whole universe.

Man is very tiny if you look at his body, man is very foolish if you look at his mind, and man is tremendously vast if you look at his consciousness. Three things meet in man. The vast, the infinite, meet in his consciousness, in his awareness. That's what you become aware of when you meditate: boundaries recede and disappear. The body does not contain you; in fact, you contain the body. Ordinarily you think, "I exist in the body." It is absolutely wrong. The body exists in you. You are vaster, you are bigger. Not only bigger than the body, you are bigger than this whole universe. It is awareness that holds all. But if you look at the body you are very tiny, and then if you go on getting identified with your body, a great desire arises to be big. That's what politics is, that's what the desire and ambition for money is, that's what you try when you use beautiful clothes to exhibit yourself: you try to hide the body, your tinyness, your smallness. You try to make it look beautiful, you try to make it precious.

It is said that once Mulla Nasruddin was in his Turkish bath, and Tamerlane, the great murderer and the great emperor and conqueror came in. Only two persons were there, Mulla Nasruddin and Tamerlane. And Tamerlane, as was his habit, asked Mulla Nasruddin, "I have heard that you are a very wise man. How much do you think is my cost, my price?" Of course, he must have been hoping that he would say, "You are priceless, sir. The whole universe is nothing before you."

But Nasruddin looked at him, brooded over it and said, "Sixty rupees."

Tamerlane was very angry and he said, "What do you mean? Sixty rupees? Even this towel I am wearing is worth more than sixty rupees!"

Nasruddin said, "That's why I said sixty rupees. I am not counting you – you are nothing – only this towel. I don't take any risks; that's why I say sixty rupees."

If you are identified with the body, of course, your value is not much – cannot be much. How much value do you think you can get out of your body if you go and sell it? If you ask the scientists they say, "Somewhere near around five rupees." Not even sixty rupees – somewhere nearer to five rupees. There is a certain amount of aluminum and iron and phosphorus and things like that; if they are all collected and sold in the market they will fetch near about five rupees – and that's true because the cost of things has gone very high.

In the first place, nobody would be ready to purchase your body. Immediately, the moment you die, everybody is ready to dispose of you some way or other: "Just finish it now."

It happened...

It is said about the great Emperor Akbar that he used to go to see a Sufi mystic, Farid, and he used to touch his feet. Now, Akbar's court people became a little jealous: "Akbar, the great emperor, touching the feet of a poor beggar?" And they told Akbar one day, "This doesn't look good, it is humiliating. You need not touch that beggar's feet. Your head is an emperor's head and you put your head on his feet?"

Akbar said, "Do one thing: take the head of a dead man and try to sell it."

Because the emperor had said, they had to try. Wherever they went people chased them out. They said, "Have you gone crazy! Get out of here! The head is stinking, and who wants this head? Get out!" They tried in all the shops, in every market in Delhi, and from everywhere they were thrown out. They came back and they said, "Nobody is ready to purchase – not only that, people don't even listen. They simply say, 'Get out of here! Have you gone mad? What will we do with a human head?'"

Akbar said, "Then what do you think? My head is just a human head; one day you will not get any price for it. So if I put this useless head at the feet of Farid, why do you think it is humiliating?"

It is said that once a great Sufi mystic was caught by a few people who wanted to sell him in a slave market. He was a very young, healthy man, radiant. So they were very happy; they were going to get a good price. They took him. He said to them, "I know that you are going to sell me, but let me tell you one thing: if you listen to me, you can get the highest price possible. I know my price, you don't know, so whenever you are ready to sell, just ask me, 'Is it the right price?'"

After just a few hours they came across a king, and the king said, "The man looks good; I will purchase him. I will give five thousand rupees." It was a lot in those days, and they were ready.

But the mystic said, "Wait, this is nothing, let the right purchaser come and I will tell you. Don't be a fool" – so they refused.

A rich man came and he offered ten thousand rupees. Now they were ready; they were not even going to ask.

But the mystic said, "Wait! Are you a fool? Have you not seen? The price is double now. Just wait."

Then came another rich man and he offered fifteen thousand rupees.

By now, those people had become aware that he was right: "We have a very precious man." And this continued the whole day.

Many people offered, but the mystic was saying, "Wait." The last offer was for fifty thousand rupees but the mystic said, "Wait!"

After that, people started going home, the market was

becoming deserted. The last man came and he was carrying just a bundle of straw. And that was the last man. The slave traders said, "Now there seems to be no purchaser, and we will again have to wait for eight days. Next week, again there will be a market."

The mystic said, "Wait, ask this man." They asked the man and he said, "I can give you this bundle of straw. I don't have anything else."

The mystic said, "That is the right price; sell me! This is exactly the right price. Now don't miss this opportunity."

The slave traders started beating their heads. They said, "We have got a madman! We have lost fifty thousand rupees and now he says, 'This is the right price!'"

But he was showing, he was indicating something: there is no price; the body is very tiny and very small. If you get identified with it, you are getting identified with straw, a bundle of straw – or as Buddha says, "A bag of skin, full of filth." If you get identified with the mind; you have a little more freedom. But mind is foolish, mind is stupid, mind is mediocre: it does not know anything about truth. It simply goes on inferring about truth, guessing. Mind is guesswork. Buddha says that if you get to really know yourself, then you are vast, infinite. Then you are divine.

I consider this universe as small as the holila fruit. I consider the lake of Anavatapta as a drop of oil with which one smears the feet. Buddha is saying: if you know man in his true reality, he is so vast that the biggest lake is just an oil drop on his feet. He is so vast that the whole universe is smaller than him.

> *I consider the various methods of salvation taught by the buddhas as a treasure created by the imagination.*

This is the sword: it cuts everything from the roots. Now he says: *I consider the various methods of salvation taught by the buddhas as a treasure created by the imagination.* All methods are created by the mind, so they cannot lead you beyond the mind. That which is created by the mind cannot lead you beyond it. To go beyond it you will have to leave all that is created by the mind. Methods are also created by mind. Yoga, Tantra, Yantra, Mantra:

all methods are mind creations, imagination – beautiful imagination, sweet dreams, golden dreams, and of course, they are created by buddhas.

To bring you out of your body, mind is used, so there are a few techniques to bring you out of the identification with the body. Then, to bring you to the very boundary of the mind, there are other methods which take you to the very brink of where mind ends. Then you have to jump out of the mind – of course, by jumping out of all methods.

> *I consider the various methods of salvation taught by the buddhas as a treasure created by the imagination. I consider the transcendental doctrine of Buddhism as a precious metal or priceless fabric seen in a dream.*

Buddha says, "Even what I am saying to you, maybe it is very precious; but it is precious metal or precious stones seen in a dream."

That's what I say to you always: that truth cannot be uttered. The moment you utter it, it becomes a lie. Truth cannot be said. The moment you say it it is almost part of a dream now, no longer truth.

The Zen Buddhists say Buddha was never born, never walked on earth, never taught a single teaching, never initiated anybody to be his sannyasin. And still they go and worship Buddha. Rinzai used to say that it looks absurd.

One skeptical philosopher came and he heard Rinzai saying that Buddha was never born. And just behind Rinzai was a great statue of Buddha. The thinker waited, and Rinzai said that Buddha never taught anything – in fact he never existed, so how could he teach? Then, when the sermon was over, Rinzai went to the statue, touched the feet and offered a few flowers. The skeptical thinker said, "Wait! Now, there is a limit to everything. This is too much. You say this man never walked on the earth; you say he never taught; you say in fact that he was never there. And now, whose feet are you touching? Whose feet are you touching, and to whom are these flowers offered?"

Rinzai laughed and he said, "I am offering these flowers to this man because he taught, and still he said, 'I have not taught you anything.' He was born and yet he said, 'That which is born is beyond birth and death.' He walked on the earth but still deep inside he remained immovable; he never walked. The wheel moved; the hub remained in its place, centered."

Buddha's teaching is tremendously contradictory. First he teaches you, "Do this, do that," and then he suddenly says, "Drop all. Now the boundary of the mind has come. Now drop this last dream too."

> *I consider the teaching of buddhas as a sky flower before my eyes.*

Have you sometimes watched, sitting by the shore, on a beach? Look into the sky and you will see flowers moving in the sky. Now scientists say they are ions. Or if you ask Wilhelm Reich, he says that they are particles of orgone energy. If you ask the eye specialists, they say that there is nothing; just the movement inside your eye. Nerves create the fallacy of something in the sky. You can press your eye with a finger and then you can see those flowers anytime. They are called sky flowers – they exist not, but you can see them. If you move your eyes they will go down and they will go up; you can play with them like a yo-yo. But they are not, they are not existential.

Buddha says: *I consider the teaching of buddhas as a sky flower before my eyes.* All teaching is meaningless. Truth cannot be taught, it can only be caught. There is no way to teach it. By teaching you can transfer words, doctrines, beliefs. Truth is never transferred that way. But being with a buddha, you can catch it, it is infectious. Hence the value of *satsang*: being with a buddha, being with a master, being with one who has become enlightened.

What does it mean, "to become enlightened"? It simply means, says Buddha:

> *I consider nirvana as awakening from a daydream or nightmare.*

He says you are living in a dream: the dream of ambition,

desire, a thousand and one types of greed, anger, lust, passion. You live in a dream. Nirvana, enlightenment, is nothing but coming out of the dream, just becoming awake. There is nothing occult in it, nothing esoteric in it. Buddha has no esoterics in his teachings; he is very simple. He says: "This is all – the man who lives in the world, the worldly man, the *samsaric* man, is in a dream, that's all – and the Buddha is one who has come out of the dream." The difference is not in their consciousness, the difference is only that the worldly man has something more than Buddha. Buddha has only awareness; the worldly man has something more than the Buddha. Buddha has only awareness; the worldly man has awareness plus dreams. And because of those dreams, the awareness becomes clouded – as if the sun is clouded and you cannot see. Clouds disappear and the sun is there. But as far as the inner light is concerned, there is no difference between a buddha and an ignorant man. They are made of same stuff.

> *I consider the struggle between heterodox and orthodox as the antics of the six [mythical] dragons.*

Buddha says it is all nonsense – the traditional and the anti-traditional, the orthodox and the heterodox, the theist and atheist, and the thousand and one types of philosophies and systems fighting with each other, arguing, proving, disproving. He says it is just a game, a mind-game, mythological. It has no significance. Don't be too entangled with theories and doctrines; they are part of the dream. Get out of the dreaming state, become more aware.

> *I consider the doctrine of sameness as the absolute ground of reality.*

This is his ultimate assertion; meditate over it. *I consider the doctrine of sameness as the absolute ground of reality.*

Buddha says things are not different, they are the same. They only look different, they only appear different. The tree there, and the rock, and you, and the animals and the stars, are not different. At the innermost core, reality is one and the same, substance is one and the same: there are no distinctions. Distinctions are dreams.

Physicists call that one reality electricity or energy. Materialists, Marxists, communists, call that reality matter. Idealists call that reality mind. Yogis call that reality consciousness. Buddha calls that reality nothingness.

Now, this word *nothingness* is very important. *Nothingness* means: no-thing-ness. No thing is. All things are just forms, dreams. We are different only in form, and forms are just dreams. It is as if out of gold you can make many sorts of ornaments. Those forms, different ornaments, are just dreams because the gold is the reality. Behind all the forms is gold; behind all the forms is one reality. Buddha says, "That sameness is the absolute ground of reality."

If you go in, you leave the form. First you leave the form of the body. Have you observed it? People who are close to me and meditating come again and again to that insight. These sayings can be understood only if you have certain insights of your own; otherwise it is impossible to understand them. When you are meditating, many times it happens that you forget your form, your body. You don't know who you are and how you look – you forget your face. In fact in deep meditation, you become completely oblivious of your body. When you close your eyes, you are formless.

Your mind also has form. You are a Hindu, Christian, Mohammedan, Jaina, Buddhist; then you have a form of the mind. You think in terms of being a Christian, you have a certain identity, the dogma defines you. But if you go still deeper, mind also disappears. Then you are no longer a Christian.

At the deepest core you are neither a body nor a mind. Then what are you?

Buddha says, "Nothingness, no-thing-ness; now you are not a thing, now you are universal." Now you are not confined in any idea: you are infinite. You are that which has always been there and will remain always. You are eternal. Then there is no birth to you and there is no death to you. You are like the sky: clouds come and go and the sky remains untouched by them. Millions of times clouds have come and gone, and the sky has remained pure and virgin. It has not been corrupted or polluted by them. You are the inner sky. When all forms disappear, the inner and the outer also disappear because they are also forms. Then there is nothing inner and nothing outer.

Oneness, sameness, Buddha does not call it God, because to call it God you may start thinking again of form. But that's exactly what the word *God* means, or should mean. God is that sameness that exists in all. God means existence, isness. The tree is, the rock is, the cloud is, man is – forms are different but isness is the same. As far as isness is concerned, a tree and you are the same. The form is different: the tree is green and you are not green, and the tree has flowers and you don't have any flowers, and the bird can fly into the sky and you cannot fly – but these are differences of the form. But isness is the same. To look into that isness is what meditation is all about. And to come to realize that isness is nirvana.

This is the last message, the last sutra of this Sutra of Forty-Two Chapters. This is the forty-second sutra, Buddha's ultimate message. I don't think you will be able to understand it right now. Intellectually of course you can understand it, but the real understanding has to be existential. That will come only if you follow the path of inner discipline to the point where you can drop it. If you follow the path of meditation to the point where even meditation becomes a hindrance, and you drop it... It is as if you move on a staircase from one floor to another, but when you have reached to the next floor you get off the staircase. You don't cling to it. All methods are staircases – or in Buddha's terminology, all methods are like boats. You cross the river, then you leave the boat and you forget all about it.

Methods have to be used and then dropped. It has to be remembered from the very beginning because there is every possibility that you may become too attached to the method. You become so attached that the method becomes a clinging: you start possessing it and it starts possessing you. Then the medicine has become a disease.

It happens: you are ill, you take medicine, then the illness goes but now you cannot leave the medicine. You have become accustomed to the medicine, to the drug. When the illness has gone, throw the medicine away immediately.

Meditation is a medicine. – you have to use it because you are ill. When wellness has come, then drop it immediately.

All devices have to be dropped one day, and all scriptures have to be dropped one day. This is the greatness of Buddha, that he says that even his teachings, his methods, have to be dropped.

When Zarathustra was saying good-bye to his disciples, the last thing that he said has to be remembered. Keep it in your heart. This is what Buddha is saying in the last sutra. Said Zarathustra to his disciples, "Now I am going and this is my last message: Beware of Zarathustra." And he left.

Beware of Zarathustra? Beware of the master because you can fall in love too much, you can become too attached. The real master is one who helps you to fall in love and then helps you to stand on your own so that you can leave the master. A real master never becomes a crutch for you. Never! Before he sees that you are clinging too much, he starts getting out of your life. The ultimate goal is freedom – freedom from all crutches, freedom from all props, freedom from every discipline, doctrine, method. Freedom from all. That's the goal.

Always remember that goal. Remembering that goal will help you not to go astray.

A small story and I will finish this discourse. It is a Hasid story: "The Three Prisoners."

After the death of Rabbi Uri of Istalisk, who was called "The Seraph," one of the Hasidim came to Rabbi Birnham and wanted to become his disciple. Rabbi Birnham asked, "What was your teacher's way of instructing you to serve?"

"His way," said the Hasid, "was to plant humanity in our hearts. That was why everyone who came to him, whether he was a nobleman or a scholar, had first to fill two large buckets at the well in the marketplace, or to do some other hard and menial labor in the street."

Rabbi Birnham said, "I shall tell you a story…

"Three men, two of them wise and one foolish, were once put in a dungeon black as night, and every day food and eating utensils were lowered down to them. The darkness and the misery of the imprisonment had deprived the fool of his last bit of sense, so that he no longer knew how to use the utensils; he could not see. One of his companions showed him, but the next day he had forgotten again so his wise companion had to teach him continually. But the third prisoner sat in silence and did not bother about the fool.

"Once the second prisoner asked him why he never offered his help. 'Look,' said the other, 'you take infinite trouble and yet you never reach the goal because every day destroys your work. But I, sitting here, am not just sitting. I am trying to bore a hole in the wall so that the light and sun can enter, and all three of us can see everything.'"

Now, there are two types of masters in the world. The first type I call the teacher. He teaches you things: disciplines, virtue, character, but next day you forget. Again he teaches you the same, and next day you forget again. The second I call the master. He does not teach you virtue, he does not teach you character, he does not teach you ordinary humility, humbleness, poverty – no. He bores a hole into your being so that light can penetrate and you can see yourself. He tries to make you aware, full of light. That's the real master. In the East we call him *satguru*, the right master. Teachers are many; *satgurus* are very few and far between. Remember this distinction.

If you are with a teacher, you may become a good man, but you cannot become enlightened. And your goodness will always remain on a volcano; it can erupt any moment. If you are with a teacher, he will teach you outward things – how to discipline yourself, how to be good, how to be a servant, how to serve people, how to be nonviolent, how to be loving, kind, compassionate. He will teach you a thousand and one things.

If you come to a master, he teaches only one thing – how to become aware, how to bore a hole into your being so light can enter into your imprisonment. And in that light, everything starts happening of its own accord.

And when things happen of their own accord, they have a beauty to them. Then there is great benediction.

Enough for today.

[illegible]

[illegible]

Now, there are two types of [illegible]. The first type [illegible]

[illegible] between [illegible]

[illegible]

[illegible]

[illegible]

[illegible]

OSHO INTERNATIONAL MEDITATION RESORT

Each year the Meditation Resort welcomes thousands of people from more than 100 countries. The unique campus provides an opportunity for a direct personal experience of a new way of living – with more awareness, relaxation, celebration and creativity. A great variety of around-the-clock and around-the-year program options are available. Doing nothing and just relaxing is one of them!

All of the programs are based on Osho's vision of "Zorba the Buddha" – a qualitatively new kind of human being who is able *both* to participate creatively in everyday life *and* to relax into silence and meditation.

Location

Located 100 miles southeast of Mumbai in the thriving modern city of Pune, India, the OSHO International Meditation Resort is a holiday destination with a difference. The Meditation Resort is spread over 28 acres of spectacular gardens in a beautiful tree-lined residential area.

OSHO Meditations

A full daily schedule of meditations for every type of person includes both traditional and revolutionary methods, and particularly the OSHO Active MeditationsTM. The daily meditation program takes place in what must be the world's largest meditation hall, the OSHO Auditorium.

OSHO Multiversity

Individual sessions, courses and workshops cover everything from creative arts to holistic health, personal transformation, relationship and life transition, transforming meditation into a lifestyle for life and work, esoteric sciences, and the "Zen" approach to sports and recreation. The secret of the OSHO Multiversity's success lies in the fact that all its programs are combined with meditation, supporting the understanding that as human beings we are far more than the sum of our parts.

OSHO Basho Spa

The luxurious Basho Spa provides for leisurely open-air swimming surrounded by trees and tropical green. The uniquely styled, spacious Jacuzzi, the saunas, gym, tennis courts...all these are enhanced by their stunningly beautiful setting.

Cuisine

A variety of different eating areas serve delicious Western, Asian and Indian vegetarian food – most of it organically grown especially for the Meditation Resort. Breads and cakes are baked in the resort's own bakery.

Night life

There are many evening events to choose from – dancing being at the top of the list! Other activities include full-moon meditations beneath the stars, variety shows, music performances and meditations for daily life.

Facilities

You can buy all of your basic necessities and toiletries in the Galleria. The Multimedia Gallery sells a large range of OSHO media products. There is also a bank, a travel agency and a Cyber Café on-campus. For those who enjoy shopping, Pune provides all the options, ranging from traditional and ethnic Indian products to all of the global brand-name stores.

Accommodation

You can choose to stay in the elegant rooms of the OSHO Guesthouse, or for longer stays on campus you can select one of the OSHO Living-In programs. Additionally there is a plentiful variety of nearby hotels and serviced apartments.

www.osho.com/meditationresort
www.osho.com/guesthouse
www.osho.com/livingin

FOR MORE INFORMATION

For any information about OSHO books, please contact:

OSHO Media International

17 Koregaon Park, Pune - 411001, MS, India

Phone: +91-20-66019999 Fax: +91-20-66019990

E-mail: distribution@osho.net

Website: http://www.osho.com

For More Information

For a full selection of OSHO multilingual online destinations, see

www.OSHO.com/AllAboutOsho

The official comprehensive website of OSHO International is

www.OSHO.com